A PASSION
FOR CHOCOLATE

ALSO BY ROSE LEVY BERANBAUM

Romantic and Classic Cakes (1981)
The Cake Bible (1988)

A PASSION FOR

CHOCOLATE

MAURICE AND JEAN-JACQUES BERNACHON

Translated and Adapted for the American Kitchen by

ROSE LEVY BERANBAUM

Photographs by Vincent Lee

WILLIAM MORROW AND COMPANY, INC.

New York

Library of Congress Cataloging-in-Publication Data

Bernachon, Maurice.
  [Passion du chocolat. English]
  A passion for chocolate / Maurice and Jean-Jacques Bernachon; translated and
adapted for the American kitchen by Rose Levy Beranbaum.
    p. cm.
  Translation of: La passion du chocolat.
  ISBN 0-688-07554-1
  1. Cookery (Chocolate) I. Bernachon, Jean-Jacques. II. Title.
TX767.C5B4713 1989
641.6′374—dc20   89-33499
                                                                CIP

Printed in the United States of America

First Edition

2 3 4 5 6 7 8 9 10

BOOK DESIGN BY RICHARD ORIOLO

BERNACHONS

To our mothers, to our wives,
to our children

BERANBAUM

To *l'esprit français*
To beauty and believers
And the bittersweetness of life

PHOTO CREDITS

ACKNOWLEDGMENTS

Recipe testers:
Nancy Blitzer, Paula Perlis, Maureen Haviland,
Denise Tillar Landis, Rodney Madden

Proofreaders:
Paula Perlis, Nancy Blitzer, David Shamah,
Lillian Wager Levy

Special thanks to my friends
chez Bernachon for sharing so much of their
knowledge and expertise, especially Raymond, a born
teacher,
and Alain, who uncomplainingly took
me under his wing.

Many thanks to the wonderful team of professionals who
produced the
exquisite photographs.
Photographer: Vincent Lee
Assistant: Eugene DeLucie
Food stylist: A. J. Battifarano
Assistant: Ellen Lucas
Prop stylist: Sara Barbaris

Editor: Maria D. Guarnaschelli,
who added her unmistakable signature
of excellence and quality

CONTENTS

CONTENTS

13

CONTENTS

LITTLE CAKES AND COOKIES

CONTENTS

15

CONTENTS

DESSERTS: MOUSSES, ICE CREAMS, SOUFFLÉS

CONFECTIONS: CHOCOLATE TRUFFLES AND CANDIES

CONTENTS

CHOCOLATE DRINKS

THE BASICS OF THE BERNACHON KITCHEN

19
CONTENTS

20
CONTENTS

DECORATIONS

If you could be a fly on the wall anyplace your imagination leads you, where would it be? For me it was chez Bernachon in Lyon, absorbing the tricks of the trade of France's most treasured *chocolatier*.

To visit a country without speaking the language is to remain with one foot in one's own. To enter into the world of Bernachon, however, required not only French but also the arcane languages of pastry and chocolate. I have never been more grateful for my knowledge of these special vocabularies, because it gave me a glimpse of baker's paradise, enabling me to gather gems of confectionary wisdom.

I am grateful to have had the opportunity to bring this jewel of a book to the American public because through it I fell in love—not only with Bernachon chocolate and the Bernachons' infinite variety of chocolate creations but also with the Bernachons themselves and their absolute dedication to excellence and quality. It has been my goal here to enable American home bakers to produce chocolate desserts and confections, in their kitchens, that are as close as humanly possible to the original Bernachon creations produced in a French commercial setting.

It was a great challenge, but the results were well worth the effort. While we may not have the glorious butter of Charentes or the pure heavy cream of Lyon, our high-protein flour makes it possible to produce a *pain chocolat* that is (dare I say?) perhaps even slightly superior to one made in France! And of course excellent bittersweet chocolate is available in this country (but one can also order Bernachon's own, directly from Lyon).

In this book I have presented myriad of Bernachon's special tips and secrets, such as aging the ganache for superior flavor, candying orange peels without the usual bitterness, baking ladyfingers on cardboard for maximum moistness. Intermingled are many of my own special techniques, which offer the same spectacular results as the sometimes more rarefied commercial methods but with greater speed and ease—such as making nougat in an electric mixer, melting chocolate in the microwave, making ganache and cream-puff pastry in a food processor.

The fine recipes in this book are the Bernachons', but the explanations and directions for the American kitchen are my contribution.

The title of this book, *A Passion for Chocolate (La Passion du Chocolat)*, perfectly describes the Bernachons. When one enters into this world of the artisan, perfumed by the pervasive aroma of rich bittersweet chocolate, one is surrounded by charm, order, camaraderie, and love of craft. Is it the nature of this delicious medium that makes everyone so cheerful, or is it the tone set by the Bernachons? Surely the two are inextricably involved.

Their world is a self-contained utopia, a labyrinth of separate but interconnected stations that produce virtually everything needed for their desserts, starting from the finest unroasted cocoa beans, through the candied fruits and preserves, ice creams and sorbets, fillings, frostings, cakes, pastries, cookies, up to the finished packaged cakes and confections. There is even a savory kitchen that prepares delicious lunches for all the workers and a few special items such as *quen-*

elles (a fish dumpling, a specialty of Lyon) for customers to purchase for take-out.

Maurice Bernachon is the essence of the Old World artisan, uncorrupted by modern time-saving devices that risk decreasing quality. He started his apprenticeship at age fourteen. Now seventy, he continues to work at the ovens every day of the week, from 6:00 A.M. until noon, rapidly making batters and controlling the placement of the baking pans with long wooden *palets*. His afternoons are spent in the office and boutique.

Never have I seen a person work with such sustained intensity and concentration, blending the attention of a beginner with the skill of long experience. I know that someday, when he is called to baker's heaven, one will hear him muttering, "In a minute; I have these two bowls of macaroons to pipe first!"

Bernachon's silvery mane has given him the name Lion of Lyon (*Lion de Lyon*), when he is not being called the king of chocolate. One sees immediately a man of great kindness and enormous integrity with a courteous disposition, the charm of sincerity, love of work, and devotion to excellence. Although he denies having ever actually "invented" anything, his creations are widely imitated throughout France.

Jean-Jacques Bernachon, Maurice's tall, dark-haired son and partner, has the demeanor of a responsible *patron*, which readily gives way to charming spontaneity and joie de vivre. When asked if the craft always interested him, he answered simply "yes," but his glowing eyes and proud smile told me in a minute that the passion is in him as well.

When he is not energetically shopping for the finest ingredients, directing the flow of activity, and surveying his efficiently run domain, Jean-Jacques is upstairs in his modern computerized office, collecting rare cookbooks and preserving antique chocolate labels which are often fine works of art. His marriage of over twenty years to the daughter of one of France's greatest chefs, Paul Bocuse, has resulted not only in two lovely daughters but in a joint business venture as well. The Bernachon-Bocuse boutique, a part of the Bernachon complex, offers special wines, *confits*, and other products with the Bocuse label.

The idea for this book was Jean-Jacques's inspiration. When asked about the poetic French names of his recipes, he shrugs with that famous Gallic nonchalance as if to say, "Nothing special—*c'est logique.*" And indeed they are. Most of the recipes are named the way French cheeses are, after the region that produces the ingredient that best characterizes them. Le Torino (the Turin): chestnuts; Le Sicilien (the Sicilian): pistachios; Le Corinthien (the Corinthian): raisins.

The Bernachon day begins at 6:00 A.M. The first person to arrive is always Monsieur Raymond, the head chocolate maker. The dipping of chocolate must take place in the very early cool hours of the day. Moments later Maurice arrives to tend his ovens. Jean-Jacques is already at the markets, searching out the best fruits for preserving and having a quick cup of coffee with Bocuse and other colleagues. Almost immediately the entire kitchen complex becomes the proverbial beehive of activity. During the busy seasons there are as many as fifty workers.

The croissants, brioches, and *petits pains au chocolat* must be baked by 7:00 A.M. for breakfast customers. Then a short break for all the workers, standing around the table laughing and dunking the fresh hot pastries into bowls of *café au lait*. After the break, the rest of the baking begins. By noon all the work is finished and much of it transferred to the boutique in front for purchase.

All workers have assigned stations, but Jean-Jacques supervises with a watchful eye—closing refrigerator doors after forgetful fledgling bakers, making sure things get rotated and don't burn in the ovens.

Each chef is respected king of his domain: Raymond, a superb *chocolatier* and teacher, supervises chocolate production. He has been with the Bernachons for nineteen years. He also works part-time as a professor at a nearby culinary institute. Several nim-

26

ble-fingered, good-natured Portuguese women work with him, preparing and dipping the vast varieties of chocolates. One, who divulged to me the secret of using the more sensitive back of the fingers to feel the temperature of chocolate, has worked alongside him for those nineteen years.

Michel is longtime chef of cake assembly and decoration; Thierry, chef of ice cream and sorbet; Roger, chef of pastry. Certain activities, however, such as the arrival of a shipment of ripe golden apricots or bright red sour cherries, require communal effort. Everyone with a free hand, including Jean-Jacques, cheerfully participates in the pitting process, still done individually with giant hairpins held in wine-cork bases. Nothing goes to waste; the pits are saved to weight down pastry shells. The fruits are preserved in huge copper vats, and then jarred and stored to be used during the rest of the year.

The manual preparation of nougat requires great strength, so it is consigned to the men. The process of pounding caramelized nuts into thin sheets provides the perfect outlet for any minor frustrations that arise even in the happiest of families. The moment the hot caramel and nut mixture is poured onto the marble slab, the signal is given and the men come running with their metal paddles to beat and flatten it vigorously before it cools, always with smiles of mad delight on their faces.

The uniform worn at Bernachon is the traditional French black and white checked pants. The workers wear blue work shirts, the chefs, including the Bernachons, white chef's jackets. All wear long white aprons, tied around the waist. The men wear low white baker's caps; the women, white cotton scarves tied neatly behind their heads. Of course the starchy white aprons quickly become streaked with chocolate. As Maurice Bernachon likes to say, shaking his head with mock regret and a twinkle in his eye, *"C'est un sale métier"* (It's a dirty profession)!

When I first arrived to work with the Bernachons, curious stares, indicating mild suspicion, followed me, an awkward stranger with a notebook, trying to be everywhere at once—to find out everything without intruding, but not yet moving in the rhythm of this harmoniously complex bakery ballet. Gradually my feet remembered where the tile floor sloped downward and I stopped stumbling and became a part of the flow of activity, learning when to ask and when to step quickly and silently out of the way. Eventually I even became bold enough to unselfconsciously grab an occasional truffle in passing. (Their dark tangy velvet centers were an ever-present temptation.)

By the end I felt *chez moi*—part of the family—nicknamed "La Petite" by Papa Bernachon. We were all friends and allies in this conspiracy to bring gustatorial joy and delight to those susceptible to it. I wanted it never to end. And because of the book it never will. It immortalizes our happy association. We hope that for you this book will be like having a part of the magically exquisite world of Bernachon chocolate in your own home—and that you will come soon to Lyon to be welcomed at its source.

INTRODUCTION

NOTES FROM ROSE

When chocolate is mixed with another ingredient or ingredients, as it is in most of the recipes in this book, it is easy and fun to use.

WORKING WITH CHOCOLATE

When chocolate is melted and not combined with another ingredient or ingredients, such as when making chocolate cigarettes and little chocolate cups, certain precautions must be taken:

- The room temperature should be between 65°F. and 70°F., and definitely not above 74°F. Humidity should be low and the room free of drafts. In conditions other than these, the chocolate may not set well and will develop bloom (a grayish streaking on the surface of the chocolate). If you wish to work with plain chocolate during the warmer months, use summer coating (also known as compound chocolate). It contains cocoa solids and sugar (as does real chocolate) but instead of cocoa butter, it contains vegetable shortening such as soya, palm kernel, or coconut oil. The flavor, however, is not as delicious.
- Chocolate, when melted, must never exceed 120°F. or flavor will be lost.

- Water—not even a drop in the form of steam—must never touch the chocolate or "seizing" will occur (the chocolate becomes stiff and unworkable). If this should occur, add fat, 1 tablespoon at a time, such as vegetable shortening, clarified butter, or cocoa butter, to help restore fluidity.
- The temperature of real chocolate (chocolate containing cocoa butter) must be controlled during melting. This is known as tempering. The methods recommended for the recipes in this book are simple but effective ones that involve either stirring unmelted chocolate into the melted chocolate until the proper temperature is reached or removing the chocolate from the heat source before the chocolate has fully melted and stirring until it is completely melted.
- Leftover chocolate can be re-melted many times, but to prevent graying and streaking, always add a few ounces of chocolate that has not been melted before (except, of course, during initial production).
- When the chocolate has set completely, it is usually firm enough to prevent finger marks from marring its surface. Chocolatiers, as an added precaution (especially if a room is not cool enough), sometimes wear white cotton gloves when working with the chocolate.

TYPES OF CHOCOLATE Any bittersweet or semisweet chocolate can be used interchangeably in all the recipes here that call for bittersweet chocolate. Lindt Excellence, which comes in 3-ounce bars, is the closest to the Bernachon chocolate, but by all means use the bittersweet or semisweet chocolate of your choice. What tastes good to you in the bar will taste the same in a ganache. If the texture is a little gritty in the bar, it will also feel that way even when mixed with heavy cream.

When couverture is called for to dip chocolate, I recommend Lindt Courante (available from Maid of Scandinavia, see Sources, page 382). If plain bittersweet or semisweet chocolate is used, the coating will be thicker. You can also achieve the same consistency by adding ½ teaspoon (.19 ounce/5.4 grams) cocoa butter (available from Maid of Scandinavia, see Sources, page 382) for every ounce of chocolate used.

Maestrani (Taam-Tov Food, Inc., page 382), a Swiss company, produces an excellent-quality kosher chocolate that is also parave (contains no dairy products).

Unsweetened Dutch-processed cocoa is the cocoa used by the Bernachons. Dutch-processed means that the cocoa has been treated with a mild alkali to mellow the flavor and make it more soluble (easy to dissolve). European cocoa is usually Dutch-processed, Hershey's and Nestle's are not. My favorite cocoa is Lindt's dark cocoa (available from Maid of Scandinavia, see Sources, page 382). Pernigotti (available from Williams-Sonoma, see Sources, page 382) is another favorite.

TYPES OF COCOA

The best way to store chocolate or cocoa is to keep it well wrapped in an airtight container (chocolate is quick to absorb other odors and must not be exposed to dampness) at a temperature of 60°F. to 75°F. with less than 50 percent relative humidity. Under these conditions dark chocolate should be keep well for at least two years. I have experienced chocolate stored at ideal conditions for several years and it seems to age like a fine wine, becoming more mellow and subtle. Milk chocolate keeps, even at optimum conditions, for only a little over one year, and white chocolate and summer coating, about one year.

STORING CHOCOLATE

European butter used for pastry has a higher butterfat content than most American brands. A new European-style butter, Plugra (containing 82 percent butterfat), has recently been produced by Hotel Bar Butter and is being distributed nationally. This butter is ideal for making puff pastry and croissants; it contributes an extraordinarily fresh butter flavor and a lighter, flakier texture.

WORKING WITH BUTTER

NOTES FROM ROSE

L'Aveline
(Very Rich Chocolate Cake:
Rum-Soaked Layer Cake of Chocolate
Génoise with Chocolate Hazelnut Filling and
Chocolate Glaze), page 51

Le Cinghalais
(Festive Cake Consisting of
Three Rum-Soaked Layers of Chocolate
Génoise Filled with Cinnamon Chocolate Ganache
and Praline Buttercream), page 67

Le Président
(Yellow Génoise Layer
Cake Filled with
Chocolate Ganache
and Brandied Cherries),
page 98

Les Truffes au Chocolat
(Chocolate Truffles),
page 265

Le Quatre-Quarts
au Chocolat
(Chocolate Pound Cake),
page 106

Le Saint-Honoré
au Chocolat
(Ring of Caramel- or
Chocolate-Glazed Cream
Puffs on Top of a
Circle of Pie Pastry,
Filled with Chocolate
Pastry Cream), page 109

Le Sévillan
(Square Layers of Yellow Génoise
with a Chocolate Filling and Frosting and an
Encasement of Hazelnuts), page 114

Le Sicilien
(Layers of Chocolate Génoise Between
Pistachio Buttercream), page 119

Le Succès
(Almond Meringue Layer Cake
Filled with Chocolate Ganache and
Dusted with Cocoa), page 125

Les Éclairs au Chocolat
(Chocolate Éclairs), page 161

Les Brownies
(Chocolate Brownies with Moist and
Chewy Centers), page 135

Les Petit Pains au Chocolat
(Little Croissant Rectangles Filled with
Bittersweet Chocolate), page 142

Les Madeleines
au Chocolat
(Little Chocolate Sponge
Cakes Shaped Like
Shells), page 159

Les Écorces d'Oranges
Confites Enrobés de
Chocolat
(Candied Orange Peel
Dipped in Chocolate),
page 248

From foreground:
Le Rochers San Antonio
(Chocolate Almond Meringues), page 197,
Les Figues (Little Sponge Cakes Filled with Chocolate
Pastry Cream, in the Shape of Figs), page 147 ,
Les Massepains au Chocolat
(Almond-Cocoa Meringues Filled with Ganache), page 192,
Les Florentins (Thin Orange-and-Citron-Infused Butter Cookies
Coated with Bittersweet Chocolate), page 204,
Les Tuiles au Chocolat (Thin Orange-Chocolate Butter
Cookies in the Shape of Roof Tiles), page 207

Les Poires Belle-Hélène
(Poached Peares Surrounded
by Vanilla Ice Cream
and Chocolate Sauce),
page 224

Les Nougats au Chocolat
(Chocolate Nougat),
page 252

Le Dauphin au Chocolat
(Soft Cocoa-Flavored Ice Cream), page 231

Les Palets d'Or
(Gold-Flecked Chocolate Coins), page 262

Les Marthas
(Little Chocolate Cups Filled with Leftover
Cakes and Creams), page 210

Fruits d'Automne
(Chocolate Candies with Chestnut Buttercream Centers
and a Coating of Marzipan), page 272

SPECIAL NOTE ON WEIGHTS AND MEASURES

Do not expect the mathematics of the metric system to correlate exactly with the avoirdupois system. The grams have been rounded off to the nearest whole number without decimal point (except for leavening, which needs to be more precise) whereas the ounces have been rounded off to the nearest quarter ounce.

MEASURING DRY INGREDIENTS

Dry ingredients should be measured in a cup with an unbroken top (no spout) designed for solids. I prefer the Foley stainless-steel set of measuring cups and spoons and the Tupperware plastic ones. (The 2-tablespoon Foley cup, however, measures less than it should.) Other measuring cups may vary in size and are generally less reliable.

The *dip and sweep* method of measuring refers to dipping the measuring cup into a bin containing the ingredient and sweeping off the excess with a long flat spatula or knife.

Sifted means that the ingredient is sifted into a cup that is sitting on a counter. The cup is never touched or shaken. Only the handle is held when the excess is swept off with a spatula or knife.

MEASURING LIQUID INGREDIENTS Liquid ingredients, including corn syrup, should be measured in a liquid measure with a spout. There is a difference in volume between liquid and solid measuring cups. The most accurate liquid measure at the present time is made by Oven Basics. One cup of water weighs exactly 8.337 ounces/236.35 grams, which is the dictionary definition of an 8-ounce cup of water. Many other brands are off by quite a bit, and the marks are not level. The measure of the liquid should be read at eye level, below the meniscus (the curved upper surface of the liquid).

SPECIAL NOTE ON WEIGHTS AND MEASURES

GRAND CAKES

L'AMANDON

ALMOND MERINGUE LAYER CAKE
WITH CHOCOLATE BUTTERCREAM FILLING AND A
GLAZE OF BITTERSWEET CHOCOLATE
AND HONEYED ALMONDS

SERVES 8 TO 10

This classic recipe consists of a slightly chewy but tender, cake-like almond meringue, fragrant with almonds and not overly sweet. The silky chocolate buttercream features pastry cream as its base. The cake's texture will be at its tenderest if prepared at least one day ahead.

COMPONENTS
Succès • *Chocolate Buttercream* •
Chopped Honeyed Almonds

DECORATION
Glaze of bittersweet chocolate (3 ounces/85 grams) *
Whole Honeyed Almonds

INGREDIENTS	MEASURE	WEIGHT	
	VOLUME	OUNCES	GRAMS
sliced blanched almonds	2 cups	6.25 ounces	180 grams
superfine sugar	¾ cup + 2 tablespoons	6.25 ounces	180 grams
7 large egg whites, room temperature	7 fluid ounces	7.25 ounces	210 grams
cream of tartar	1 teaspoon		3 grams

Two 17 by 12-inch baking sheets, buttered and floured or lined with parchment, marked with three 8-inch circles.

Preheat the oven to 350°F.

In a food processor, combine the almonds and ¾ cup sugar and process until the almonds are finely grated.

In a mixing bowl beat the egg whites until foamy, add the cream of tartar, and beat until soft peaks form when the beater is raised slowly. Gradually add the remaining 2 tablespoons sugar, beating until stiff peaks form when the beater is raised slowly.

Fold in the grated almond mixture.

Using a 1-gallon zip-seal bag with one corner cut off or a pastry bag fitted with a large plain number 6 (½-inch) tip, pipe the batter onto the prepared baking sheets to form three 8-inch circles, starting at the outer perimeter and spiraling inward toward the center. Using a small metal spatula, fill in any gaps with leftover batter and smooth the surface. Bake for 15 to 20 minutes, or just until the discs begin to brown. Remove baking sheets to a rack. Loosen the succès from the sheets and allow them to cool completely on the sheets before transferring to a work surface or serving plate. They will have expanded to about 9 inches.

To obtain a perfect circle, invert a cake pan over each succès and trim any excess with a sharp knife.

The almond meringue layers are called succès. They are similar to meringue except that half the sugar (by weight) is replaced with nuts. The result is a delicious nutty flavor and a soft but slightly chewy texture. Unlike meringue, succès is neither crisp nor very sweet. Use superfine sugar for best texture. It is not actually necessary to use flour on the baking pan to keep it from sticking; however, the flour does have the desirable effect of keeping the succès from spreading.

(Recipe makes three discs. Freeze one well wrapped, up to 2 months, for future use.)

CHOCOLATE BUTTERCREAM

INGREDIENTS	MEASURE	WEIGHT	
	VOLUME	OUNCES	GRAMS
milk	2½ *cups*	21.25 *ounces*	605 *grams*
1 vanilla bean, * **split**			
salt	¾ *teaspoon*		5 *grams*
5 large egg yolks	3 *fluid ounces*	3.25 *ounces*	93 *grams*
superfine sugar	¾ *cup*	5.25 *ounces*	150 *grams*
all-purpose flour	½ *cup (dip and sweep)*	2.5 *ounces*	70 *grams*
bittersweet chocolate, chopped	½ (3-ounce) *bar*	1.5 *ounces*	43 *grams*
unsalted butter, softened	⅓ *cup*	2.5 *ounces*	75 *grams*

*You may substitute 1 teaspoon vanilla extract for the vanilla bean, but the bean offers a fuller, more aromatic flavor. If you are using extract, add it after the buttercream has cooled. If using a Tahitian bean, use only ½ bean.

In a saucepan, place 2 cups of the milk, the vanilla bean, and the salt. Bring it to a full boil, and remove it from the heat.

In a medium bowl, whisk together the egg yolks and sugar until thoroughly combined. Whisk in the flour, and then the remaining ½ cup of cold milk (to prevent curdling). Whisking constantly, gradually add the hot milk mixture. Return the mixture to the saucepan and bring to a boil, whisking constantly. Simmer for 3 minutes, whisking constantly. Remove from the heat and add the chocolate. Stir gently until completely melted and smooth.

Transfer to a bowl, press plastic wrap directly onto the surface of the pastry cream (to prevent a skin from forming), and cool unrefrigerated. In a small bowl, mash the butter with a fork to ensure that it is soft and creamy. Remove the vanilla bean, and when the cream is almost cold, gently whisk in the butter until smooth. Return plastic to the surface. Allow to cool. Store refrigerated.

NOTE   Pastry cream must not be cold when butter is added or it will separate. If separation should occur, warm the bottom of the bowl over hot water for 2 to 3 seconds before continuing to beat. Overbeating will also cause cream to break down.

HONEYED ALMONDS

INGREDIENTS	MEASURE	WEIGHT	
	VOLUME	OUNCES	GRAMS
water	1¼ cups	10.5 ounces	295 grams
sugar	1 cup	7 ounces	200 grams
½ vanilla bean, split			
honey	2 teaspoons	0.5 ounces	14 grams
sliced blanched almonds	1 cup	3 ounces	85 grams

A greased baking sheet.

Preheat oven to 400°F.

In a large saucepan, combine the water, sugar, vanilla bean, and honey. Bring it to a boil, stirring constantly.

Stir in the almonds and let boil undisturbed for 3 minutes.

Using a strainer, drain the almonds, discarding the syrup. Also, discard the vanilla bean or rinse it, allow it to dry, and reserve it for another use. Place the almonds in one layer on the baking sheet and bake, gently stirring them occasionally, for 6 to 10 minutes, or until golden in color. Cool. Stored in an airtight container, they will keep for several weeks at room temperature, several months refrigerated.

Reserve ⅓ cup of the almonds for decoration and coarsely chop the remainder.

ASSEMBLING THE CAKE

Place one disc of succès on a cardboard round or serving plate, and top with the chocolate buttercream. Sprinkle with the chopped honeyed almonds, and place the second disc on top, flat side up. Refrigerate for at least 1 hour.

Break the remaining 3 ounces/85 grams chocolate into squares and place in the top of a double boiler set over very hot water (but no hotter than 160°F.). The water must not simmer or touch the bottom of the double boiler insert.

Stir until the chocolate begins to melt. Return it to low heat if the water cools, but be careful that it does not get too hot. Stir 10 minutes, or until almost smooth. (The chocolate may be melted in a microwave oven if stirred every 15 seconds.) Using either method, remove from the heat source before fully melted and stir, using residual heat to complete the melting. Pour immediately on top of the succès, spreading evenly with a metal spatula.

Garnish with the ⅓ cup of honeyed whole almonds.

Use a heated knife to score the surface of the chocolate glaze (this will keep it from cracking). The knife can be heated by running it under hot water. Slice with a serrated knife.

TO SERVE

1 week refrigerated. Remove from the refrigerator at least 1 hour before serving.

KEEPS

L'ANTILLAIS

ALMOND MERINGUE LAYER CAKE WITH HAZELNUT RUM GANACHE AND RUM-SOAKED RAISINS

SERVES 8 TO 10

Rum-flavored ganache gives this lovely cake its name—rum comes from the Antilles islands in the West Indies. The cake is at its most tender texture if prepared at least 1 day ahead.

COMPONENTS
Succès • *Antilles Ganache* • *Raisins soaked in dark rum*

DECORATION
Optional glaze of bittersweet chocolate
(3 ounces/85 grams)

RAISINS

INGREDIENTS	MEASURE	WEIGHT	
	VOLUME	OUNCES	GRAMS
raisins soaked in dark rum (optional)	*2 tablespoons*	*1 ounce*	*28 grams*

At least 2 hours and up to 24 hours ahead, place the raisins in a small bowl and pour in enough rum to cover. Cover tightly with plastic wrap and set aside.

SUCCÈS

INGREDIENTS	MEASURE	WEIGHT	
	VOLUME	OUNCES	GRAMS
sliced blanched almonds	*2 cups*	*6.25 ounces*	*180 grams*
superfine sugar	*¾ cup + 2 tablespoons*	*6.25 ounces*	*180 grams*
7 large egg whites, room temperature	*7 fluid ounces*	*7.25 ounces*	*210 grams*
cream of tartar	*1 teaspoon*		*3 grams*

Two 17 by 12-inch baking sheets, buttered and floured or lined with parchment, marked with three 8-inch circles.

Preheat the oven to 350°F.

In a food processor, place the almonds and ¾ cup sugar and process until the almonds are finely grated.

In a mixing bowl beat the egg whites until foamy, add the cream of tartar, and beat until soft peaks form when the beater is raised slowly. Gradually beat in the remaining 2 tablespoons sugar until stiff peaks form when the beater is raised slowly. Fold in the grated almond mixture.

Using a 1-gallon zip-seal bag with one corner cut off, or a pastry bag, fitted with a large plain number 6 (½-inch) tip, pipe the batter onto the prepared baking sheets to form three 8-inch circles, starting with the outer perimeter and spiraling inward toward the center. Use a small metal spatula to fill in any gaps with leftover batter and to smooth the surface. Bake for 15 to 20 minutes, or just until the discs begin to brown. Remove baking sheets to racks. Loosen the succès from the sheets and allow them to cool completely on the sheets before transferring to a work surface or serving plate. They will have expanded to about 9 inches.

To obtain a perfect circle, invert a cake pan over each succès and trim any excess with a sharp knife.

NOTE FROM ROSE

Use superfine sugar for the best texture. It is not actually necessary to use flour on the baking pan to keep it from sticking; however, the flour does have the desirable effect of keeping the succès from spreading.

(Recipe makes three discs. Freeze one well wrapped, up to 2 months, for future use.)

ANTILLES GANACHE

INGREDIENTS	MEASURE	WEIGHT	
	VOLUME	OUNCES	GRAMS
hazelnuts	1 ¼ *cups*	6 *ounces*	170 *grams*
baking soda	¼ *cup*	2 *ounces*	60 *grams*
bittersweet chocolate	5 *(3-ounce) bars*	15 *ounces*	425 *grams*
heavy cream	1 *liquid cup*	8 *ounces*	232 *grams*
dark rum	¼ *cup*	2 *ounces*	55 *grams*

BLANCH THE HAZELNUTS

In a medium saucepan, place 3 cups of water and bring it to a boil. Add the nuts and the baking soda and boil for 3 minutes. Test a nut by running it under cold water. If the skin is not easy to remove with slight pressure from your fingers, return to the heat for a minute or so more. Drain well. Peel the nuts.

Toast the hazelnuts in a 350°F. oven for 10 to 15 minutes or until golden brown. Cool completely and chop fine, but not powder-fine. (Use the medium grater on a food processor and then pulse with the metal blade.) Set aside.

Break the chocolate into pieces and process in a food processor until very fine.

Heat the cream to the boiling point, and with the motor running, pour it through the feed tube in a steady stream. Process a few seconds until smooth. Cool slightly before adding the rum and the hazelnuts. Pulse just to combine. Transfer to a bowl and cool uncovered for several hours, until it reaches frosting consistency. In cool weather, ganache can remain unrefrigerated for at least 3 days or as long as 2 weeks. At room temperature it remains spreadable.

ASSEMBLING THE CAKE

Place one disc of succès on a cardboard round or serving plate, and cover it with an even layer of about two thirds of the ganache. Sprinkle with the drained raisins. Place the second disc on top, flat side up. Refrigerate for at least 1 hour or up to 4 hours. With a long metal spatula, spread the remaining ganache evenly on top of the succès, and set aside.

If you are glazing the cake, break the chocolate into squares and place them in the top of a double boiler set over very hot water (but no hotter than 160°F.). The water must not simmer or touch the bottom of the double boiler insert.

Stir until the chocolate begins to melt. Return the pan to low heat if the water cools, but be careful that it does not get too hot. Stir 10 minutes, or until smooth. (The chocolate may be melted in a microwave oven if stirred every 15 seconds.) Using either method, remove from the heat source before fully melted and stir, using residual heat to complete the melting. Allow the chocolate to cool until tepid, and pour at once onto the ganache, spreading it evenly with a long metal spatula.

TO SERVE

Use a heated knife to score the surface of the chocolate glaze (this will keep it from cracking). The knife can be heated by running it under hot water. Slice with a serrated knife.

KEEPS

Airtight, 1 week refrigerated. Remove from the refrigerator at least 1 hour before serving.

NOTE FROM ROSE

The Bernachons like to make this cake in the autumn and winter because the assertive rum and chocolate flavors are more appropriate with heavier, cool-weather food.

L'ARLEQUIN AU CHOCOLAT

LARGE CIRCLE OF CREAM-PUFF PASTRY FILLED WITH CHOCOLATE PASTRY CREAM AND CHOCOLATE WHIPPED CREAM, DUSTED WITH COCOA AND POWDERED SUGAR

SERVES 8 TO 10

This is the Bernachon version of the famous French dessert called the Paris-Brest. The Bernachons have given it the fanciful name in deference to its crown shape (a harlequin wears a crown).

The Bernachons' recipe for cream-puff pastry has less milk and butter than most, and more egg, which makes it both full-flavored and crisper. They offer this spectacular dessert in winter.

COMPONENTS
*Cream-Puff Pastry • Chocolate Pastry Cream •
Chocolate Whipped Cream*

DECORATION
Powdered sugar and cocoa

CREAM-PUFF PASTRY

INGREDIENTS	MEASURE	WEIGHT	
	VOLUME	OUNCES	GRAMS
milk	⅔ cup	5.5 ounces	160 grams
unsalted butter, room temperature	5 tablespoons	2.5 ounces	71 grams
sugar	1½ teaspoons		7 grams
salt	½ teaspoon		
all-purpose flour	1 cup (lightly spooned)	4.25 ounces	121 grams
5 large eggs	1 liquid cup	10 ounces	284 grams (weighed in the shells)
1 large egg for glaze, lightly beaten			
slivered almonds	scant ½ cup	1.75 ounces	50 grams

One 17 by 12-inch baking sheet, lined with parchment or greased.

Preheat the oven to 400°F.

In a medium saucepan, combine the milk, butter, sugar, and salt, and bring the mixture to a full rolling boil. Remove it immediately from the heat, and add the flour all at once. Stir with a wooden spoon until the mixture forms a ball, leaves the sides of the pan, and clings slightly to the spoon. Return it to low heat and cook, stirring and mashing continuously, for about 3 minutes (to cook the flour). Without scraping the pan, transfer the mixture to the bowl of a food processor fitted with the metal blade.

Process 15 seconds with the feed tube open (to allow steam to escape). With the motor running, pour in the eggs and continue processing for 30 seconds. The mixture should be smooth, shiny, and too soft to hold peaks. (If using an electric mixer, allow the flour mixture to cool for 5 minutes in the bowl. Then beat in the eggs, one at a time, beating after each addition until incorporated.)

If you are using parchment, place a small dot of cream-puff pastry at each corner to attach it to the baking sheet.

47

GRAND CAKES

Spoon the batter into a large ring, about 9 inches in diameter, on the baking sheet. Bake 45 minutes. Remove the pastry from the oven and brush immediately with the beaten egg. Place the almonds on top, and return it to the oven for about 5 minutes or until the almonds and the ring are a deep golden brown.

Use a long metal spatula or knife to dislodge the pastry ring and two pancake turners to lift it onto the rack; cool completely. If you are not using the ring right away, it can be stored in an airtight plastic bag up to 1 week refrigerated, 6 months frozen. Recrisp it in a warm oven, then cool and fill it before serving.

NOTE   To keep the pastry from falling, do not open the oven door until shortly before the end of the baking time.

CHOCOLATE PASTRY CREAM

INGREDIENTS	MEASURE	WEIGHT	
	VOLUME	OUNCES	GRAMS
milk	2 ½ cups	21.25 ounces	605 grams
1 vanilla bean, split *			
salt	¾ teaspoon		5 grams
5 large egg yolks	3 liquid ounces	3.25 ounces	92 grams
superfine sugar	¾ cup	5.25 ounces	150 grams
all-purpose flour	⅓ cup (dip and sweep)	1.75 ounces	50 grams
bittersweet chocolate, coarsely chopped	½ (3-ounce) bar	1.5 ounces	43 grams

*You may substitute 1 teaspoon vanilla extract for the vanilla bean, but the bean offers a fuller, more aromatic flavor. If you are using extract, add it after the pastry cream has cooled. If using a Tahitian bean, use only ½ bean.

In a saucepan, place 2 cups of the milk, the vanilla bean, and the salt. Bring to a full boil, and remove the pan from the heat.

In a medium bowl, whisk together the egg yolks and sugar until thoroughly combined. Whisk in the flour, and then the remaining ½ cup of cold milk (to

prevent curdling). Whisking constantly, gradually add the hot milk.

Return the mixture to the saucepan and bring it to a boil, whisking constantly. Simmer for 3 minutes, whisking constantly. Remove from the heat and add the chocolate. Stir gently until completely melted and smooth.

Transfer the mixture to a bowl, press plastic wrap directly onto the surface of the pastry cream (to prevent a skin from forming), and cool. Remove the vanilla bean and return the plastic to the surface.

Airtight, 5 days refrigerated.　　　　　　　**KEEPS**

CHOCOLATE WHIPPED CREAM

INGREDIENTS	MEASURE	WEIGHT	
	VOLUME	OUNCES	GRAMS
heavy cream	*2 cups*	*16.25 ounces*	*464 grams*
unsweetened cocoa	*½ cup (lightly spooned)*	*1.75 ounces*	*50 grams*
superfine sugar	*⅔ cup*	*4.5 ounces*	*132 grams*
vanilla	*1 teaspoon*		*4 grams*

In a large mixing bowl place all the ingredients and refrigerate for at least 1 hour (to dissolve the cocoa). (Chill beater alongside bowl.)

Beat until stiff peaks form when the beater is raised. Keep chilled until ready to use.

With a serrated knife, cut the crown in half horizontally. Using a large spoon or a pastry bag fitted with a large tube, spread the pastry cream onto the bottom half of the pastry.　　**ASSEMBLING THE CAKE**

Fit a large pastry bag with a large star tube, fill it with the chocolate whipped cream, and pipe it over the pastry cream.

Place the upper half of the pastry crown gently on top. Dust first with a few tablespoons of powdered sugar and then with a few tablespoons of cocoa.

To facilitate cutting, and to avoid squashing the piped cream fillings, cut the upper part of the crown into servings before placing it on top. This will be hidden by the powdered sugar.

This impressive dessert is a party favorite. Those who have loved it in its classic vanilla version will adore this chocolate one.

L'AVELINE

Very Rich Chocolate Cake: Rum-Soaked Layer Cake of Chocolate Génoise with Chocolate Hazelnut Filling and Chocolate Glaze

SERVES 8 TO 10

This glorious Bernachon classic is widely copied throughout France. It is named after the Avellino region near Naples, in Italy, which produces some of the world's finest hazelnuts. The dense, moist, chocolate intensity of this cake would please the most hopeless of chocaholics.

This is the cake to make when you want to

impress, impress, impress!

COMPONENTS
Chocolate Génoise • *Rum Syrup* • *Président Ganache*

DECORATION
Optional glaze of bittersweet chocolate
(9 ounces/255 grams); 20 toasted blanched hazelnuts
(6 ounces/170 grams)

CHOCOLATE GÉNOISE

INGREDIENTS	MEASURE	WEIGHT	
	VOLUME	OUNCES	GRAMS
unsalted butter	*2 tablespoons*	*1 ounce*	*30 grams*
vanilla	*1 teaspoon*		*4 grams*
4 large eggs	*¾ liquid cup*	*8 ounces*	*227 grams*
		(weighed in the shell)	
superfine sugar	*½ cup*	*3.5 ounces*	*100 grams*
honey (optional)	*2 teaspoons*	*0.5 ounce*	*14 grams*
sifted cake flour	*1 cup*	*3.5 ounces*	*100 grams*
unsweetened cocoa	*3 tablespoons*	*0.5 ounce*	*18 grams*

One 9 by 5 by 3-inch (8-cup) loaf pan, greased, bottom lined with parchment or wax paper, then greased again and floured.

Preheat the oven to 400°F.

In a small saucepan, melt the butter, and add the vanilla. Set aside to keep warm.

In a large mixing bowl set over a pan of simmering water, heat the eggs, sugar, and optional honey for extra moistness, until just lukewarm, stirring constantly to prevent curdling. (The eggs may also be heated by placing them *still in their shells* in a large mixing bowl in an oven with a pilot light for 3 hours or up to overnight.) Using the whisk attachment, beat the mixture on high speed for 5 minutes or until tripled in volume. (A hand beater may be used, but it will be necessary to beat for at least 10 minutes.)

While the eggs are beating, sift together the flour and cocoa.

Remove 1 cup of the egg mixture and thoroughly whisk it into the warm melted butter.

Sift half the flour mixture over the remaining egg mixture, and fold it in *gently* but rapidly with a large balloon whisk, slotted skimmer, or rubber spatula until almost all the flour has disappeared. Repeat with the remaining flour, folding just until the flour has disappeared completely. Fold in the butter mixture until just incorporated.

Pour immediately into the prepared pan, and bake 20 to 30 minutes or until the cake has started to shrink slightly from the sides of the pan. (No need for a cake tester. Once the sides shrink, the cake is done.) Avoid opening the oven door before the minimum time or the cake could fall. Toward the end of the baking time, open the door slightly, and if at a quick glance the cake does not appear done, close the door at once and check again in 5 minutes.

Loosen the side of the cake with a small metal spatula and unmold at once onto a lightly greased rack. Reinvert to cool.

Génoise cuts more easily when made ahead and **NOTE** chilled.

RUM SYRUP

INGREDIENTS	MEASURE	WEIGHT	
	VOLUME	OUNCES	GRAMS
water	*3 fluid ounces (¼ cup + 2 tablespoons)*	*3 ounces*	*90 grams*
sugar	*¼ cup + 3 tablespoons*	*3 ounces*	*90 grams*
dark rum	*3 fluid ounces (¼ cup + 2 tablespoons)*	*3 ounces*	*90 grams*

In a small saucepan with a tight-fitting lid, bring the water and sugar to a rolling boil, stirring constantly. Cover immediately, remove from the heat, and allow to cool completely. Stir in the rum. Store, airtight, refrigerated, up to 1 month.

PRÉSIDENT GANACHE

INGREDIENTS	MEASURE	WEIGHT	
	VOLUME	OUNCES	GRAMS
hazelnuts	*1¾ cups*	*8.5 ounces*	*241 grams*
baking soda	*¼ cup*	*2 ounces*	*60 grams*
bittersweet chocolate	*5⅔ (3-ounce) bars*	*17 ounces*	*482 grams*
crème fraîche (page 348) or heavy cream*	*2 cups*	*16 ounces*	*464 grams*

*The crème fraîche imparts a pleasing tang.

BLANCH THE HAZELNUTS In a medium saucepan, place 3 cups of water and bring it to a boil. Add the nuts and the baking soda, and boil for 3 minutes. Test a nut by running it under cold water. If the skin is not easy to remove with slight pressure from your fingers, return to the heat for a minute or so more. (*Note:* If you are also using hazelnuts for decoration, blanch, peel, and toast them along with the rest and reserve.) Drain well. Peel.

Toast the hazelnuts in a 350°F. oven for 10 to 15 minutes or until golden brown. Cool completely and chop fine, but not powder-fine. (Use the medium grater on a food processor and then pulse with the metal blade.) Set aside.

Break the chocolate into pieces and process in a food processor until very fine. Heat the cream to the boiling point, and with the motor running, pour it through the feed tube in a steady stream. Process a few seconds until smooth. Add the hazelnuts and pulse just to combine. Transfer to a bowl and cool for several hours, until frosting consistency.

ASSEMBLING THE CAKE Trim the bottom and top crusts of the génoise.

With a serrated knife, cut the génoise horizontally into four layers. Spread a little ganache on a cardboard rectangle cut slightly larger than the cake. Using a straight-sided cookie sheet or pancake turners, lift the widest layer onto the cardboard. Sprinkle with one

A PASSION FOR CHOCOLATE

fourth the syrup, and spread with about ¾ cup of the ganache. Continue in the same way with the remaining layers. Refrigerate for 1 hour.

Use the remaining ganache to frost the entire cake. Allow it to rest at room temperature for at least 1 hour before glazing.

TO GLAZE Place the cake on a rack set over a cookie sheet (to catch the dripping chocolate).

Break the chocolate into squares and place them in the top of a double boiler set over very hot water (but no hotter than 160°F.). The water must not simmer or touch the bottom of the double boiler insert.

Stir until the chocolate begins to melt. Return it to low heat if the water cools, but be careful that it does not get too hot. (The chocolate may be melted in a microwave oven if stirred every 15 seconds.) Using either method, remove it from the heat source before fully melted and stir, using the residual heat to complete the melting. Allow the chocolate to cool just until tepid, then pour it over the cake, spreading it quickly and evenly with a metal spatula. If any spots on the sides remain unglazed, use a small metal spatula to lift up some glaze that has fallen onto the baking sheet and apply it to the uncovered area.

Lift the rack and tap it lightly on the counter to settle the glaze (and remove the excess). Using a broad spatula or pancake turner, lift the cake from the rack and set it on a serving plate. (Glaze dulls if refrigerated.)

TO SERVE Use a heated knife to score the surface of the chocolate glaze (this will keep it from cracking). The knife can be heated by running it under hot water. Slice with a serrated knife or a sharp knife dipped in hot water. If desired, garnish with whole hazelnuts.

NOTE FROM ROSE The Bernachons traditionally use the Ganache Président for this cake, but they sometimes vary it, as in the color photograph, by preparing a second contrasting recipe of Praline Buttercream. Add one tablespoon of praline paste, available in specialty stores, to ¾ cup buttercream, and use it in place of the ganache for one of the layers. If the praline paste is very thick, it is best to soften it by beating it with a tablespoon of softened butter, as overbeating will thin out the buttercream.

KEEPS Airtight, 5 days refrigerated, but it's best not to glaze until serving day. Remove from the refrigerator at least 1 hour before serving.

A PASSION FOR CHOCOLATE

LA BÛCHE DE NOËL

ROLLED YELLOW GÉNOISE
FILLED WITH CHOCOLATE PASTRY CREAM

SERVES 16

It wouldn't be Christmas in France without the classic yule log. This delicious rendition features ganache for the "bark" and a mixture of ganache and pastry cream for the filling. For an enchanting presentation, garnish the log with little marzipan mushrooms and figures available in specialty stores at Christmastime.

COMPONENTS
Génoise • *Dark rum (optional, ⅓ cup)* • *Ganache* • *Pastry Cream*

GÉNOISE

INGREDIENTS	MEASURE	WEIGHT	
ROOM TEMPERATURE	VOLUME	OUNCES	GRAMS
unsalted butter	*3 tablespoons*	*1.5 ounces*	*40 grams*
vanilla	*1 teaspoon*		*4 grams*
4 extra-large eggs	*7 fluid ounces*	*9 ounces*	*260 grams (weighed in the shells)*
superfine sugar	*½ cup + 1 tablespoon*	*4 ounces*	*114 grams*
honey (optional)	*2 teaspoons*	*0.5 ounce*	*14 grams*
sifted cake flour	*1⅓ cups*	*4.5 ounces*	*130 grams*

One 17 by 12-inch jelly-roll pan, greased, bottom lined with parchment or foil (extending slightly over the sides), and then greased again and floured.

Preheat the oven to 400°F.

In a small saucepan, melt the butter and add the vanilla. Set aside to keep warm.

In a large mixing bowl set over a pan of simmering water, heat the eggs, sugar, and optional honey for extra moistness, until just lukewarm, stirring constantly to prevent curdling. (The eggs may also be heated by placing them *still in their shells* in a large mixing bowl in an oven with a pilot light for 3 hours or up to overnight.) Using the whisk attachment, beat the mixture on high speed for 5 minutes or until tripled in volume. (A hand beater may be used, but it will be necessary to beat for at least 10 minutes.)

Remove 1 cup of the egg mixture and thoroughly whisk it into the warm melted butter.

Sift half the flour over the remaining egg mixture, and fold it in *gently* but rapidly with a large balloon whisk, slotted skimmer, or rubber spatula until almost all the flour has disappeared. Repeat with the remaining flour, folding just until the flour has disappeared completely. Fold in the butter mixture until just incorporated.

Pour immediately into the prepared pan, and bake 10 minutes or until the cake is golden brown.

As soon as the cake is done, loosen the sides of the cake with a small metal spatula, and unmold at once onto a clean towel which has been lightly sprinkled with powdered sugar. Starting from one long edge, roll the cake, towel and all, and allow to cool completely.

GANACHE

INGREDIENTS	MEASURE	WEIGHT	
	VOLUME	POUNDS/OUNCES	GRAMS
bittersweet chocolate	*9 (3-ounce) bars*	*1 pound 11 ounces*	*765 grams*
crème fraîche (page 348) or heavy cream	*2¾ cups*	*1 pound 6 ounces*	*638 grams*

Break the chocolate into pieces and process in a food processor until very fine.

Heat the crème fraîche or heavy cream to the boiling point, and with the motor running, pour it through the feed tube in a steady stream. Process a few seconds until smooth. Transfer to a bowl and cool for several hours, until frosting consistency. In cool weather ganache can remain unrefrigerated for at least 3 days or as long as 2 weeks. At room temperature it remains spreadable.

PASTRY CREAM

INGREDIENTS	MEASURE	WEIGHT	
	VOLUME	POUNDS/OUNCES	GRAMS
milk	*2½ cups*	*1 pound 5.25 ounces*	*605 grams*
1 vanilla bean, split *			
salt	*¾ teaspoon*		*5 grams*
5 large egg yolks	*3 fluid ounces*	*3.25 ounces*	*93 grams*
superfine sugar	*¾ cup*	*5.25 ounces*	*150 grams*
all-purpose flour	*⅓ cup (dip and sweep)*	*1.75 ounces*	*50 grams*

*You may substitute 1 teaspoon vanilla extract for the vanilla bean, but the bean offers a fuller, more aromatic flavor. If you are using extract, add it after the pastry cream has cooled. If using a Tahitian bean, use only ½ bean.

In a saucepan, place 2 cups of the milk, the vanilla bean, and the salt. Bring to a full boil, then remove it from the heat.

In a medium bowl, whisk together the egg yolks and sugar until thoroughly combined. Whisk in the flour, and then the remaining ½ cup of cold milk (to prevent curdling). Whisking constantly, gradually add the hot milk.

Return the mixture to the saucepan and bring to a boil, whisking constantly. Simmer for 3 minutes, whisking constantly.

Transfer the mixture to a bowl, press plastic wrap directly onto the surface of the pastry cream to prevent a skin from forming, and cool. Store refrigerated up to 5 days. Remove the vanilla bean before serving.

ASSEMBLING THE CAKE Gently unroll the génoise, and sprinkle it with the rum if you are using it.

Stir one third of the ganache into the pastry cream. Spread it evenly over the génoise, and roll it tightly from the long end, using the towel to help begin the roll. Wrap the rolled cake in aluminum foil, and refrigerate for 1 hour to firm.

Use a sharp knife dipped into hot water to cut the ends of the roll on an angle. Place these cut sections on top of the roll to simulate knots on a log. Use a long metal spatula to frost the entire roll with the remaining ganache. The tines of a fork are perfect for creating the appearance of bark. Make circular marks in the frosting covering the cut ends to resemble the rings of a log. Refrigerate until shortly before serving.

TO SERVE Use a serrated knife or a sharp knife dipped in hot water.

NOTE An orange syrup may be used instead of rum: Heat 2 tablespoons of sugar with ¼ cup freshly squeezed orange juice until the sugar dissolves.

KEEPS Airtight, 5 days refrigerated. Remove at least 1 hour before serving.

A PASSION FOR CHOCOLATE

LE CARAQUE

ELEGANT CAKE CONSISTING OF THREE
CHERRY-SOAKED LAYERS OF CHOCOLATE GÉNOISE
WITH PRALINE BUTTERCREAM FILLING
AND CHOCOLATE FROSTING

SERVES 8 TO 10

This lovely cake combines the flavors of chocolate, cherry, and

hazelnut. Its name honors Caracas, where great-tasting,

high-quality cocoa is produced.

COMPONENTS
Chocolate Génoise • *Cherry Syrup* •
Praline Buttercream

DECORATION
Ganache piping, chocolate petals
(page 371) or curls (page 367), or gold leaf (page 381)

CHOCOLATE GÉNOISE

INGREDIENTS	MEASURE	WEIGHT	
	VOLUME	OUNCES	GRAMS
unsalted butter	3 tablespoons	1.5 ounces	43 grams
vanilla	1 ½ teaspoons		6 grams
6 large eggs	9.5 fluid ounces	12 ounces	340 grams (weighed in the shells)
superfine sugar	¾ cup	5.25 ounces	150 grams
honey (optional)	1 tablespoon	0.75 ounce	21 grams
sifted cake flour	1 ½ cups	5.25 ounces	150 grams
unsweetened cocoa	¼ cup (lightly spooned)	0.75 ounce	21 grams

One 8 by 8 by 2-inch square pan, greased, bottom lined with parchment or wax paper, then greased again and floured.

Preheat the oven to 400°F.

In a small saucepan, melt the butter and add the vanilla. Set aside to keep warm.

In a large mixing bowl set over a pan of simmering water, heat the eggs, sugar, and optional honey until just lukewarm, stirring constantly to prevent curdling. (The eggs may also be heated by placing them *still in their shells* in a large mixing bowl in an oven with a pilot light for 3 hours or up to overnight.) Using the whisk attachment, beat the mixture on high speed for 5 minutes or until tripled in volume. (A hand beater may be used, but it will be necessary to beat for at least 10 minutes.)

While the eggs are beating, sift together the flour and cocoa.

Remove 1 cup of the egg mixture and thoroughly whisk it into the warm melted butter.

Sift half the flour mixture over the remaining egg mixture, and fold it in *gently* but rapidly with a large balloon whisk, slotted skimmer, or rubber spatula until almost all the flour has disappeared. Repeat with the remaining flour, folding just until the flour has disappeared completely. Fold in the butter mixture until just incorporated.

A PASSION FOR CHOCOLATE

Pour immediately into the prepared pan, and bake 25 to 30 minutes or until the cake has started to shrink slightly from the sides of the pan. (No need for a cake tester. Once the sides shrink, the cake is done.) Avoid opening the oven door before the minimum time or the cake could fall. Toward the end of the baking time, open the door slightly, and if at a quick glance the cake does not appear done, close the door at once and check again in 5 minutes.

Loosen the sides of the cake with a small metal spatula, and unmold at once onto a lightly greased rack. Reinvert to cool.

CHERRY SYRUP

INGREDIENTS	MEASURE	WEIGHT	
	VOLUME	OUNCES	GRAMS
Cherry Marnier, maraschino or cherry liqueur	3 fluid ounces	3 ounces	90 grams
water	3 fluid ounces	3 ounces	90 grams
sugar	½ cup	3.5 ounces	100 grams

In a small saucepan with a tight-fitting lid, bring the sugar and water to a rolling boil, stirring constantly. Cover immediately, remove from the heat, and allow to cool completely. Stir in the Cherry Marnier or liqueur.

PRÉSIDENT GANACHE

INGREDIENTS	MEASURE	WEIGHT	
	VOLUME	OUNCES	GRAMS
hazelnuts	1 cup	5 ounces	142 grams
baking soda	¼ cup	2 ounces	60 grams
bittersweet chocolate	3⅓ (3-ounce) bars	10 ounces	284 grams
crème fraîche (page 348) or heavy cream	1 cup + 2 tablespoons	9 ounces	260 grams

BLANCH THE HAZELNUTS	In a medium saucepan, place 3 cups of water and bring it to a boil. Add the nuts and the baking soda, and boil for 3 minutes. Test a nut by running it under cold water. If the skin is not easy to remove, return to the heat for a minute or so more. Drain well. Peel.

Toast the hazelnuts in a 350°F. oven for 10 to 15 minutes or until golden brown. Cool completely and chop fine, but not powder-fine. (Use the medium grater on a food processor and then pulse with the metal blade.) Set aside.

Break the chocolate into pieces and process in a food processor until very fine. Heat the cream to the boiling point, and with the motor running, pour it through the feed tube in a steady stream. Process a few seconds until smooth. Add the hazelnuts and pulse just to combine. Transfer to a bowl and cool for several hours, until frosting consistency. In cool weather ganache can remain unrefrigerated for at least 3 days or as long as 2 weeks. At room temperature it remains spreadable.

BUTTERCREAM

INGREDIENTS	MEASURE	WEIGHT	
	VOLUME	OUNCES	GRAMS
milk	1 1/4 cups	10.5 ounces	303 grams
1/2 vanilla bean, split*			
salt	1/4 teaspoon		
2 extra-large egg yolks	3 tablespoons	1.5 ounces	47 grams
superfine sugar	1/4 cup + 2 tablespoons	2.5 ounces	75 grams
all-purpose flour	1/4 cup (dip and sweep)	1.25 ounces	35 grams
unsalted butter, softened	3 tablespoons	1.5 ounces	40 grams
praline paste	1 1/2 table-spoons	1 ounce	25 grams

*You may substitute 1/2 teaspoon vanilla extract for the vanilla bean, but the bean offers a fuller, more aromatic flavor. If you are using extract, add it after the buttercream has cooled. If using a Tahitian bean, use only 1/4 bean.

In a saucepan, place 1 cup of the milk, the vanilla bean, and the salt. Bring it to a full boil, then remove from the heat.

In a medium bowl, whisk together the egg yolks and sugar until thoroughly combined. Whisk in the flour, and then the remaining ¼ cup of cold milk (to prevent curdling). Whisking constantly, gradually add the hot milk. Return the mixture to the saucepan and bring to a boil, whisking constantly. Simmer for 3 minutes, whisking constantly.

Transfer the mixture to a bowl, press plastic wrap directly onto the surface (to prevent a skin from forming), and cool unrefrigerated. Whisk together the butter and praline paste until smooth and creamy. When the cream is almost cold, remove the vanilla bean and whisk in the butter and praline paste just until smooth. Return the plastic to the surface.

Pastry cream must not be cold when butter is added or it will separate. If separation should occur, warm the bottom of the bowl over hot water for 2 or 3 seconds before continuing to beat it. Overbeating will also cause cream to break down.   **NOTE**

If you are planning to decorate with piped ganache, set aside ½ cup of it.   **ASSEMBLING THE CAKE**

Trim bottom and top crusts of the génoise. Cut the génoise horizontally into three layers. Spread a small amount of ganache on a cardboard square cut a little larger than the finished cake, or spread it directly onto a serving plate.

Using a straight-sided cookie sheet or pancake turners, lift one génoise layer onto the cardboard or plate. Sprinkle with one third of the syrup, and spread with about 1 cup of the ganache (1 ¼ cups if not using ganache for piping).

Place the second layer on top of the ganache, and sprinkle it with another third of the syrup. Spread all the buttercream evenly over that, and top with the last génoise layer. Sprinkle it with the remaining syrup, and refrigerate for 1 hour.

Frost the entire cake with the remaining ganache. If desired, use reserved ganache to pipe decorations, using a number 22 star tube. The cake can also be decorated with chocolate curls (page 367), large chocolate petals (page 371), or flecks of gold leaf (page 381). This cake is excellent for any special occasion or dinner party because the flavors only improve when combined ahead.

TO SERVE Use a serrated knife or a sharp knife dipped in hot water.

KEEPS Airtight, 5 days refrigerated. Remove at least 1 hour before serving.

LE CINGHALAIS

FESTIVE CAKE CONSISTING OF THREE RUM-SOAKED LAYERS OF CHOCOLATE GÉNOISE FILLED WITH CINNAMON CHOCOLATE GANACHE AND PRALINE BUTTERCREAM

SERVES 8 TO 10

Cinghalais is the name of a dialect spoken in Ceylon, where marvelous-quality light cocoa and cinnamon are grown. Cinnamon pervades the chocolate ganache, the flavor coming through behind the chocolate. The ganache filling is somehow strongly reminiscent of the best chocolate puddings of childhood—in a very grownup setting!

COMPONENTS
Chocolate Génoise • *Rum Syrup* •
Ceylonese Ganache • *Praline Buttercream*

DECORATION
Optional glaze of bittersweet chocolate
(9 ounces/255 grams)

CHOCOLATE GÉNOISE

INGREDIENTS	MEASURE	WEIGHT	
	VOLUME	OUNCES	GRAMS
unsalted butter	¼ cup	2 ounces	60 grams
vanilla	1½ teaspoons		6 grams
7 large eggs	1½ liquid cups	14 ounces	400 grams
		(weighed in the shells)	
superfine sugar	¾ cup + 2 tablespoons	6 ounces	170 grams
honey (optional)	1 tablespoon	.75 ounce	21 grams
unsweetened cocoa	⅓ cup (lightly spooned)	1 ounce	30 grams
sifted cake flour	1¾ cups	6.25 ounces	180 grams

One 10 by 3-inch round springform pan, greased, bottom lined with parchment or wax paper, then greased again and floured.

Preheat the oven to 400°F.

In a small saucepan, melt the butter and add the vanilla. Set it aside to keep warm.

In a large mixing bowl set over a pan of simmering water, heat the eggs, sugar, and optional honey for extra moisture until just lukewarm, stirring constantly to prevent curdling. (The eggs may also be heated by placing them *still in their shells* in a large mixing bowl in an oven with a pilot light for 3 hours or up to overnight.) Using the whisk attachment, beat the mixture on high speed for 5 minutes or until tripled in volume. (A hand beater may be used, but it will be necessary to beat for at least 10 minutes.)

While the eggs are beating, sift together the cocoa and flour.

Remove 1 cup of the egg mixture and thoroughly whisk it into the warm melted butter.

Sift half the flour mixture over the remaining egg mixture, and fold it in *gently* but rapidly with a large balloon whisk, slotted skimmer, or rubber spatula until almost all the flour has disappeared. Repeat with the remaining flour, folding until the flour has disappeared completely. Fold in the butter mixture until just incorporated.

Pour immediately into the prepared pan, and bake 25 to 35 minutes or until the cake has started to shrink slightly from the sides of the pan. (No need for a cake tester. Once the sides shrink, the cake is done.) Avoid opening the oven door before the minimum time or the cake could fall. Toward the end of the baking time, open the door slightly, and if at a quick glance the cake does not appear done, close the door at once and check again in 5 minutes.

Loosen the sides of the cake with a small metal spatula, and unmold at once onto a lightly greased rack. Reinvert to cool.

RUM SYRUP

| INGREDIENTS | MEASURE | WEIGHT | |
	VOLUME	OUNCES	GRAMS
water	*3 tablespoons*	*1.5 ounces*	*43 grams*
sugar	*¼ cup*	*1.75 ounces*	*50 grams*
dark rum	*3 tablespoons*	*1.5 ounces*	*43 grams*

In a small saucepan with a tight-fitting lid, bring the water and sugar to a rolling boil, stirring constantly. Cover immediately, remove from the heat, and allow to cool completely. Stir in the rum.

CEYLONESE GANACHE

| INGREDIENTS | MEASURE | WEIGHT | |
	VOLUME	OUNCES	GRAMS
bittersweet chocolate	*4 (3-ounce) bars*	*12 ounces*	*340 grams*
cinnamon	*½ teaspoon*		
heavy cream*	*1½ liquid cups*	*12 ounces*	*340 grams*

*The Bernachons use crème fraîche for this ganache, but I find the combination with the cinnamon too tart for my taste.

Break the chocolate into pieces and process with the cinnamon in a food processor until very fine. Heat the cream to the boiling point, and with the motor running, pour it through the feed tube in a steady stream. Process a few seconds until smooth. Transfer to a bowl and cool for several hours, until frosting consistency. In cool weather ganache can remain unrefrigerated for at least 3 days or as long as 2 weeks. At room temperature it remains spreadable.

PRALINE BUTTERCREAM

INGREDIENTS	MEASURE	WEIGHT	
	VOLUME	OUNCES	GRAMS
milk	1 ¼ cups	10.5 ounces	303 grams
½ vanilla bean, split*			
salt	¼ teaspoon		
2 extra-large egg yolks	3 tablespoons	1.5 ounces	47 grams
superfine sugar	¼ cup + 2 tablespoons	2.5 ounces	75 grams
all-purpose flour	¼ cup (dip and sweep)	1.25 ounces	35 grams
unsalted butter, softened	3 tablespoons	1.5 ounces	40 grams
praline paste	1 ½ tablespoons	1 ounce	25 grams

*You may substitute ½ teaspoon vanilla extract for the vanilla bean, but the bean offers a fuller, more aromatic flavor. If you are using extract, add it after the buttercream has cooled. If using a Tahitian bean, use only ¼ bean.

In a saucepan, place 1 cup of the milk, the vanilla bean, and the salt. Bring it to a full boil, then remove from the heat.

In a medium bowl, whisk together the egg yolks and sugar until thoroughly combined. Whisk in the flour, and then the remaining ¼ cup of cold milk (to prevent curdling). Whisking constantly, gradually add the hot milk. Return the mixture to the saucepan and bring to a boil, whisking constantly. Simmer for 3 minutes, whisking constantly.

Transfer the mixture to a bowl, press plastic wrap directly onto the surface (to prevent a skin from forming), and cool unrefrigerated. Whisk together the butter and praline paste until smooth and creamy. When the cream is almost cold, remove the vanilla bean and whisk in the butter and praline paste just until smooth. Return the plastic to the surface.

70

Pastry cream must not be cold when butter is added or it will separate. If separation should occur, warm the bottom of the bowl over hot water for 2 or 3 seconds before continuing to beat it. Overbeating will also cause cream to break down.

If you are planning to decorate with piped ganache, set aside ½ cup of it.

Cut the génoise horizontally into three layers. Spread a small amount of ganache on a cardboard round cut a little larger than the finished cake.

Using pancake turners or the removable bottom of a quiche pan, lift one génoise layer onto the cardboard. Sprinkle with one third of the syrup, and spread with the praline buttercream.

Place the second layer on top of the buttercream, and sprinkle it with another third of the syrup. Spread with about 1 cup of the ganache (1 ¼ cups if not using ganache for piping), and top with the last génoise layer. Sprinkle it with the remaining syrup, and refrigerate for 1 hour.

Frost the entire cake with the remaining ganache.

Place the cake on a rack set over a cookie sheet (to catch the dripping chocolate).

Break the chocolate into squares and place them in the top of a double boiler set over very hot water (but no hotter than 160°F.). The water must not simmer or touch the bottom of the double boiler insert.

Stir until the chocolate begins to melt. Return the pan to low heat if the water cools, but be careful that it does not get too hot. (The chocolate may be melted in a microwave oven if stirred every 15 seconds.) Using either method, remove it from the heat source before fully melted and stir, using the residual heat to complete the melting. Allow the chocolate to cool until tepid, then pour it over the cake, spreading it evenly with a metal spatula. If any spots on the sides remain unglazed, use a small metal spatula to lift up some glaze that has fallen onto the baking sheet and apply it to the uncovered area.

If desired, use reserved ganache to pipe decorations, using a number 22 star tube. Lift rack and tap

71

lightly on the counter to settle the glaze. Using a broad spatula or pancake turner, lift the cake from the rack and set it on a serving plate. (Glaze dulls if refrigerated.)

TO SERVE Use a heated knife to score the surface of the chocolate glaze (this will keep it from cracking). The knife can be heated by running it under hot water. Continue dipping the knife in hot water while slicing the cake.

KEEPS Airtight, 5 days refrigerated, but it's best not to glaze it until serving day. Remove the cake from the refrigerator at least 1 hour before serving.

NOTE FROM ROSE Cinnamon ganache is one of my favorite chocolate fillings, praline buttercream perhaps my favorite of all buttercreams. The combined effect makes it well worth the extra effort of preparing two separate fillings.

LE CORINTHIEN

THREE RAISIN-FILLED LAYERS OF YELLOW GÉNOISE BETWEEN HAZELNUT CHOCOLATE GANACHE

SERVES 8 TO 10

Rum-soaked raisins add a lovely flavor and moistness to this cake. The name of the cake was inspired by the small dark raisins that come from Corinth, Greece.

COMPONENTS
Génoise • *Antilles Ganache* • *Rum Syrup*

DECORATION
Optional glaze of bittersweet chocolate (9 ounces/255 grams); unsweetened cocoa (page 365) or chocolate petals (page 371).

INGREDIENTS	MEASURE	WEIGHT	
	VOLUME	OUNCES	GRAMS
bittersweet chocolate	2 (3-ounce) bars	6 ounces	170 grams
dark raisins	⅓ cup	1.75 ounces	50 grams
dark rum	3 tablespoons	1.5 ounces	43 grams

At least 2 hours ahead, place the raisins in a small bowl and pour the rum over them. Cover tightly with plastic wrap and set aside.

GÉNOISE

INGREDIENTS	MEASURE	WEIGHT	
	VOLUME	OUNCES	GRAMS
unsalted butter	¼ cup	2 ounces	60 grams
vanilla	1½ teaspoons		6 grams
7 large eggs	1½ liquid cups	14 ounces	400 grams (weighed in the shells)
superfine sugar	¾ cup + 2 tablespoons	6 ounces	170 grams
honey (optional)	1 tablespoon	.75 ounce	21 grams
sifted cake flour	2 cups	7 ounces	200 grams

One 10 by 3-inch baking pan or springform pan, greased, bottom lined with parchment or wax paper, and then greased again and floured.

Preheat the oven to 400°F.

In a small saucepan, melt the butter and add the vanilla. Set aside to keep warm.

In a large mixing bowl set over a pan of simmering water, heat the eggs, sugar, and optional honey for extra moistness until just lukewarm, stirring constantly to prevent curdling. (The eggs may also be heated by placing them *still in their shells* in a large mixing bowl in an oven with a pilot light for 3 hours or up to overnight.) Using the whisk attachment, beat the mixture on high speed for 5 minutes or until tri-

A PASSION FOR CHOCOLATE

pled in volume. (A hand beater may be used, but it will be necessary to beat for at least 10 minutes.)

Remove 1 cup of the egg mixture and thoroughly whisk it into the warm melted butter.

Sift half the flour over the remaining egg mixture, and fold it in *gently* but rapidly with a large balloon whisk, slotted skimmer, or rubber spatula until almost all the flour has disappeared. Repeat with the remaining flour, folding just until the flour has disappeared completely. Fold in the butter mixture until just incorporated.

Pour immediately into the prepared pan, and bake 20 to 30 minutes or until the cake is golden brown and has started to shrink slightly from the sides of the pan. (No need for a cake tester. Once the sides shrink, the cake is done.) Avoid opening the oven door before the minimum time or the cake could fall. Toward the end of the baking time, open the door slightly, and if at a quick glance the cake does not appear done, close the door at once and check again in 5 minutes.

Loosen the sides of the cake with a small metal spatula, and unmold at once onto a lightly greased rack. Reinvert to cool.

Génoise cuts more easily when made ahead and **NOTE** chilled.

RUM SYRUP

INGREDIENTS	MEASURE	WEIGHT	
	VOLUME	OUNCES	GRAMS
water	3 tablespoons	1.5 ounces	43 grams
sugar	¼ cup	1.75 ounces	50 grams
dark rum	3 tablespoons	1.5 ounces	43 grams

In a small saucepan with a tight-fitting lid, bring the water and sugar to a rolling boil, stirring constantly. Cover immediately, remove from the heat, and allow to cool completely. Stir in the rum.

GRAND CAKES

INGREDIENTS	MEASURE	WEIGHT	
	VOLUME	OUNCES	GRAMS
hazelnuts	1 ¼ cups	6 ounces	170 grams
baking soda	¼ cup	2 ounces	60 grams
bittersweet chocolate	5 (3-ounce) bars	15 ounces	425 grams
heavy cream	1 liquid cup	8 ounces	232 grams
dark rum	¼ cup	2 ounces	55 grams

BLANCH THE HAZELNUTS In a medium saucepan, place 3 cups of water and bring it to a boil. Add the nuts and the baking soda and boil for 3 minutes. Test a nut by running it under cold water. If the skin is not easy to remove with slight pressure from the fingers, return to the heat for a minute or so more. Drain well. Peel.

Toast the hazelnuts in a 350°F. oven for 10 to 15 minutes or until golden brown. Cool completely and chop fine, but not powder-fine. (Use the medium grater on a food processor and then pulse with the metal blade.) Set aside.

Break the chocolate into pieces and process in a food processor until very fine.

Heat the cream to the boiling point, and with the motor running, pour it through the feed tube in a steady stream. Process a few seconds until smooth. Cool slightly before adding the rum and the hazelnuts. Pulse just to combine. Transfer to a bowl and cool for several hours, until frosting consistency.

ASSEMBLING THE CAKE If you are planning to decorate with piped ganache, set aside ½ cup of it.

Trim the bottom and top crusts of the génoise. Using a serrated knife, cut the génoise horizontally into three layers. Spread a small amount of ganache on a cardboard round cut a little larger than the finished cake.

Using pancake turners or the removable bottom of a quiche pan, lift one génoise layer onto the cardboard. Sprinkle it with one third of the syrup, and spread with about 1 cup of the ganache (1¼ cups if not using ganache for piping). Sprinkle on half of the drained raisins.

Place the second layer on top of the ganache, and sprinkle it with another third of the syrup. Spread with another cup of the ganache (1¼ cups if not using ganache for piping). Sprinkle on the remaining drained raisins, and top with the last génoise layer. Sprinkle it with the remaining syrup, and refrigerate for 1 hour.

Frost the entire cake with the remaining ganache.

Refrigerate for about 10 minutes to firm the ganache before glazing. (Ganache should not be too cold, however, or the glaze will set too quickly before an even coat can be achieved.)

TO GLAZE

Place the cake on a rack set over a cookie sheet (to catch the dripping chocolate).

Break the chocolate into squares and place them in the top of a double boiler set over very hot water (but no hotter than 160°F.). The water must not simmer or touch the bottom of the double boiler insert.

Stir until the chocolate begins to melt. Return the pan to the heat if the water cools, but be careful that it does not get too hot. (The chocolate may be melted in a microwave oven if stirred every 15 seconds.) Using either method, remove it from the heat source before fully melted and stir, using the residual heat to complete the melting. Allow the chocolate to cool until tepid, then pour it over the cake, quickly spreading it evenly with a metal spatula. If any spots on the sides remain unglazed, use a small metal spatula to lift up some glaze that has fallen onto the baking sheet and apply it to the uncovered area.

Lift rack and tap it lightly on the counter to settle the glaze. Using a broad spatula or a pancake turner, lift the cake from the rack and set it on a serving plate. (Glaze dulls if refrigerated.) If desired, use reserved ganache to pipe decorations, using a number 22 star tube.

TO SERVE

Use a heated knife to score the surface of the chocolate glaze. This will keep it from cracking. The knife can be heated by running it under hot water. Continue dipping the knife in hot water while slicing.

KEEPS   Airtight, 5 days refrigerated, but it's best not to glaze it until serving day. Remove the cake from the refrigerator at least 1 hour before serving.

A PASSION FOR CHOCOLATE

LE DAUPHINOIS

THREE LAYERS OF YELLOW GÉNOISE FILLED WITH WALNUTS AND MOCHA GANACHE

SERVES 8 TO 10

Walnuts, coffee, rum, and chocolate are the delectable flavors of this cake. Its name is derived from the renowned walnuts of Grenoble, in the Dauphiné region of France. Walnuts have a natural way of accentuating the flavor of chocolate. The mocha ganache has a wonderfully intense coffee flavor, strongly reminiscent of the popular Höpje candies of my childhood.

COMPONENTS
Génoise • *Mocha Ganache* • *Rum Syrup* • *Walnuts*

DECORATION
Chopped walnuts and walnut halves

INGREDIENTS	MEASURE	WEIGHT	
ROOM TEMPERATURE	VOLUME	OUNCES	GRAMS
unsalted butter	¼ *cup*	2 *ounces*	60 *grams*
vanilla	1½ *teaspoons*		6 *grams*
7 large eggs	1½ *liquid cups*	14 *ounces*	400 *grams*
			(weighed in the shells)
superfine sugar	¾ *cup + 2 tablespoons*	6 *ounces*	170 *grams*
honey (optional)	1 *tablespoon*	.75 *ounce*	21 *grams*
sifted cake flour	2 *cups*	7 *ounces*	200 *grams*

One 10 by 3-inch round baking pan or springform pan, greased, bottom lined with parchment or wax paper, and then greased again and floured.

Preheat the oven to 400°F.

In a small saucepan, melt the butter and add the vanilla. Set aside to keep warm.

In a large mixing bowl set over a pan of simmering water, heat the eggs, sugar, and optional honey for extra moistness, until just lukewarm, stirring constantly to prevent curdling. (The eggs may also be heated by placing them *still in their shells* in a large mixing bowl in an oven with a pilot light for 3 hours or up to overnight.) Using the whisk attachment, beat the mixture on high speed for 5 minutes or until tripled in volume. (A hand beater may be used, but it will be necessary to beat for at least 10 minutes.)

Remove 1 cup of the egg mixture and thoroughly whisk it into the warm melted butter.

Sift half the flour over the remaining egg mixture, and fold it in *gently* but rapidly with a large balloon whisk, slotted skimmer, or rubber spatula until almost all the flour has disappeared. Repeat with the remaining flour, folding just until the flour has disappeared completely. Fold in the butter mixture until just incorporated.

Pour immediately into the prepared pan, and bake 20 to 30 minutes or until the cake is golden brown and has started to shrink slightly from the sides of the pan. (No need for a cake tester. Once the sides shrink, the cake is done.) Avoid opening the oven door before the minimum time or the cake could fall. Toward the end of the baking time, open the door slightly, and if at a quick glance the cake does not appear done, close the door at once and check again in 5 minutes.

Loosen the sides of the cake with a small metal spatula, and unmold at once onto a lightly greased rack. Reinvert to cool.

Génoise cuts more easily when made ahead and chilled. **NOTE**

RUM SYRUP

INGREDIENTS	MEASURE	WEIGHT	
	VOLUME	OUNCES	GRAMS
water	3 tablespoons	1.5 ounces	43 grams
sugar	¼ cup	1.75 ounces	50 grams
dark rum	3 tablespoons	1.5 ounces	43 grams

In a small saucepan with a tight-fitting lid, bring the water and sugar to a rolling boil, stirring constantly. Cover immediately, remove from the heat, and allow to cool completely. Stir in the rum.

MOCHA GANACHE

INGREDIENTS	MEASURE	WEIGHT	
	VOLUME	OUNCES	GRAMS
bittersweet chocolate	4 (3-ounce) bars	12 ounces	340 grams
Medaglia d'Oro instant espresso powder	2 tablespoons		
crème fraîche (page 348) or heavy cream	1 ½ cups	12 ounces	340 grams

Break the chocolate into pieces and process, together with the coffee, in a food processor until very fine. Heat the cream to the boiling point, and with the motor running, pour it through the feed tube in a steady

81

GRAND CAKES

stream. Process a few seconds until smooth. Transfer to a bowl and cool for several hours, until frosting consistency. In cool weather ganache can remain unrefrigerated for at least 3 days or up to 2 weeks. At room temperature it remains spreadable.

WALNUT FILLING AND DECORATION

| INGREDIENTS | MEASURE | WEIGHT | |
	VOLUME	OUNCES	GRAMS
walnut halves	*2⅔ cups*	*13 ounces*	*370 grams*

Reserve 10 walnut halves and chop the remainder medium-fine.

Measure 1¾ cups (7 ounces/200 grams) chopped nuts and set aside for the filling. Use the remainder for the sides.

ASSEMBLING THE CAKE Trim the bottom and top crusts of the génoise. Using a serrated knife, cut the génoise horizontally into three layers. Spread a small amount of ganache on a cardboard round cut a little larger than the finished cake.

Using pancake turners or the removable bottom of a quiche pan, lift one génoise layer onto the cardboard. Sprinkle with one third of the syrup, and spread with about ⅔ cup of the ganache. Sprinkle on half of the chopped walnuts reserved for the filling.

Place the second layer on top of the ganache and sprinkle it with another third of the syrup. Spread with another ⅔ cup of the ganache. Sprinkle on the remaining chopped walnuts reserved for the filling, and top with the last génoise layer. Sprinkle it with the remaining syrup, and refrigerate for 1 hour.

Frost the entire cake with the remaining ganache. Garnish the sides of the cake with the remaining chopped walnuts, and the top with the reserved walnut halves.

TO SERVE Use a serrated knife or a sharp knife dipped in hot water.

KEEPS Airtight, 5 days refrigerated. Remove from the refrigerator at least 1 hour before serving.

LA MILLE-FEUILLE
AU CHOCOLAT

LARGE ROUND OF PUFF PASTRY
FILLED WITH CHOCOLATE PASTRY CREAM AND
GLAZED WITH BITTERSWEET CHOCOLATE

SERVES 6 TO 8

The Bernachon version of this classic French puff pastry is uncharacteristically round in shape, and the traditional pastry cream varied with bittersweet chocolate. If you don't wish to make puff pastry from scratch, by all means use frozen puff pastry when available, but only if it has been prepared with butter. You will need 1 1/4 pounds/570 grams.

COMPONENTS
Classic Puff Pastry • *Chocolate Pastry Cream*

DECORATION
Glaze of bittersweet chocolate (6 ounces/170 grams)

INGREDIENTS	MEASURE	WEIGHT	
ROOM TEMPERATURE	VOLUME	OUNCES	GRAMS
unsalted butter	*1 cup*	*8 ounces*	*227 grams*
all-purpose unbleached flour, preferably Heckers	*2 cups minus 2 tablespoons (dip and sweep)*	*8 ounces*	*227 grams*
salt	*½ teaspoon*		*3.5 grams*
ice water	*½ cup*	*4 ounces*	*118 grams*

Three 10- to 12-inch baking discs or sheets

THE DOUGH Remove 1 ounce (2 tablespoons) of butter from the 8 ounces and refrigerate the remainder. Place the butter in a mixing bowl and add 7 ounces (1⅔ cups) of the flour and the salt. Rub this mixture between your fingers until it is very fine and grainy and no lumps of butter are discernible (about 5 minutes). Add 6 tablespoons of the water and stir gently with a fork to incorporate it. The dough should be soft and clumpy. If necessary, add the remaining water by droplets.

Empty the dough out onto a floured surface and gently knead it, just until the dough holds together and looks fairly smooth. It should not become too elastic or it will be difficult to roll. Cover the dough and allow it to rest 20 minutes at room temperature, or up to 24 hours well wrapped and refrigerated.

THE BUTTER BLOCK Place the remaining 1 ounce (3 tablespoons) of flour on a sheet of plastic wrap, and place the remaining 7 ounces of butter on top. Sprinkle a little of the flour on top of the butter and cover it with the plastic wrap. Pound the butter lightly with a rolling pin to flatten and soften it, then knead it together, using the plastic wrap and your knuckles to avoid touching the butter directly. Work quickly. As soon as the flour is incorporated, shape the butter into a 4½-inch square (no thicker than ¾ inch). At this point the butter should

84

be cool but workable—60°F. Use it at once or keep it cool. Butter must not be colder than 60°F. when rolled into pastry or it will break through the dough and not distribute evenly.

 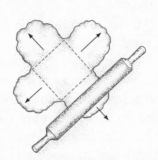 

Roll out the dough on a well-floured surface to form a 6-inch square. Place the butter block diagonally in the center of the dough square, and lightly mark the dough at the edges of the butter with the dull side of a knife. Remove the butter and roll out each marked corner of the dough to form flaps. The dough will be slightly elastic. Moisten these flaps lightly with water and replace the butter on the dough, wrapping securely. Stretch the flaps slightly to reach across the dough package. **THE DOUGH PACKAGE**

On a well-floured surface, keeping the dough seam side up, gently roll the package into a rectangle measuring 6 by 12 inches. Brush off all flour from the surface of the dough, and fold it into thirds as you would fold a business letter. This is the first "turn." Before each subsequent turn, move the dough so the closed end is on your left. Clean the work surface, reflour, and roll and fold a second time exactly the same way, but turn the dough over occasionally to keep seams and edges even. Be sure to roll into all four corners of the dough and use a pastry scraper to even the edges.

Mark the dough with two fingertips, or knuckles if you have long nails, to indicate that two turns have been completed. Wrap the dough in plastic wrap, then foil, and refrigerate for 30 to 40 minutes. The dough must not chill for longer than 40 minutes, or the butter will never distribute evenly.

Continue to roll and turn the dough, marking the

turns with fingertips and resting 30 minutes between turns, until six turns have been completed. It is best to do only one turn at a time now, as the dough will become elastic and the best results are obtained when the dough is not forced and the layers are not pressed together.

Allow the finished pastry to rest, refrigerated, for at least 2 hours.

NOTES FROM ROSE

Puff pastry that is given six "turns" has 729 layers. Unbleached all-purpose flour has more gluten-forming protein and is necessary to provide the extra support for the thin, fragile layers of butter and dough. Heckers flour has an especially high protein content of 13. (The protein count is indicated on the side of the flour bag.)

Single turns, as opposed to the newer double turns, make it easier to control the shaping and layering of the pastry, and it will rise more evenly when baked. Although the actual working time is short, you will need to be around for a 4-hour period to complete the turns. The temperature of the butter is critical to making the best puff pastry. It should be cold but malleable.

It is best if the pastry is used by the next day, or it may be frozen for months.

TO BAKE THE PASTRY

Divide the pastry into three equal parts, and on a floured surface roll each into a circle about 9 inches in diameter and ⅛ inch thick. Transfer the pastry to lightly moistened baking sheets, and use an inverted pan and sharp knife to trim it for perfectly shaped rounds. Prick the pastry all over with a fork, cover it with a clean dish towel, and allow to rest for 1 hour, refrigerated.

NOTE FROM ROSE

Freezing the shaped pastry for 15 minutes before baking helps to retain its shape.

Bake in a preheated 400°F. oven for 15 minutes, or until the pastry just begins to brown. Cool completely.

A PASSION FOR CHOCOLATE

CHOCOLATE PASTRY CREAM

INGREDIENTS MEASURE		WEIGHT	
	VOLUME	POUNDS/OUNCES	GRAMS
milk	*5 cups*	*2 pounds 10.5 ounces*	*1 kilogram 210 grams*
2 vanilla beans, split*			
salt	*1½ teaspoons*		*10 grams*
bittersweet chocolate, chopped	*1 (3-ounce) bar*	*3 ounces*	*85 grams*
10 large egg yolks	*¾ liquid cup*	*6.5 ounces*	*186 grams*
superfine sugar	*1½ cups*	*10.5 ounces*	*300 grams*
all-purpose flour	*¾ cup + 1 tablespoon (lightly spooned)*	*3.5 ounces*	*100 grams*

*You may substitute 2 teaspoons vanilla extract for the vanilla bean but the beans offer a fuller, more aromatic flavor. If you are using extract, add it after the pastry cream has cooled. If using a Tahitian bean, use only 1 bean.

In a saucepan, place 4 cups of the milk, the vanilla beans, and the salt. Bring to a full boil, remove from the heat, and add the chocolate.

In a medium bowl, whisk together the egg yolks and sugar until thoroughly combined. Whisk in the flour, and then the remaining 1 cup of cold milk (to prevent curdling). Whisking constantly, gradually add the hot milk mixture.

Return the mixture to the saucepan and bring to a boil, whisking constantly. Simmer for 3 minutes, whisking constantly.

Transfer the mixture to a bowl, press plastic wrap directly onto the surface of the pastry cream (to prevent a skin from forming), and cool. Store refrigerated up to 5 days. Remove the vanilla beans before serving. Return plastic to the surface.

ASSEMBLING THE PASTRY

Place a disc of puff pastry on a serving plate, and spread it with an even layer of half the pastry cream. Place a second pastry disc on top, and spread on the remaining pastry cream. Top with the third pastry disc. Refrigerate for 30 minutes to 1 hour to set the pastry cream.

TO GLAZE Break the chocolate into squares and place them in the top of a double boiler set over very hot water (but no hotter than 160°F.). The water must not simmer or touch the bottom of the double boiler insert.

Stir until the chocolate begins to melt. Return the pan to the heat if the water cools, but be careful that it does not get too hot. (The chocolate may be melted in a microwave oven if stirred every 15 seconds.) Using either method, remove it from the heat source before fully melted and stir, using the residual heat to complete the melting. Allow the chocolate to cool until tepid, then pour it over the cake, spreading it evenly with a metal spatula.

Serve at once, or allow the cake to sit at room temperature for no more than 4 hours.

TO SERVE Use a serrated knife.

NOTE FROM ROSE For the crispiest pastry, it is best to assemble the pastry no more than 4 hours before serving. The pastry cream, of course, can be prepared a day ahead and refrigerated. Longer than that it becomes a little difficult to spread.

LA MOKATINE

CRISP MERINGUE DISCS ENCASING A CREAMY COFFEE-FLAVORED GANACHE

SERVES 8 TO 10

This elegant but easy-to-make cake is great for do-ahead entertaining as the two components can be made well in advance. The meringues keep airtight for months at room temperature and the ganache also keeps for months in the freezer.

COMPONENTS
Meringue • *Mocha Ganache*

DECORATION
Glaze of bittersweet chocolate (3 ounces/85 grams)

MERINGUE

INGREDIENTS	MEASURE	WEIGHT	
	VOLUME	POUNDS/OUNCES	GRAMS
6 extra-large egg whites, room temperature	6.5 fluid ounces	7 ounces	200 grams
cream of tartar	¾ teaspoon		
superfine sugar	2⅔ cups	1 pound 2.5 ounces	525 grams

Two 10- to 12-inch baking rounds or sheets, buttered and floured or lined with parchment.

Preheat the oven to 300°F.

In a mixing bowl beat the egg whites until foamy. Add the cream of tartar and beat until soft peaks form when the beater is raised slowly. Gradually add 2 tablespoons of the sugar, beating until stiff peaks form when the beater is raised slowly. With a large rubber spatula, gently fold in the remaining sugar.

Using a 1-gallon zip-seal bag with a corner cut off or a pastry bag fitted with a large plain number 6 (½-inch) tip, pipe the meringue onto the prepared baking sheets, forming two 10-inch circles, starting with the outer perimeter and spiraling inward toward the center. Using a small metal spatula, fill in any gaps with leftover meringue. Pipe any remaining meringue into puffs on a separate baking sheet.

Bake about 25 minutes, or until the meringue is crisp but not beginning to brown and can be removed easily from the baking sheets with the aid of a thin metal spatula or pancake turner.

MOCHA GANACHE

INGREDIENTS	MEASURE	WEIGHT	
	VOLUME	OUNCES	GRAMS
bittersweet chocolate	4 (3-ounce) bars	12 ounces	340 grams
Medaglia d'Oro instant espresso powder	2 tablespoons		
crème fraîche (page 348) or heavy cream	1½ cups	12 ounces	340 grams

Break the chocolate into pieces and process, with the espresso powder, in a food processor until very fine. Heat the cream to the boiling point, and with the motor running, pour it through the feed tube in a steady stream. Process a few seconds until smooth. Transfer to a bowl and cool for several hours, until frosting consistency. In cool weather ganache can remain unrefrigerated for at least 3 days or up to 2 weeks. At room temperature it remains spreadable.

Spread a small amount of mocha ganache onto a serving plate. Place one disc of meringue on top of this and top with about two thirds of the ganache. Place the second disc on top, flat side up. Refrigerate for at least 1 hour.

ASSEMBLING THE CAKE

Using a long metal spatula, spread the remaining ganache evenly on top of the meringue, and refrigerate for about 10 minutes to firm the ganache before glazing. (Ganache should not be too cold, however, or the glaze will set too quickly before an even coat can be achieved.)

Break the chocolate into squares and place in the top of a double boiler set over very hot water (but no hotter than 160°F.). The water must not simmer or touch the bottom of the double boiler insert.

TO GLAZE

Stir until the chocolate begins to melt. Return it to low heat if the water cools, but be careful that it does not get too hot. Stir 10 minutes or until smooth. (The chocolate may be melted in a microwave oven if stirred every 15 seconds.) Using either method, remove it from the heat source before fully melted and stir, using residual heat to complete the melting. Allow the chocolate to cool until tepid and pour at once onto the ganache, spreading it quickly and evenly with a long metal spatula.

Use a heated knife to score the surface of the chocolate glaze (this will keep it from cracking). The knife can be heated by running it under hot water. Slice with a serrated knife.

TO SERVE

KEEPS The meringue can be made months ahead and stored airtight. The ganache can be refrigerated for up to 1 week, or frozen for months. Once assembled, the cake is best stored at room temperature and eaten the same day.

NOTE FROM ROSE   The crispy sweet meringue perfectly complements the creamy bittersweet chocolate filling. This dessert is a perfection of simplicity. If you have frozen or refrigerated the ganache and it is a little too stiff to spread at room temperature, soften it by gently stirring it in a double boiler over simmering water. This can also be done in a microwave on high power, stirring every 5 seconds. In any case, it is important to stir only as much as necessary to equalize the melting process or the ganache will aerate and lighten in color. Chocolate coffee beans provide a perfect decoration for the top.

L'OPÉRA

MERINGUE NUT LAYER CAKE FILLED WITH MOCHA BUTTERCREAM AND MOCHA GANACHE

SERVES 8 TO 10

This cake is for the passionate coffee lover. Tender, nutty discs of succès are contrasted with a silky mocha buttercream and an intensely coffee ganache. The textures and flavors of this cake are truly something to sing about!

COMPONENTS
Succès • *Mocha Buttercream* • *Mocha Ganache*

DECORATION
Optional glaze of bittersweet chocolate (9 ounces/255 grams)

SUCCÈS

INGREDIENTS	MEASURE	WEIGHT	
	VOLUME	OUNCES	GRAMS
sliced almonds	*2 cups*	*6.25 ounces*	*180 grams*
superfine sugar	*¾ cup + 2 tablespoons*	*6.25 ounces*	*180 grams*
7 large egg whites, room temperature	*7 fluid ounces*	*7.25 ounces*	*210 grams*
cream of tartar	*1 teaspoon*		*3 grams*

Two baking sheets, buttered and floured or lined with parchment, marked with three 8-inch circles.

Preheat the oven to 350°F.

In a food processor, place the almonds and ¾ cup sugar and process until the almonds are finely grated.

In a mixing bowl beat the egg whites until foamy, add the cream of tartar, and beat until soft peaks form when the beater is raised slowly. Gradually add the remaining 2 tablespoons sugar, beating until stiff peaks form when the beater is raised slowly. Fold in the grated almond mixture.

Using a 1-gallon zip-seal bag with a corner cut off, or a pastry bag fitted with a large plain number 6 (½-inch) tip, pipe the batter onto the prepared baking sheets to form three 8-inch circles, starting with the perimeter and spiraling inward toward the center. Using a small metal spatula, fill in any gaps with leftover batter and smooth the surface. Bake for 15 to 20 minutes, or just until the discs begin to brown. Loosen the succès from the baking sheets and allow them to cool completely on sheets or racks before transferring to a work surface or serving plate. They will have expanded to about 9 inches.

To obtain a perfect circle, invert a cake pan over the succès and trim any excess with a sharp knife.

NOTES FROM ROSE

Use superfine sugar for the best texture. It is not actually necessary to use flour on the baking pan to keep it from sticking; however, the flour does keep the succès from spreading.

MOCHA BUTTERCREAM

INGREDIENTS	MEASURE	WEIGHT	
	VOLUME	OUNCES	GRAMS
milk	1 ¼ *cups*	10.5 *ounces*	303 *grams*
½ *vanilla bean, split* *			
salt	¼ *teaspoon*		
2 *extra-large egg yolks*	3 *tablespoons*	1.5 *ounces*	47 *grams*
superfine sugar	¼ *cup + 2 tablespoons*	2.5 *ounces*	75 *grams*
all-purpose flour	¼ *cup (dip and sweep)*	1.25 *ounces*	35 *grams*
unsalted butter, softened	3 *tablespoons*	1.5 *ounces*	40 *grams*
Medaglia d'Oro instant espresso powder	1 *tablespoon*		

*You may substitute ½ teaspoon vanilla extract for the vanilla bean, but the bean offers a fuller, more aromatic flavor. If you are using extract, add it after the buttercream has cooled. If using a Tahitian bean, use only ¼ bean.

In a saucepan, place 1 cup of the milk, the vanilla bean, and the salt. Bring it to a full boil, then remove from the heat.

In a medium bowl, whisk together the egg yolks and sugar until thoroughly combined. Whisk in the flour, and then the remaining ¼ cup of cold milk (to prevent curdling). Whisking constantly, gradually add the hot milk. Return the mixture to the saucepan and bring to a boil, whisking constantly. Simmer for 3 minutes, whisking constantly.

Transfer the mixture to a bowl, press plastic wrap directly onto the surface of the pastry cream (to prevent a skin from forming), and cool unrefrigerated. In a small bowl, mash the butter with a fork to ensure that it is soft and creamy throughout. Remove the vanilla bean, and when the cream is almost cold, whisk in the butter just until smooth. Dissolve the instant espresso powder in ½ teaspoon boiling water, and gently whisk this into the buttercream. Return the plastic to the surface. Store refrigerated.

Mocha Ganache

INGREDIENTS	MEASURE	WEIGHT	
	VOLUME	OUNCES	GRAMS
bittersweet chocolate	4 (3-ounce) bars	12 ounces	340 grams
Medaglia d'Oro instant espresso powder	2 tablespoons		
crème fraîche (page 348) or heavy cream	1½ cups	12 ounces	340 grams

Break the chocolate into pieces and process, with the espresso powder, in a food processor until very fine. Heat the cream to the boiling point, and with the motor running, pour it through the feed tube in a steady stream. Process a few seconds until smooth. Transfer to a bowl and cool for several hours, until frosting consistency. In cool weather ganache can remain unrefrigerated for at least 3 days or as long as 2 weeks. At room temperature it remains spreadable.

ASSEMBLING THE CAKE Place one disc of succès on a cardboard round or serving plate and top with the mocha buttercream. Place the second disc on top, flat side up, and top with an even layer of half the ganache. Place the third disc on top, flat side up, and refrigerate for at least 1 hour.

Frost the entire cake with the remaining ganache. Refrigerate for about 10 minutes to firm the ganache before glazing. (Ganache should not be too cold, however, or the glaze will set too quickly before an even coat can be achieved.)

TO GLAZE Place the cake on a rack set over a cookie sheet (to catch the dripping chocolate).

Break the chocolate into squares and place them in the top of a double boiler set over very hot water (but no hotter than 160°F). The water must not simmer or touch the bottom of the double boiler insert.

Stir until the chocolate begins to melt. Return the pan to low heat if the water cools, but be careful that it does not get too hot. Stir 10 minutes or until smooth. (The chocolate may be melted in a microwave oven if stirred every 15 seconds.) Using either method, remove it from the heat source before fully melted and stir, using residual heat to complete the melting. Allow the chocolate to cool until tepid, then pour it over the cake, spreading it evenly with a metal spatula. If any spots on the sides remain unglazed, use a small metal spatula to lift up some glaze that has fallen onto the baking sheet, and apply it to the uncovered area.

Lift rack and tap it lightly on the counter to settle the glaze. Using a broad spatula or pancake turner, lift the cake from the rack and set it on a serving plate. (Glaze dulls if refrigerated.)

TO SERVE Use a heated knife to score the surface of the chocolate glaze (this will keep it from cracking). The knife can be heated by running it under hot water. Slice with a serrated knife.

KEEPS Airtight, 5 days refrigerated, but it's best not to glaze it until serving day. Remove the cake from the refrigerator at least 1 hour before serving.

LE PRÉSIDENT

Yellow Génoise Layer
Cake Filled with Chocolate Ganache
and Brandied Cherries

SERVES 8 TO 10

This spectacular creation is the signature cake of the house of Bernachon, where it was originally called Le Montmorency, in honor of the Montmorency cherries it features. The new name was born when Bernachon made the cake for Valéry Giscard d'Estaing when he was president of France.

The Bernachons have a special machine that produces exceptionally fine chocolate ruffles. In a home situation, I recommend using chocolate cigarettes or curls. Either way, the cake will be equally and wondrously delicious.

COMPONENTS
*Génoise • Cherry liqueur • Brandied cherries •
Président Ganache*

DECORATION
Chocolate cigarettes (12 ounces/340 grams
bittersweet chocolate) (page 369)

INGREDIENTS	MEASURE	WEIGHT	
	VOLUME	OUNCES	GRAMS
Cherry Marnier, maraschino or cherry liqueur	1/2 cup	4 ounces	113 grams
10 griottes *or brandied cherries, drained and coarsely chopped**			

*Pitted tart French cherries, packed in liqueur, available in specialty stores.

Génoise

INGREDIENTS	MEASURE	WEIGHT	
ROOM TEMPERATURE	VOLUME	OUNCES	GRAMS
unsalted butter	1/4 cup	2 ounces	60 grams
vanilla	1 1/2 teaspoons		
7 large eggs	1 1/2 liquid cups	14 ounces	400 grams (weighed in the shells)
superfine sugar	3/4 cup + 2 tablespoons	6 ounces	170 grams
honey (optional)	1 tablespoon	.75 ounce	21 grams
sifted cake flour	2 cups	7 ounces	200 grams

One 10 by 3-inch round baking pan or springform pan, greased, bottom lined with parchment or wax paper, and then greased again and floured.

Preheat the oven to 400°F.

In a small saucepan, melt the butter and add the vanilla. Set aside to keep warm.

In a large mixing bowl set over a pan of simmering water, heat the eggs, sugar, and optional honey for extra moistness, until just lukewarm, stirring constantly to prevent curdling. (The eggs may also be heated by placing them *still in their shells* in a large mixing bowl in an oven with a pilot light for 3 hours or up to overnight.) Using the whisk attachment, beat the mixture on high speed for 5 minutes or until tripled in volume. (A hand beater may be used, but it will be necessary to beat for at least 10 minutes.)

Remove 1 cup of the egg mixture and thoroughly whisk it into the warm melted butter.

Sift half the flour over the remaining egg mixture, and fold it in *gently* but rapidly with a large balloon whisk, slotted skimmer, or rubber spatula until almost all the flour has disappeared. Repeat with the remaining flour, folding just until the flour has disappeared completely. Fold in the butter mixture until just incorporated.

Pour immediately into the prepared pan, and bake 20 to 30 minutes or until the cake is golden brown and has started to shrink slightly from the sides of the pan. (No need for a cake tester. Once the sides shrink, the cake is done.) Avoid opening the oven door before the minimum time or the cake could fall. Toward the end of the baking time, open the door slightly, and if at a quick glance the cake does not appear done, close the door at once and check again in 5 minutes.

Loosen the sides of the cake with a small metal spatula, and unmold at once onto a lightly greased rack. Reinvert to cool.

NOTE: Génoise cuts more easily when made ahead and chilled.

PRÉSIDENT GANACHE

INGREDIENTS	MEASURE	WEIGHT	
	VOLUME	OUNCES	GRAMS
hazelnuts	*1 cup*	*5 ounces*	*142 grams*
baking soda	*¼ cup*	*2 ounces*	*60 grams*
bittersweet chocolate	*3⅓ (3-ounce) bars*	*10 ounces*	*284 grams*
crème fraîche (page 348) or heavy cream	*1 cup + 2 tablespoons*	*9 ounces*	*260 grams*

BLANCH THE HAZELNUTS In a medium saucepan, place 3 cups of water and bring it to a boil. Add the nuts and the baking soda, and boil for 3 minutes. Test a nut by running it under cold water. If the skin is not easy to remove with slight pressure from the fingers, return to the heat for a minute or so more. Drain well. Peel.

Toast the hazelnuts in a 350°F. oven for 10 to 15 minutes or until golden brown. Cool completely and chop fine, but not powder-fine. (Use the medium grater on a food processor and then pulse with the metal blade.) Set aside.

Break the chocolate into pieces and process in a food processor until very fine. Heat the cream to the boiling point, and with the motor running, pour it through the feed tube in a steady stream. Process a few seconds until smooth. Add the hazelnuts and pulse just to combine. Transfer to a bowl and cool for several hours, until frosting consistency. In cool weather ganache can remain unrefrigerated for at least 3 days or as long as 2 weeks. At room temperature it remains spreadable.

Trim the bottom and top crusts of the génoise.

With a serrated knife, cut the génoise horizontally into three layers. Spread a small amount of ganache on a cardboard round cut a little larger than the finished cake, or spread it directly onto a serving plate.

Using a straight-sided cookie sheet or pancake turners, lift one génoise layer onto the cardboard or plate. Sprinkle with one third of the liqueur, and spread with about ¾ cup of the ganache. Scatter the chopped cherries on top.

Place the second layer on top of the ganache, and sprinkle it with another third of the liqueur. Spread with about ¾ cup of the ganache, and top with the last génoise layer. Sprinkle it with the remaining liqueur and refrigerate for 1 hour.

Frost the entire cake with the remaining ganache. Decorate with short chocolate cigarettes or curls.

ASSEMBLING THE CAKE

Tweezers work well to place the chocolate cigarettes without breaking them or smudging the surface.

NOTE FROM ROSE

Use a serrated knife or a sharp knife dipped in hot water.

TO SERVE

Airtight, 5 days refrigerated. Remove from the refrigerator at least 1 hour before serving.

KEEPS

LA POMPONNETTE

RUM BABA FILLED WITH CHOCOLATE WHIPPED CREAM

SERVES 10 TO 12

This traditional baba au rhum is a rum-soaked crown filled with a deliciously untraditional chocolate whipped cream.

COMPONENTS

Baba • *Chocolate Whipped Cream*
• *Rum Syrup*

INGREDIENTS	MEASURE	WEIGHT	
	VOLUME	OUNCES	GRAMS
water	2 tablespoons		
sugar	1 tablespoon	0.5 ounce	15 grams
fresh yeast or	2 packed teaspoons	0.5 ounce	11 grams
dry yeast, not rapid-rise	1 ½ teaspoons		4.5 grams
bread flour	2 cups (lightly spooned)	8.75 ounces	250 grams
5 large eggs	1 liquid cup	10 ounces (weighed in the shells)	284 grams
unsalted butter	9 tablespoons	4.5 ounces	125 grams
salt	¾ teaspoon		6 grams
golden raisins	1 cup	5 ounces	142 grams

One lightly buttered 6-cup ring mold.

In a small bowl combine the water (100°F. if using fresh yeast, 110°F. if using dry), ½ teaspoon of the sugar, and the yeast. If you are using fresh yeast, crumble it slightly while adding. Set aside in a draft-free spot for 10 to 20 minutes. By this time, the mixture should be full of bubbles. If not, the yeast is too old to be useful. **PROOF THE YEAST**

In a mixing bowl, combine the flour, eggs, and yeast mixture. Beat (number 6 on a KitchenAid mixer) about 1 minute, or until smooth and well combined. Cut the butter into thin slices and place on top of the dough. Cover with plastic wrap and allow it to rise for 2 hours.

Sprinkle the salt, remaining sugar, and raisins over the dough and mix on low speed just until incorporated and the dough is smooth.

Scrape the mixture into the prepared mold, filling it only half full. Cover it loosely with lightly buttered plastic wrap, and allow it to rise in a warm draft-free area 1 or 2 hours, or until the dough reaches the top of the mold.

Preheat the oven to 450°F. Bake the baba 5 minutes, lower the temperature to 350°F., and continue baking 20 to 25 minutes or until golden brown and a skewer inserted in the center comes out clean.

RUM SYRUP

INGREDIENTS	MEASURE	WEIGHT	
	VOLUME	POUNDS/OUNCES	GRAMS
sugar	*2 cups*	*14 ounces*	*400 grams*
water	*4 cups*	*2 pounds 1.25 ounces*	*944 grams*
dark rum	*½ cup*	*3.75 ounces*	*110 grams*

Prepare shortly before using and keep warm: In a medium saucepan, bring the sugar and water to a full rolling boil, stirring constantly. Remove from the heat and cool for a few minutes before adding the rum.

Unmold the baba onto a rack, and place it in a large pan or on foil (to catch the dripping syrup). Poke it all over with a cake tester or skewer, and spoon on the hot syrup until as much as possible of it is absorbed (a poultry baster works well). Reserve the extra syrup. Allow it to rest for several hours, until firm enough to transfer to a serving plate.

CHOCOLATE WHIPPED CREAM

INGREDIENTS	MEASURE	WEIGHT	
	VOLUME	OUNCES	GRAMS
heavy cream	*1 cup*	*8 ounces*	*232 grams*
unsweetened cocoa	*¼ cup (lightly spooned)*	*0.75 ounce*	*25 grams*
superfine sugar	*⅓ cup*	*2.25 ounces*	*66 grams*
vanilla	*½ teaspoon*		

A PASSION FOR CHOCOLATE

In a large mixing bowl, place all the ingredients and stir well. Refrigerate for at least 1 hour to dissolve the cocoa (chill the beater alongside bowl).

Beat until stiff peaks form when the beater is raised. Keep chilled until ready to use.

Spoon chocolate whipped cream into the center, or pipe with a star tube of your choice. **ASSEMBLING THE BABA**

Slice with a serrated knife. Serve with a dollop of the chocolate whipped cream on the side. Pass around the leftover syrup to pour over the slices if desired. **SERVE**

Airtight, 4 days refrigerated. Remove from the refrigerator at least 30 minutes before serving. **KEEPS**

LE QUATRE-QUARTS AU CHOCOLAT

CHOCOLATE POUND CAKE

SERVES 8 TO 10

This is the Bernachon chocolate version of the classic French pound cake that is prepared by housewives throughout France. For the best texture, a syrup (see the note) is highly recommended.

INGREDIENTS	MEASURE	WEIGHT	
	VOLUME	OUNCES	GRAMS
unsalted butter	1¼ cups	10 ounces	284 grams
sifted cake flour	2 cups	7 ounces	200 grams
unsweetened cocoa	½ cup (lightly spooned)	1.75 ounces	50 grams
baking powder	1½ teaspoons		7 grams
4 extra-large eggs, separated			
yolks	⅓ liquid cup	2.75 ounces	79 grams
whites	4.5 fluid ounces	4.75 ounces	135 grams
superfine sugar	1¼ cups	8.75 ounces	250 grams
salt	pinch		
cream of tartar	½ teaspoon		

One 9 by 5 by 3-inch (8-cup) loaf pan, greased, bottom lined with parchment or wax paper, then greased again and floured.

Preheat the oven to 400°F.

Melt the butter and allow it to cool until no longer warm.

Whisk together the cake flour, cocoa, and baking powder until well combined.

In a mixing bowl, with the whisk attachment, beat the yolks with all but 2 tablespoons of the sugar until the mixture is very thick and light in color.

Using a large rubber spatula, fold in the butter.

Sift the flour mixture over the egg mixture in two stages, continuing to fold until totally incorporated.

In a mixing bowl beat the egg whites with the pinch of salt until foamy. Add the cream of tartar, and beat until soft peaks form when the beater is raised slowly. Add the reserved 2 tablespoons of sugar, beating until very stiff peaks form when the beater is raised slowly.

Fold the whites into the batter in two stages, until uniformly combined.

Scrape the batter into the prepared pan. Bake 40 minutes, or until a wooden toothpick inserted in the center comes out clean and the cake springs back when lightly pressed in the center. If necessary, tent the cake with foil after about 25 minutes to prevent overbrowning.

Let the cake cool in the pan on a rack for 10 minutes. Then loosen the sides with a small metal spatula and invert onto a greased metal rack. Reinvert so that the top is up, and cool completely before wrapping airtight.

NOTE FROM ROSE

Although not strictly traditional, a simple sugar syrup flavored with Kahlúa does wonders for taste and texture: In a small pan, stir together ⅓ cup water and 2 tablespoons sugar. Bring to a full rolling boil, cover, and remove from the heat. When the syrup is cool, add 2 tablespoons Kahlúa. When the cake is removed from the oven, poke holes all over with a thin metal or wooden skewer and brush half the syrup over the top. Cool the cake 10 minutes and then invert it onto a lightly greased rack. Brush the bottom and sides with the remaining syrup. Reinvert onto a rack, top side up, to finish cooling. Allow the cake to rest, airtight, for at least 2 hours to distribute the syrup evenly.

TO SERVE Slice with a serrated knife.

KEEPS The texture is the most moist the same day or up to one day after.

A PASSION FOR CHOCOLATE

LE SAINT-HONORÉ AU CHOCOLAT

RING OF CARAMEL- or CHOCOLATE-GLAZED CREAM PUFFS ON TOP OF A ROUND OF PIE PASTRY, FILLED WITH CHOCOLATE PASTRY CREAM

SERVES 8 TO 10

Gâteau St. Honoré is one of the great French classics, consisting of a pastry base surrounded by cream puffs topped with a crunchy burnishing of caramel, the centers filled with whipped-cream–lightened pastry cream. The Bernachon version of this classic is further lightened and enhanced by replacing the pastry cream with chocolate whipped cream.

COMPONENTS
Pâte Brisée • Cream-Puff Pastry • Caramel • Chocolate Whipped Cream

PÂTE BRISÉE

INGREDIENTS	MEASURE	WEIGHT	
	VOLUME	OUNCES	GRAMS
unsalted butter	*9 tablespoons*	*4.5 ounces*	*125 grams*
all-purpose flour	*1¾ cups (dip and sweep)*	*8.75 ounces*	*250 grams*
salt	*¼ teaspoon*		
1 extra-large egg		*2.25 ounces*	*65 grams*
ice water	*1 to 2 tablespoons*		

One 12-inch or larger baking round or sheet.

Cut the butter into small pieces and allow it to soften slightly.

In a bowl, combine the flour, salt, and butter. Rub between the fingertips until coarse and crumbly—don't overdo or it will be too tender.

Add the egg and mix lightly with the fingertips or a fork until the flour mixture is moistened. Sprinkle on the water, 1 teaspoon at a time, until all the particles are moistened and the mixture begins to hold together. Dump the dough out onto a work surface and "*fraiser*": smear it in front of you with the palm of the hand, two or three times, but don't overwork it. The dough should feel slightly elastic. Flatten it into two discs, one a little larger than the other, wrap in plastic, and let it rest, refrigerated, for at least 2 hours.

Freeze the smaller disc for future use. Roll out the larger disc about ⅛ inch thick, 10 inches in diameter. Transfer it to a baking sheet and prick the bottom. Cover with plastic wrap and refrigerate until the cream-puff pastry has been prepared (up to 1 day ahead).

CREAM-PUFF PASTRY

INGREDIENTS	MEASURE	WEIGHT	
	VOLUME	OUNCES	GRAMS
milk	⅔ *cup*	5.5 *ounces*	160 *grams*
unsalted butter	5 *tablespoons*	2.5 *ounces*	71 *grams*
sugar	1½ *teaspoons*		7 *grams*
salt	½ *teaspoon*		
all-purpose flour	1 *cup (lightly spooned)*	4.25 *ounces*	121 *grams*
5 large eggs	1 *liquid cup*	10 *ounces* (weighed in the shells)	284 *grams*

One baking sheet, greased or lined with parchment.

Preheat the oven to 400°F.

In a medium saucepan, combine the milk, butter, sugar, and salt, and bring the mixture to a full rolling boil. Remove immediately from the heat, and add the flour all at once. Stir with a wooden spoon until the mixture forms a ball, leaves the sides of the pan, and clings slightly to the spoon. Return to low heat and cook, stirring and mashing continuously, for about 3 minutes (to cook the flour). Without scraping the pan, transfer the mixture to the bowl of a food processor fitted with the metal blade.

Process 15 seconds with the feed tube open (to allow steam to escape). With the motor running, pour in the eggs and continue processing for 30 seconds. The mixture should be smooth, shiny, and too soft to hold peaks. (If using an electric mixer, allow the flour mixture to cool for 5 minutes in the bowl. Then beat in the eggs, one at a time, beating after each addition until incorporated.)

Fill a pastry bag, fitted with a number 6 (½-inch) tip, with the mixture. Pipe a ring on top of the pâte brisée pastry disc—not too close to the outer edge, as the cream-puff pastry will expand and the pastry base will shrink slightly on baking. Pipe a second ring inside and touching the first one.

If you are using parchment, place a small dot of

the cream-puff pastry at each corner to attach it to the baking sheet. With the remaining pastry, pipe puffs 1½ inches in diameter at least 1 inch apart. (Twelve to fourteen puffs are needed for the cake. Extra puffs can be stored in an airtight plastic bag or container up to 1 week refrigerated, 6 months frozen.)

Bake the puffs and the pastry round for about 20 minutes, or until the puffs are golden brown and do not yield to pressure when squeezed gently. Remove the pastry round and cool it on a rack. Leave the puffs in the turned-off oven for 1 hour, using a wooden spoon to prop the oven door slightly ajar. Then remove the puffs to a rack and cool completely. If necessary, trim any excess pastry base with a sharp knife while the pastry is still hot.

NOTE   To prevent the puffs from collapsing, do not open the oven door until shortly before the end of the baking time.

CHOCOLATE WHIPPED CREAM

INGREDIENTS	MEASURE	WEIGHT	
	VOLUME	OUNCES	GRAMS
heavy cream	*2 cups*	*16 ounces*	*464 grams*
unsweetened cocoa	*½ cup (lightly spooned)*	*1.75 ounces*	*50 grams*
superfine sugar	*⅔ cup*	*4.5 ounces*	*132 grams*
vanilla	*1 teaspoon*		

In a large mixing bowl, place all the ingredients and stir well. Refrigerate for at least 1 hour to dissolve the cocoa (chill beater alongside bowl).

When you are ready to assemble the cake, beat until stiff peaks form when the beater is raised. Refrigerate.

CARAMEL*

INGREDIENTS	MEASURE	WEIGHT	
	VOLUME	OUNCES	GRAMS
sugar	1 cup	7 ounces	200 grams
water	⅓ liquid cup	2.75 ounces	80 grams
cream of tartar	⅛ teaspoon		

In a small heavy saucepan, combine all the ingredients and cook over medium-low heat, stirring constantly, to dissolve the sugar. Increase the heat and boil without stirring until pale amber (350°F. to 360°F.). Remove the pan from the heat and set the bottom of the pan in cold water to stop the cooking.

ASSEMBLING THE ST. HONORÉ

Holding a puff with tongs or fingertips, carefully dip the bottom into the caramel and attach it to the cream-puff ring. Continue with the remaining puffs until the ring is complete. Drizzle the remaining caramel over the tops of the puffs.

Fill the center of the ring with the chocolate whipped cream, using a large star tip if desired for a special decorative effect.

Refrigerate uncovered until serving time.

VARIATION*: Chocolate

In place of the caramel, place about 6 ounces of bittersweet chocolate in the top of a double boiler set over very hot water (no hotter than 160°F). The water must not simmer or touch the bottom of the top part of the double boiler. Stir until the chocolate begins to melt. Return the double boiler to low heat if the water cools, but be careful that it does not get too hot. The chocolate may be melted in a microwave oven if it is stirred every 15 seconds. With either method, remove the chocolate from the heat source before it is fully melted, and stir, having the residual heat complete the melting. Proceed with the recipe, using this instead of caramel.

TO SERVE

Slice with a serrated knife.

The texture is at its best for no more than 4 hours.

NOTES
FROM ROSE

When baking the pâte brisée pastry base with the cream-puff pastry piped on top, as it expands the ring of cream puff sometimes slips a little from the pastry, which tends to contract. If you prefer, you can bake the two separately and attach the ring with caramel or melted chocolate.

For a special effect, puff pastry (page 311) may be used in place of the pâte brisée. This is a wonderfully impressive dessert. Although it is composed of several elements, each is easy and the final result stunning.

When making caramel, if you have a microwave oven, pour the caramel into a heat-proof glass measure. If it cools and becomes too thick, a few seconds in the microwave are the ideal way to reheat it.

LE SÉVILLAN

SQUARE LAYERS OF YELLOW GÉNOISE WITH A CHOCOLATE FILLING AND FROSTING AND AN ENCASEMENT OF NUTS OF YOUR CHOICE

SERVES 8 TO 10

The faintly orangey and indescribable tones of Grand Marnier blend magnificently with golden honeyed génoise and chocolate ganache. This splendid cake is decoratively topped with chocolate cigarettes, which are said to have been invented in Seville, Spain.

COMPONENTS
Génoise • *Grand Marnier Syrup* • *Ganache*

DECORATION
Chocolate cigarettes (9 ounces bittersweet chocolate) or grated chocolate, chopped nuts such as hazelnuts or almonds (¾ cup/3 ounces/85 grams)

GÉNOISE

INGREDIENTS	MEASURE	WEIGHT	
ROOM TEMPERATURE	VOLUME	OUNCES	GRAMS
unsalted butter	*3 tablespoons*	*1.5 ounces*	*40 grams*
vanilla	*1 teaspoon*		*4 grams*
4 extra-large eggs	*7 fluid ounces*	*9 ounces*	*260 grams*
			(weighed in the shells)
superfine sugar	*½ cup + 1 tablespoon*	*4 ounces*	*114 grams*
honey (optional)	*2 teaspoons*	*0.5 ounce*	*14 grams*
sifted cake flour	*2 cups*	*7 ounces*	*200 grams*

One 8 by 8 by 2-inch square baking pan, greased, bottom lined with parchment or wax paper, and then greased again and floured.

Preheat the oven to 400°F.

In a small saucepan, melt the butter and add the vanilla. Set aside to keep warm.

In a large mixing bowl set over a pan of simmering water, heat the eggs, sugar, and optional honey (for extra moistness) until just lukewarm, stirring constantly to prevent curdling. (The eggs may also be heated by placing them *still in their shells* in a large mixing bowl in an oven with a pilot light for 3 hours or up to overnight.) Using the whisk attachment, beat the mixture on high speed for 5 minutes or until tripled in volume. (A hand beater may be used, but it will be necessary to beat for at least 10 minutes.)

Remove 1 cup of the egg mixture and thoroughly whisk it into the warm melted butter.

Sift half the flour over the remaining egg mixture, and fold it in *gently* but rapidly with a large balloon whisk, slotted skimmer, or rubber spatula until almost all the flour has disappeared. Repeat with the remaining flour, folding just until the flour has disappeared completely. Fold in the butter mixture until just incorporated.

Pour immediately into the prepared pan, and bake 20 to 30 minutes or until the cake is golden brown and has started to shrink slightly from the sides of the pan. (No need for a cake tester. Once the sides shrink, the cake is done.) Avoid opening the oven door before the minimum time or the cake could fall. Toward the end of the baking time, open the door slightly, and if at a quick glance the cake does not appear done, close the door at once and check again in 5 minutes.

Loosen the sides of the cake with a small metal spatula, and unmold at once onto a lightly greased rack. Reinvert it to cool.

Génoise cuts more easily when made ahead and **NOTE** chilled.

GRAND MARNIER SYRUP

INGREDIENTS	MEASURE	WEIGHT	
	VOLUME	OUNCES	GRAMS
water	*¼ cup*	*2 ounces*	*60 grams*
sugar	*⅓ cup*	*2 ounces*	*60 grams*
Grand Marnier	*¼ cup*	*2 ounces*	*60 grams*

In a small saucepan with a tight-fitting lid, bring the sugar and water to a rolling boil, stirring constantly. Cover immediately, remove from the heat, and allow to cool completely. Stir in the Grand Marnier.

GANACHE

INGREDIENTS	MEASURE	WEIGHT	
	VOLUME	OUNCES	GRAMS
bittersweet chocolate	*4 (3-ounce) bars*	*12 ounces*	*340 grams*
crème fraîche (page 348) or heavy cream	*1 ¼ cups*	*10 ounces*	*290 grams*

Break the chocolate into pieces and process in a food processor until very fine.

Heat the crème fraîche to the boiling point, and with the motor running, pour it through the feed tube

117

in a steady stream. Process a few seconds until smooth. Transfer to a bowl and cool for several hours, until frosting consistency. In cool weather ganache can remain unrefrigerated for at least 3 days or as long as 2 weeks. At room temperature it remains spreadable.

ASSEMBLING THE CAKE

Trim the bottom and top crusts of the génoise.

Using a serrated knife, cut the génoise horizontally into three layers. Spread a small amount of ganache on a cardboard square cut a little larger than the finished cake, or spread it directly onto a serving plate.

Using a flat cookie sheet or pancake turners, lift one génoise layer onto the cardboard or plate. Sprinkle with one third of the syrup and spread with about 1 cup of the ganache.

Place the second layer on top of the ganache, and sprinkle it with another third of the syrup. Spread with about 1 cup of the ganache, and top with the last génoise layer. Sprinkle it with the remaining syrup, and refrigerate for 1 hour.

Frost the entire cake with the remaining ganache. Decorate it with chocolate cigarettes or curls, and with chopped nuts on the side.

TO SERVE

Slice with a serrated knife or a sharp knife that has been dipped into hot water.

NOTES FROM ROSE

To make extra long cigarettes, insert one smaller end into a second larger one in a telescoping fashion.

For a special striped effect, lay strips of wax paper over the top of the cake, sprinkle with powdered sugar, and carefully remove the strips.

KEEPS

Airtight, 5 days refrigerated. Remove from the refrigerator at least 1 hour before serving.

LE SICILIEN

LAYERS OF CHOCOLATE
GÉNOISE BETWEEN PISTACHIO
BUTTERCREAM

SERVES 8 TO 10

As a child I often agonized between my two favorite ice cream flavors: pistachio and chocolate. If only I had known then how wonderful they are together!

This cake, which features the pistachio nut, is named for the region that is said to produce the most fabulous variety.

COMPONENTS
Chocolate Génoise • *Kirsch Syrup* •
Pistachio Buttercream • *Ganache*

DECORATION
Chopped pistachio nuts and/or pistachio marzipan (8 ounces),
a few thin chocolate cigarettes

CHOCOLATE GÉNOISE

INGREDIENTS	MEASURE	WEIGHT	
	VOLUME	OUNCES	GRAMS
unsalted butter	*3 tablespoons*	*1.5 ounces*	*43 grams*
vanilla	*1½ teaspoons*		*6 grams*
6 large eggs	*9.5 fluid ounces*	*12 ounces*	*340 grams* (weighed in the shells)
superfine sugar	*¾ cup*	*5.25 ounces*	*150 grams*
honey (optional)	*1 tablespoon*	*.75 ounce*	*21 grams*
sifted cake flour	*1½ cups*	*5.25 ounces*	*150 grams*
unsweetened cocoa	*¼ cup (lightly spooned)*	*0.75 ounce*	*21 grams*

One 8 by 8 by 2-inch baking pan, greased, bottom lined with parchment or wax paper, then greased again and floured.

Preheat the oven to 400°F.

In a small saucepan, melt the butter, and add the vanilla. Set aside to keep warm.

In a large mixing bowl set over a pan of simmering water, heat the eggs, sugar, and optional honey for extra moistness until just lukewarm, stirring constantly to prevent curdling. (The eggs may also be heated by placing them *still in their shells* in a large mixing bowl in an oven with a pilot light for 3 hours or up to overnight.) Using the whisk attachment, beat the mixture on high speed for 5 minutes or until tripled in volume. (A hand beater may be used, but it will be necessary to beat for at least 10 minutes.)

While eggs are beating, sift together the flour and cocoa.

Remove 1 cup of the egg mixture, and thoroughly whisk it into the warm melted butter.

Sift half the flour mixture over the remaining egg mixture, and fold it in *gently* but rapidly with a large balloon whisk, slotted skimmer, or rubber spatula until almost all the flour has disappeared. Repeat with the remaining flour, folding just until the flour has disappeared completely. Fold in the butter mixture until just incorporated.

Pour immediately into the prepared pan, and bake 25 to 30 minutes or until the cake has started to shrink slightly from the sides of the pan. (No need for a cake tester. Once the sides shrink, the cake is done.) Avoid opening the oven door before the minimum time or the cake could fall. Toward the end of the baking time, open the door slightly, and if at a quick glance the cake does not appear done, close the door at once and check again in 5 minutes.

Loosen the sides of the cake with a small metal spatula, and unmold at once onto a lightly greased rack. Reinvert to cool.

KIRSCH SYRUP

INGREDIENTS	MEASURE	WEIGHT	
	VOLUME	OUNCES	GRAMS
water	¼ cup	2 ounces	60 grams
sugar	⅓ cup	2 ounces	60 grams
kirsch	¼ cup	2 ounces	60 grams

In a small saucepan with a tight-fitting lid, bring the water and sugar to a rolling boil, stirring constantly. Cover immediately, remove from the heat, and allow to cool completely. Stir in the kirsch.

INGREDIENTS MEASURE		WEIGHT	
	VOLUME	POUNDS/OUNCES	GRAMS
milk	2 ½ cups	1 pound 5.25 ounces	605 grams
1 vanilla bean, split*			
salt	¾ teaspoon		5 grams
5 large egg yolks	3 fluid ounces	3.25 ounces	93 grams
superfine sugar	¾ cup	5.25 ounces	150 grams
all-purpose flour	½ cup (dip and sweep)	2.5 ounces	71 grams
unsalted butter, softened	⅓ cup	2.5 ounces	75 grams
pistachio extract or	1 teaspoon		
shelled unsalted pistachio nuts, ground†	⅓ cup	1.75 ounces	50 grams

*You may substitute 1 teaspoon vanilla extract for the vanilla bean, but the bean offers a fuller, more aromatic flavor. If you are using extract, add it after the buttercream has cooled. If using a Tahitian bean, use only ½ bean.
†If you are using pistachio nuts instead of the extract, remove the skins by baking the nuts in a 350°F. oven for 5 to 10 minutes, or until the skins separate from the nuts when scratched lightly with a fingernail. In a food processor or nut grinder, grind the nuts very fine.

In a saucepan, place 2 cups of the milk, the vanilla bean, and the salt. Bring it to a full boil, then remove from the heat.

In a medium bowl, whisk together the egg yolks and sugar until thoroughly combined. Whisk in the flour, and then the remaining ½ cup of cold milk (to prevent curdling). Whisking constantly, gradually add the hot milk. Return the mixture to the saucepan and bring to a boil, whisking constantly. Simmer for 3 minutes, whisking constantly.

Transfer the mixture to a bowl, press plastic wrap directly onto the surface (to prevent a skin from forming), and cool unrefrigerated. In a small bowl, mash the butter with a fork to ensure that it is soft and creamy throughout. When the cream is almost cold, remove the vanilla bean and gently whisk in the butter just until smooth. Divide the buttercream into two equal batches, and add the pistachio extract or ground pistachio nuts to one. Re-cover with plastic wrap.

Pastry cream must not be cold when butter is added **NOTE** or it will separate. If separation should occur, warm the bottom of the bowl over hot water for 2 to 3 seconds before continuing to beat. Overbeating will also cause cream to break down.

GANACHE

INGREDIENTS	MEASURE	WEIGHT	
	VOLUME	OUNCES	GRAMS
bittersweet chocolate	*1⅓ (3-ounce) bars*	*4 ounces*	*113 grams*
crème fraîche (page 348) or heavy cream	*⅓ cup*	*2.5 ounces*	*77 grams*

Break the chocolate into pieces and process in a food processor until very fine.

Heat the crème fraîche to the boiling point, and with the motor running, pour it through the feed tube in a steady stream. Process a few seconds until smooth. Transfer to a bowl and cool for several hours, until frosting consistency. In cool weather ganache can remain unrefrigerated for at least 3 days or as long as 2 weeks. At room temperature it remains spreadable.

Trim the bottom and top crusts of the génoise. **ASSEMBLING**
Using a serrated knife, cut the génoise horizon- **THE CAKE** tally into four layers. Spread a small amount of ganache on a cardboard square cut a little larger than the finished cake, or spread it directly onto a serving plate.

Using a flat cookie sheet or pancake turners, lift one génoise layer onto the cardboard or plate. Sprinkle with one fourth of the syrup, and spread with the pistachio buttercream.

Place the second layer on top, and sprinkle it with another fourth of the syrup. Spread with the plain buttercream, and top with the third layer of génoise.

Sprinkle it with another fourth of the syrup, and spread with about 1 ¼ cups ganache.

Place the fourth génoise layer on top, sprinkle with the remaining syrup, and refrigerate for 1 hour. Frost the entire cake with the remaining ganache.

TO DECORATE WITH MARZIPAN Knead ½ teaspoon of pistachio extract or a few drops of green food coloring into ¾ cup + 1 tablespoon (8 ounces/227 grams) of marzipan.* Roll out between sheets of plastic wrap to form an 8-inch square. Slip the marzipan onto a cookie sheet and trim the edges. Freeze for at least 5 minutes, or until firm enough to handle easily. Remove the plastic wrap and place the marzipan on top of cake.

For an unusual decorative effect, dust the top lightly with powdered sugar, heat a metal skewer or spatula until red hot, and press it gently against the marzipan. The sugar in the marzipan will caramelize and brown, creating interesting markings. Alternatively, decorate with the thinnest possible chocolate cigarettes.

TO SERVE Slice with a serrated knife.

KEEPS Airtight, 5 days refrigerated. Remove from the refrigerator at least 1 hour before serving.

NOTE FROM ROSE A few teaspoons of melted cocoa butter, kneaded into the marzipan just before rolling, gives it a beautifully smooth and supple texture. Start by adding 1 teaspoon and if the marzipan is still a bit stiff, add more, a teaspoon at a time.

*See sources, page 382.

LE SUCCÈS

ALMOND MERINGUE LAYER
CAKE FILLED WITH CHOCOLATE GANACHE
AND DUSTED WITH COCOA

SERVES 8 TO 10

This cake is the Bernachons' hands-down favorite (mine too!). This is the cake Maurice's mother made for him when he was a child. He especially loves the marriage of almonds and bittersweet chocolate, and the fact that there is no alcohol to interfere with the pure taste of the cocoa. The cake will have the tenderest texture if prepared at least 1 day ahead.

COMPONENTS
Succès • *Ganache*

DECORATION
Unsweetened cocoa

SUCCÈS

INGREDIENTS	MEASURE	WEIGHT	
	VOLUME	OUNCES	GRAMS
sliced almonds	2 cups	6.25 ounces	180 grams
superfine sugar	¾ cup + 2 tablespoons	6.25 ounces	180 grams
7 large egg whites, room temperature	7 fluid ounces	7.25 ounces	210 grams
cream of tartar	1 teaspoon		3 grams

Two baking sheets, buttered and floured or lined with parchment, marked with three 8-inch circles.

Preheat the oven to 350°F.

In a food processor, place the almonds and ¾ cup sugar and process until the almonds are finely grated.

In a mixing bowl, beat the egg whites until foamy, add the cream of tartar, and beat until soft peaks form when the beater is raised slowly. Gradually add the remaining 2 tablespoons sugar, beating until stiff peaks form when the beater is raised slowly. Fold in the grated almond mixture.

Using a 1-gallon zip-seal bag with one corner cut off, or a pastry bag fitted with a large plain number 6 (½-inch) tip, pipe the batter onto the prepared baking sheets to form three 8-inch circles, starting with the perimeter and spiraling inward toward the center. Use a small metal spatula to fill in any gaps with leftover batter and to smooth the surface. Bake for 15 to 20 minutes, or just until the discs begin to brown.

Remove baking sheets to a rack. Loosen the succès from the sheets, and allow them to cool completely on the sheets before transferring to a work surface or serving plate. They will have expanded to about 9 inches.

To obtain a perfect circle, invert a cake pan over the succès and trim any excess with a sharp knife.

NOTES FROM ROSE Use superfine sugar for the best texture. It is not actually necessary to use flour on the baking pan to keep it from sticking; however, the flour does have the desirable effect of keeping the succès from spreading.

The recipe makes three discs. Freeze one for another use, or, if desired, to make a higher cake as in the photo, make extra ganache (1 pound chocolate; 1⅔ cups cream) and use the third disc to create another layer. The original version makes a very low, European-style cake.

GANACHE

INGREDIENTS	MEASURE	WEIGHT	
	VOLUME	OUNCES	GRAMS
bittersweet chocolate	*4 (3-ounce) bars*	*12 ounces*	*340 grams*
crème fraîche (page 348) or heavy cream	*1¼ cups*	*10 ounces*	*290 grams*

Break the chocolate into pieces and process in a food processor until very fine.

Heat the crème fraîche to the boiling point, and with the motor running, pour it through the feed tube in a steady stream. Process a few seconds until smooth. Transfer to a bowl and cool for several hours, until frosting consistency. In cool weather ganache can remain unrefrigerated for at least 3 days or as long as 2 weeks. At room temperature it remains spreadable.

ASSEMBLING THE CAKE

Place one disc of succès on a cardboard round or serving plate, and top with an even layer of about two thirds of the chocolate ganache. Place the second disc on top, flat side up. Refrigerate for at least 1 hour.

Using a long metal spatula, spread the remaining ganache evenly on top of the succès and a thin layer around the sides.

Place a few tablespoons of cocoa in a flour dredger or fine strainer, and sprinkle it evenly over the top of the succès. For decorative markings, lightly press a cake rack on top of the cocoa and lift away carefully.

TO SERVE

Slice with a serrated knife.

KEEPS

Airtight, 5 days refrigerated. Remove from the refrigerator at least 1 hour before serving.

LE TORINO

YELLOW GÉNOISE LAYER CAKE
FILLED WITH CHESTNUT BUTTERCREAM
AND CHOCOLATE GANACHE

SERVES 8 TO 10

This autumn and winter cake is named for the region of Italy that produces the finest chestnuts. The perfect marriage of chestnuts and rum stands up to the prevailing flavor of the chocolate in the ganache.

COMPONENTS
*Génoise • Rum Syrup •
Chestnut Buttercream • Ganache •*

DECORATION
Almond paste (7 ounces/200 grams) • 12 marrons glacés
(whole candied chestnuts) • Optional: piped melted
bittersweet chocolate (page 378)

GÉNOISE

INGREDIENTS	MEASURE	WEIGHT	
ROOM TEMPERATURE	VOLUME	OUNCES	GRAMS
unsalted butter	*¼ cup*	*2 ounces*	*60 grams*
vanilla	*1 ½ teaspoons*		*6 grams*
7 large eggs	*1 ½ liquid cups*	*14 ounces*	*400 grams (weighed in the shells)*
superfine sugar	*¾ cup + 2 tablespoons*	*6 ounces*	*170 grams*
honey (optional)	*1 tablespoon*	*.75 ounce*	*21 grams*
sifted cake flour	*2 cups*	*7 ounces*	*200 grams*

One 10 by 3-inch round baking pan or springform pan, greased, bottom lined with parchment or wax paper, and then greased again and floured.

Preheat the oven to 400°F. In a small saucepan, melt the butter and add the vanilla. Set aside to keep warm.

In a large mixing bowl set over a pan of simmering water, heat the eggs, sugar, and optional honey for extra moistness until just lukewarm, stirring constantly to prevent curdling. (The eggs may also be heated by placing them *still in their shells* in a large mixing bowl in an oven with a pilot light for 3 hours or up to overnight.) Using the whisk attachment, beat the mixture on high speed for 5 minutes or until tripled in volume. (A hand beater may be used, but it will be necessary to beat for at least 10 minutes.)

Remove 1 cup of the egg mixture and thoroughly whisk it into the warm melted butter.

Sift half the flour over the remaining egg mixture, and fold it in *gently* but rapidly with a large balloon whisk, slotted skimmer, or rubber spatula until almost all the flour has disappeared. Repeat with the remaining flour. Fold in the butter mixture until just incorporated.

Pour immediately into the prepared pan, and bake 20 to 30 minutes or until the cake is golden brown and has started to shrink slightly from the sides of the pan. Avoid opening the oven door before the minimum time or the cake could fall. Toward the end of the baking time, open the door slightly, and if at a quick glance the cake does not appear done, close the door at once and check again in 5 minutes.

Loosen the sides of the cake with a small metal spatula, and unmold at once onto a lightly greased rack. Reinvert to cool.

NOTE Génoise cuts more easily when made ahead and chilled.

RUM SYRUP

INGREDIENTS	MEASURE	WEIGHT	
	VOLUME	OUNCES	GRAMS
water	3 tablespoons	1.5 ounces	43 grams
sugar	¼ cup	1.75 ounces	50 grams
dark rum	3 tablespoons	1.5 ounces	41 grams

In a small saucepan with a tight-fitting lid, bring the water and sugar to a rolling boil, stirring constantly. Cover immediately, remove from the heat, and allow to cool completely. Stir in the rum.

CHESTNUT BUTTERCREAM

INGREDIENTS	MEASURE	WEIGHT	
	VOLUME	OUNCES	GRAMS
milk	1 cup	8.5 ounces	242 grams
1-inch piece of vanilla bean*			
salt	⅛ teaspoon		
2 extra-large egg yolks		1.25 ounces	37 grams
superfine sugar	3 tablespoons + 1½ teaspoons	2 ounces	57 grams
all-purpose flour	3 tablespoons	0.5 ounce	18 grams
unsalted butter, softened	2 tablespoons	0.5 ounce	18 grams
crème de marrons (chestnut cream)†	1 cup	8 ounces	225 grams

*You may substitute ¼ teaspoon vanilla extract for the vanilla bean, but the bean offers a fuller, more aromatic flavor. If you are using extract, add it after the buttercream has cooled. If using a Tahitian bean, use only ½ inch.
†Available in specialty food stores.

A PASSION FOR CHOCOLATE

In a saucepan, place ¾ cup of the milk, the vanilla bean, and the salt. Bring it to a full boil, then remove from the heat.

In a medium bowl, whisk together the egg yolks and sugar until thoroughly combined. Whisk in the flour, and then the remaining cold milk (to prevent curdling). Whisking constantly, gradually add the hot milk.

Return the mixture to the saucepan and bring it to a boil, whisking constantly. Simmer for 3 minutes, whisking constantly.

Transfer the mixture to a bowl, press plastic wrap directly onto the surface (to prevent a skin from forming), and cool unrefrigerated. In a small bowl, whisk together the butter and *crème de marrons*. When the cream is almost cold, remove the vanilla bean, and gently whisk in the butter and *crème de marrons* just until smooth. Return plastic to the surface. Store refrigerated.

GANACHE

INGREDIENTS	MEASURE	WEIGHT	
	VOLUME	OUNCES	GRAMS
bittersweet chocolate	*2 (3-ounce) bars*	*6 ounces*	*170 grams*
crème fraîche (page 348) or heavy cream	*⅔ cup*	*5 ounces*	*150 grams*

Break the chocolate into pieces and process in a food processor until very fine.

Heat the crème fraîche to the boiling point, and with the motor running, pour it through the feed tube in a steady stream. Process a few seconds until smooth. Transfer to a bowl and cool for several hours, until frosting consistency. In cool weather ganache can remain unrefrigerated for at least 3 days or as long as 2 weeks. At room temperature it remains spreadable.

ASSEMBLING
THE CAKE

Trim the bottom and top crusts of the génoise.

Using a serrated knife, cut the génoise horizontally into three layers. Spread a small amount of ganache on a cardboard round cut a little larger than the finished cake, or spread it directly onto a serving plate.

Using a flat cookie sheet or pancake turners, lift one génoise layer onto the cardboard or plate. Sprinkle with one third of the syrup, and spread with about one third of the chestnut buttercream. Set aside three of the most attractive marrons glacés, and crumble the rest on top of the buttercream.

Place the second layer of génoise on top, and sprinkle it with another third of the syrup. Spread with the ganache, and top with the last génoise layer. Sprinkle it with the remaining syrup, and frost the entire cake with the remaining chestnut buttercream. Refrigerate for 1 hour.

Roll the almond paste between sheets of plastic wrap or on a surface sprinkled with powdered sugar. Using a zigzag pastry cutter or wheel, cut a circle about 12 inches in diameter. Slide your hands, palms down, under the almond paste and lift it onto the cake. With a circular motion, smooth the top into place. Decorate the cake with the reserved chestnuts and, if desired, designs of piped chocolate.

TO SERVE

Slice with a serrated knife.

KEEPS

Airtight, 2 days refrigerated. Remove from the refrigerator at least 1 hour before serving.

NOTES
FROM ROSE

A few teaspoons of melted cocoa butter, kneaded into the marzipan just before rolling, gives it a beautifully smooth and supple texture. Start by adding 1 teaspoon and if the marzipan is still a bit stiff, add more, a teaspoon at a time. A decoratively embossed rolling pin can be used to create interesting designs on the surface of the almond paste.

The marriage of chestnut, rum, and chocolate was indeed one made in heaven. This is a cold-weather dessert not only because of the strong, deep flavors but also, logically, because cold weather is chestnut harvesting time.

LITTLE CAKES AND COOKIES

LES BROWNIES

CHOCOLATE BROWNIES WITH MOIST AND CHEWY CENTERS

MAKES 16 BROWNIES

This fabulous brownie recipe was given to the Bernachons by two American women who taught cooking in Lyon, France. The brownies are medium chocolate in color, and slice easily yet somehow stay (miraculously) moist and chewy. My dear friend Nancy Blitzer applauds these as the best of more than fifty brownie recipes she has tested in her kitchen. In fact, everyone who tastes these brownies proclaims them the best.

| INGREDIENTS | MEASURE | | WEIGHT |
	VOLUME	OUNCES	GRAMS
bittersweet chocolate	1⅔ (3-ounce) bars	5 ounces	142 grams
unsalted butter	6 tablespoons	3 ounces	85 grams
sifted all-purpose flour	1¼ cups	5 ounces	142 grams
baking powder	½ teaspoon		
salt	½ teaspoon		
superfine sugar	¾ cup + 2 tablespoons	6 ounces	175 grams
2 extra-large eggs	½ liquid cup	4.5 ounces	130 grams (weighed in the shells)
walnuts, coarsely chopped	1 scant cup	3.5 ounces	100 grams

One 8-inch square baking pan, greased, lined with parchment or wax paper, then greased again and floured.

Preheat the oven to 350°F.

Break the chocolate into squares and place them, together with the butter, in the top of a double boiler set over very hot water (but no hotter than 160°F.). The water must not simmer or touch the bottom of the double boiler insert.

Stir until the chocolate begins to melt. Return the pan to low heat if the water cools, but be careful that it does not get too hot. (The chocolate and butter may be melted in a microwave oven if stirred every 15 seconds.) Using either method, remove it from the heat source before fully melted and stir, using the residual heat to complete the melting. Allow the chocolate to cool just until no hotter than lukewarm.

In a small bowl, whisk together the flour, baking powder, and salt.

Gradually add the sugar, eggs, and then the flour mixture to the chocolate. Mix until well incorporated. Stir in the nuts.

Scrape the batter into the prepared pan and bake

A PASSION FOR CHOCOLATE

30 to 35 minutes, or until a toothpick inserted in the center comes out almost clean. The brownies should still be slightly moist in the center.

Loosen the sides with a small metal spatula and unmold onto a lightly greased cookie sheet. Reinvert onto a lightly greased second cookie sheet. When cool, use a serrated or sharp knife to cut the brownies into 2-inch squares. Wrap each brownie in plastic wrap to preserve moisture.

Saran wrap is ideal for wrapping the brownies because it is an airtight plastic with no microscopic "breathing" holes (unlike many other brands).

You can turn brownies into an elegant dessert by serving them with vanilla ice cream (page 357) and chocolate sauce (page 346).

NOTES FROM ROSE

LES BRIOCHINS

BABY BRIOCHES FILLED
WITH BITTERSWEET CHOCOLATE

MAKES 10 ROLLS

Little rolls of fine-textured, buttery brioche encase dark bittersweet chocolate. Brioche dough is easy to make and the deliciously oven-fresh results are well worth the effort.

COMPONENTS
Rectangles of bittersweet chocolate • *Brioche*

Brioche

INGREDIENTS MEASURE		WEIGHT	
ROOM TEMPERATURE	VOLUME	POUNDS/OUNCES	GRAMS
water	*2 table-spoons*	*1 ounce*	*30 grams*
superfine sugar	*2½ table-spoons*	*1 ounce*	*30 grams*
fresh yeast* or	*2 packed teaspoons*	*0.5 ounce*	*11 grams*
dry yeast, not rapid-rise	*1½ teaspoons*		*4.5 grams*
bread flour	*4 cups (lightly spooned)*	*1 pound 1.5 ounces*	*500 grams*
salt	*1¾ teaspoons*	*0.5 ounce*	*12 grams*
10 large eggs	*2 liquid cups*	*1 pound 4 ounces (weighed in the shells)*	*570 grams*
unsalted butter	*1¾ cups*	*14 ounces*	*400 grams*
1 extra-large egg for glaze, lightly beaten			

*In cool weather use 16 grams fresh (1 packed tablespoon) or 7 grams dry (1 package, 2¼ teaspoons).

PROOF THE YEAST

In a small bowl combine the water (100°F. if using fresh yeast, 110°F. if using dry), ½ teaspoon of the sugar, and the yeast. If using fresh yeast, crumble it slightly while adding. Set aside in a draft-free spot for 10 to 20 minutes. By this time, the mixture should be full of bubbles. If not, the yeast is too old to be useful.

In a mixing bowl, on low speed mix together the flour, salt, the proofed yeast, remaining sugar, and 6 of the eggs. When the ingredients are incorporated, add the remaining eggs, one at a time. Raise speed to medium (4 on a KitchenAid mixer), and beat about 5 minutes or until the dough is smooth, shiny, and very elastic. Using your fingertips, gently mix in the butter, 1 tablespoon at a time. The dough will be very soft and sticky.

Sprinkle the dough lightly with flour (to keep a crust from forming). Cover the bowl tightly and allow the dough to rise at room temperature for 1½ hours.

With lightly greased hands or a rubber spatula, very gently deflate the dough by stirring it or flattening it and turning it over a few times. Sprinkle lightly with flour, cover tightly, and refrigerate for 6 hours or up to 2 days, gently deflating the dough every 45 minutes during the first 4 hours, after which it becomes cold enough to prevent rising. Wrap it loosely but securely in plastic wrap and then foil, and refrigerate.

INGREDIENTS	MEASURE	WEIGHT	
ROOM TEMPERATURE	VOLUME	OUNCES	GRAMS
*bittersweet chocolate**	*10 (½-ounce) bars*	*5 ounces*	*142 grams*

*Lindt 3-ounce bars are divided into six main sections, each one weighing ½ ounce.

On a floured surface, roll the dough out to form a long rectangle about 4 inches wide and ⅛ inch thick. Cut the dough into ten pieces. Place a ½-ounce bar of chocolate on each piece of dough, close to one of the 4-inch edges. Moisten the opposite edge with a little water, and roll the dough around the chocolate, pressing the moistened edge against the dough to make it adhere well.

Place the briochins, seam side down and widely spaced, on a buttered baking sheet. Cover them with lightly greased plastic wrap, and allow them to rise at room temperature for 1 hour.

Preheat the oven to 425°F.

Brush the briochins with the lightly beaten egg. Bake them for 10 minutes, then reduce the temperature to 350°F. and continue baking for another 5 minutes or until golden brown. Use a pancake turner to remove them to racks for cooling.

A PASSION FOR CHOCOLATE

For the best flavor and texture, it is important to keep the yeast from over-raising the dough, by deflating it at regular intervals. (Bernachon calls this very important process *remprage*. It prevents the dough from over-rising, which could spoil its texture and impart a sour flavor.) Making the dough a day ahead of baking produces the most buttery flavor.

LES PETITS PAINS
AU CHOCOLAT

LITTLE CROISSANT RECTANGLES
FILLED WITH BITTERSWEET CHOCOLATE

MAKES 16 CROISSANTS

Good news! It is possible to make superlative croissant dough in your own kitchen! Croissant dough is actually a puff pastry dough with yeast added.

Affectionately called *pain chocolat,* there is nothing better than a freshly baked, airy, crisp croissant wrapped around a little rectangle of chocolate, still slightly melted and warm from the oven. One of the joys I experienced while working with the Bernachons was the *petit pain* that was waiting for me every morning on a little marble-topped table just outside the kitchens, accompanied by a steaming cup of *café au lait.*

COMPONENTS
Bittersweet chocolate bars • Croissants

INGREDIENTS MEASURE	WEIGHT		
	VOLUME	POUNDS/OUNCES	GRAMS
water	2 tablespoons	1 ounce	30 grams
superfine sugar	1 tablespoon + 2 tea-spoons	0.75 ounce	20 grams
fresh yeast or	2 packed teaspoons	0.5 ounce	11 grams
dry yeast, not rapid-rise	1½ teaspoons		4.5 grams
unbleached all-purpose flour*	3½ cups (dip and sweep)	1 pound 1.5 ounces	500 grams
salt	1¾ teaspoons	0.5 ounce	12 grams
warm milk	1⅓ cups	11 ounces	314 grams
unsalted butter	1 cup + 1½ tablespoons	8.75 ounces	250 grams
bittersweet chocolate	2⅔ (3-ounce) bars	8 ounces	227 grams
1 large egg, lightly beaten			

*Heckers flour is the perfect choice here because of its high protein count, producing a very light dough.

Three 11 by 17-inch baking sheets, buttered.

In a small bowl combine the water (100°F. if using fresh yeast, 110°F. if using dry), ½ teaspoon of the sugar, and the yeast. If using fresh yeast, crumble it slightly while adding. Set aside in a draft-free spot for 10 to 20 minutes. By this time, the mixture should be full of bubbles. If not, the yeast is too old to be useful.

PROOF THE YEAST

Reserve 3 tablespoons (1 ounce/28 grams) of the flour, and in a large mixing bowl, mix together the remaining flour, salt, and remaining sugar. Add a scant cup of the warm milk and the yeast mixture, and stir just until the dough is smooth, adding more milk if necessary. Place it in a clean, lightly buttered bowl, cover the bowl with plastic wrap, and allow the dough to rise at room temperature for 1½ hours (in summer or if the kitchen is very warm, only 45 minutes). To

143

ensure that the yeast is distributed evenly, while the dough is rising, one or two times gently deflate it by tossing it over and flattening it gently with your hands.

Place the remaining 1 ounce (3 tablespoons) of flour on a sheet of plastic wrap and place the butter on top. Sprinkle a little of the flour on top of the butter, and cover with the plastic wrap. Pound the butter lightly with a rolling pin to flatten and soften it, then knead together the butter and flour, using the plastic wrap and your knuckles to avoid touching the butter directly. Work quickly. As soon as the flour is incorporated, shape it into a 5-inch square (no thicker than ¾ inch). At this point the butter should be cool but workable—60°F. Use at once or keep it cool. The butter must not be colder than 60°F. when rolled into the pastry or it will break through the dough and not distribute evenly.

THE DOUGH PACKAGE Roll out the dough on a well-floured surface to form an 8-inch square. Place butter square diagonally in center of dough square, and lightly mark dough at edges of butter with the dull side of a knife. Remove butter and roll each marked corner of the dough out to form a flap. Dough will be slightly elastic. Moisten these flaps lightly with water and replace butter on dough, wrapping securely. Stretch flaps slightly to reach across the dough package. Wrap loosely in plastic wrap and refrigerate for 30 minutes.

On a well-floured surface, keeping dough seam side up, gently roll dough package into a rectangle measuring 8 by 12 inches. Brush off all flour from the surface of the dough, and fold dough into thirds as you would fold a business letter. This is the first "turn."

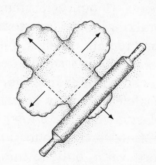
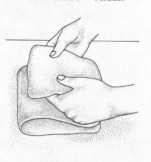

A PASSION FOR CHOCOLATE

Before each subsequent turn, move the dough so that the closed end is on your left. Clean the surface, reflour, and roll and fold a second time exactly the same way—but turn the dough over occasionally to keep seams and edges even. Be sure to roll into all four corners of the dough and use a pastry scraper to even the edges.

Mark dough with two fingertips, or knuckles if you have long nails, to indicate that two turns have been completed. Wrap with plastic wrap, then foil, and refrigerate for 30 to 40 minutes. The dough must not chill for longer than 40 minutes, or the butter will never distribute evenly.

Continue to roll and turn dough, marking the turns with fingertips and resting 30 minutes between turns, until a total of four turns have been completed. It is best to do only one turn at a time now, as the dough will become elastic and the best results are obtained when dough is not forced and layers not pressed together.

Wrap the dough in plastic wrap, then foil, and refrigerate overnight.

The next day, remove the dough and allow it to sit at room temperature for 10 to 15 minutes or until soft enough to roll.

Give the dough one more turn, then cut it in half and roll it out to form two rectangles, each 18 by 6 by 1/8 inch thick. Cut each rectangle in half the long way. You will now have four 18 by 3-inch strips. Cut each into four pieces, measuring about 4 by 3 inches.

Using a sharp knife, break the chocolate bars along each vertical seam so that each bar yields six little bars; you will have a total of sixteen. (The 3-ounce European chocolate bars are the ideal size for this.)

Lay a piece of chocolate on each piece of dough so that the length of the chocolate is parallel to the longer edge of the dough, and starting from a long side, roll up the dough so that it encloses the chocolate. Moisten the end of the dough with a bit of water, and place them on the buttered pastry sheets, seam side down, 2 inches apart. Cover lightly with plastic wrap.

Allow the *pains* to rise for 1 hour at room temperature. They will become slightly puffy and lighter when touched with the fingertip, but they will not increase very much in size.

Preheat the oven to 475°F. Brush the *pains* with the lightly beaten egg. Bake for 5 minutes, then lower the heat to 400°F. and continue baking for 7 to 10 minutes or until golden brown and done. (Check by cutting into one to see if the dough in the center is cooked.) Remove immediately from the sheets and cool on racks.

NOTE Check carefully toward the end of the baking time, as some may be done before others.

KEEPS Airtight, 2 days at room temperature, 3 months frozen. Reheat for 3 to 5 minutes in a 300°F. oven to crisp the outside, freshen the inside, and soften the chocolate.

VARIATION *Croissants:* This same wonderful dough can be used to make twenty-four croissants by cutting and shaping in the following way:

Roll out dough to form a rectangle about 12 by 36 inches and ⅛ thick. Cut it into two long pieces (each will be 6 by 36 inches). Cut each piece into twelve triangles (each one will measure 3 inches at its base).

Roll each triangle, starting at the base and working toward the point. It helps to hold the point in place in order to achieve a tight roll. (Believe me, this is an acquired skill—I noticed out of the corner of my eye all the chefs smiling at my clumsy efforts to achieve it. The *pain chocolat* shape is a lot easier!) Place them on buttered pastry sheets and proceed as above.

NOTES FROM ROSE When making the dough, it is important that the butter remain cool though malleable. Beating it with a rolling pin helps to soften it without melting it.

The frozen *pains chocolat* taste like fresh-baked when reheated (but do not use a microwave oven, as they could toughen and will not crisp).

If oven space does not allow for adequate air circulation between the pans, bake one sheet at a time.

LES FIGUES

LITTLE SPONGE CAKES
FILLED WITH CHOCOLATE PASTRY CREAM,
IN THE SHAPE OF FIGS

MAKES ABOUT 15 CAKES

For moist, light airiness and charm, there is nothing to compare to fresh homemade biscuit, a butterless European-type sponge cake. These little creations are called "figs" because each is piped to resemble a fig. When you bite into these plump delicacies, you'll find a delightful surprise of chocolate pastry cream inside.

The biscuit recipe comes from my book *The Cake Bible*, as this batter most reliably holds its shape for piping in a home kitchen. One tablespoon of honey, however, replaces the tablespoon of water, for additional moistness.

COMPONENTS
Biscuit • *Bittersweet chocolate* •
Chocolate Pastry Cream

INGREDIENTS	MEASURE	WEIGHT	
	VOLUME	OUNCES	GRAMS
6 large eggs, separated			
yolks	3.5 *fluid ounces*	4 ounces	112 grams
whites	¾ *liquid cup*	6.25 ounces	180 grams
superfine sugar	¾ *cup*	5.25 ounces	150 grams
vanilla	2½ *teaspoons*		10 grams
honey	1 *tablespoon*	0.75 ounce	21 grams
sifted cake flour	1½ *cups*	5.25 ounces	150 grams
cream of tartar	¾ *teaspoon*		

Two large baking sheets, buttered and floured or lined with parchment or foil.

Preheat the oven to 400°F.

In a large mixing bowl, beat the yolks and ½ cup of the sugar on high speed for 5 minutes, or until the mixture is very thick and forms ribbons when dropped from the beater. Lower the speed and beat in the vanilla and honey. Increase to high speed and beat for 30 seconds or until thick again. Sift the flour over the yolk mixture without mixing it in, and set aside.

In another large mixing bowl beat the whites until foamy. Add the cream of tartar and beat until soft peaks form when the beater is raised. Gradually beat in the remaining ¼ cup sugar, beating until very stiff peaks form when the beater is raised slowly. Add one third of the whites to the yolk mixture, and with a large rubber spatula fold until all the flour is incorporated. Gently fold in the remaining whites. Working quickly so that the batter does not lose volume, scoop the batter into a pastry bag, or a 1-gallon zip-seal bag with one corner cut off, fitted with a number 9 (¾-inch) round tip and pipe about thirty fig-shaped forms, about 2 inches at their widest point and 3 inches in length (higher at one end and pointed at the other). Space them at least 1 inch apart, as they will spread slightly.*

Bake 10 to 15 minutes, or until light golden brown and springy to the touch. Cool for a few minutes on the baking sheets, on wire racks. Remove from the baking sheets and finish cooling on the wire racks. Store airtight for 1 day or frozen until ready to fill.

The Bernachons pipe this batter onto ⅛-inch-thick heavy-duty cardboard. Jean-Jacques explained that cardboard does not absorb heat the way metal would, so the biscuit cooks from the top only and remains moister. **NOTE FROM ROSE**

CHOCOLATE PASTRY CREAM

INGREDIENTS	MEASURE	WEIGHT	
	VOLUME	POUNDS/OUNCES	GRAMS
milk	2½ cups	1 pound 5.25 ounces	605 grams
1 vanilla bean, split*			
salt	¾ teaspoon		5 grams
bittersweet chocolate, coarsely chopped	½ (3-ounce) bar	1.5 ounces	43 grams
5 large egg yolks	3 liquid ounces	3.25 ounces	92 grams
superfine sugar	¾ cup	5.25 ounces	150 grams
all-purpose flour	⅓ cup (dip and sweep)	1.75 ounces	50 grams

*You may substitute 1 teaspoon vanilla extract for the vanilla bean, but the bean offers a fuller, more aromatic flavor. If you are using extract, add it after the pastry cream has cooled. If using a Tahitian bean, use only ½ bean.

In a saucepan, place 2 cups of the milk, the vanilla bean, and the salt. Bring to a full boil, and remove from the heat.

*To pipe the fig shape, hold the pastry bag at a 45° to 90° angle to the work surface, with the tip facing away from you and raised slightly above the surface. Hold the tip in place as you squeeze, allowing the batter to fan out forward and sideways. Gradually relax the pressure as you lower the tube to the surface, tapering off the batter to a point.

In a medium bowl, whisk together the egg yolks and sugar until thoroughly combined. Whisk in the flour, and then the remaining ½ cup of cold milk (to prevent curdling). Whisking constantly, gradually add the hot milk.

Return the mixture to the saucepan and bring it to a boil, whisking constantly. Simmer for 3 minutes, whisking constantly. Remove from the heat and add the chocolate. Stir gently until completely melted and smooth.

Transfer the mixture to a bowl, press plastic wrap directly onto the surface (to prevent a skin from forming), and cool. Remove the vanilla bean and return plastic to the surface. Store, airtight, refrigerated.

NOTE The "figs" will be less fragile if allowed to cool for several hours before hollowing.

ASSEMBLING THE "FIGS" Using a small sharp knife and without damaging the outside, carefully make an inch-long hollow in the flat side of each "fig."

Using a small spoon or a pastry bag fitted with a round tip, fill these cavities with pastry cream. Spread a thin coating of pastry cream all over the flat (filled) side of two "figs," and press them together to form a whole "fig." Repeat with the remainder.

Dust with powdered sugar, and use a small sharp knife to make about six long lines on the back of each to further enhance the illusion of a fig.

KEEPS Best eaten the same day they are prepared. They can be stored, refrigerated, for 24 hours if wrapped airtight to prevent the biscuit from drying out.

LES BOMBALES AU CHOCOLAT

LITTLE ROUND SPONGE CAKES FILLED WITH CHOCOLATE PASTRY CREAM

MAKES ABOUT 30 CAKES

A fine bittersweet chocolate coating provides crunch for the soft light biscuit rounds filled with silken chocolate pastry cream.

COMPONENTS
Biscuit • *Chocolate Pastry Cream*

DECORATION
Glaze of bittersweet chocolate
(6 ounces/170 grams)

BISCUIT

INGREDIENTS	MEASURE	WEIGHT	
	VOLUME	OUNCES	GRAMS
6 large eggs, separated			
yolks	3.5 *fluid ounces*	4 *ounces*	112 *grams*
whites	¾ *liquid cup*	6.25 *ounces*	180 *grams*
superfine sugar	¾ *cup*	5.25 *ounces*	150 *grams*
vanilla	2½ *teaspoons*		10 *grams*
honey	1 *tablespoon*	0.75 *ounce*	21 *grams*
sifted cake flour	1½ *cups*	5.25 *ounces*	150 *grams*
cream of tartar	¾ *teaspoon*		

Two large baking sheets, buttered and floured or lined with parchment or foil.

Preheat the oven to 400°F.

In a large mixing bowl, beat the yolks and ½ cup of the sugar on high speed for 5 minutes, or until the mixture is very thick and forms ribbons when dropped from the beater. Lower the speed and beat in the vanilla and honey. Increase to high speed and beat for 30 seconds or until thick again. Sift the flour over the yolk mixture without mixing it in, and set aside.

In another large mixing bowl beat the whites until foamy. Add the cream of tartar and beat until soft peaks form when the beater is raised. Gradually beat in the remaining ¼ cup sugar, beating until very stiff peaks form when the beater is raised slowly. Add one third of the whites to the yolk mixture, and with a large rubber spatula fold until all the flour is incorporated. Gently fold in the remaining whites. Working quickly so that the batter does not lose volume, scoop the batter into a pastry bag, or a 1-gallon zip-seal bag with one corner cut off, fitted with a number 6 (½-inch) round tip and pipe about sixty 1-inch discs about ⅜-inch high onto the prepared baking sheets. Space them at least 1 inch apart, as they will spread slightly.

Bake 10 to 15 minutes, or until light golden brown and springy to the touch. Cool for a few minutes on the baking sheets, on wire racks. Remove from the baking sheets and finish cooling on the wire racks. Store airtight for 1 day or freeze until ready to fill.

NOTE FROM ROSE

The Bernachons pipe this batter onto ⅛-inch-thick heavy-duty cardboard. Jean-Jacques explained that cardboard does not absorb heat the way metal does, so the biscuit cooks from the top only and remains moister. Using baking sheets manufactured with double thickness and a layer of air between also works well. Or use two baking sheets—one on top of the other—as insulation.

CHOCOLATE PASTRY CREAM

INGREDIENTS MEASURE		WEIGHT	
	VOLUME	POUNDS/OUNCES	GRAMS
milk	2½ cups	1 pound 5.25 ounces	605 grams
1 vanilla bean, split*			
salt	¾ teaspoon		5 grams
5 large egg yolks	3 liquid ounces	3.25 ounces	92 grams
superfine sugar	¾ cup	5.25 ounces	150 grams
all-purpose flour	⅓ cup (dip and sweep)	1.75 ounces	50 grams
bittersweet chocolate, coarsely chopped	½ (3-ounce) bar	1.5 ounces	43 grams

*You may substitute 1 teaspoon vanilla extract for the vanilla bean, but the bean offers a fuller, more aromatic flavor. If you are using extract, add it after the pastry cream has cooled. If using a Tahitian bean, use only ½ bean.

In a saucepan, place 2 cups of the milk, the vanilla bean, and the salt. Bring it to a full boil.

In a medium bowl, whisk together the egg yolks and sugar until thoroughly combined. Whisk in the flour, and then the remaining ½ cup of cold milk (to prevent curdling). Whisking constantly, gradually add the hot milk.

Return the mixture to the saucepan and bring it to a boil, whisking constantly. Simmer for 3 minutes, whisking constantly. Remove from the heat and add the chocolate. Stir gently until completely melted and smooth.

Transfer the mixture to a bowl, press plastic wrap directly onto the surface (to prevent a skin from forming), and cool. Remove the vanilla bean and return plastic to the surface. Store refrigerated up to 5 days.

ASSEMBLING THE BOMBALES Using a sharp melon baller or small sharp knife, carefully hollow out the center of each little disc without damaging the outside.

Using a small spoon or a pastry bag fitted with a round tip, fill these cavities with the pastry cream.

Spread a thin coating of pastry cream on the base of a disc and attach it to the base of a second disc. Repeat with the remaining discs.

NOTE The biscuit rounds will be less fragile if allowed to cool for several hours before hollowing.

TO GLAZE Break the chocolate into squares and place them in the top of a double boiler set over very hot water (but no hotter than 160°F.). The water must not simmer or touch the bottom of the double boiler insert.

Stir until the chocolate begins to melt. Return the pan to low heat if the water cools, but be careful that it does not get too hot. (The chocolate may be melted in a microwave oven if stirred every 15 seconds.) Using either method, remove it from the heat source before it is fully melted and stir, using residual heat to complete the melting. Allow it to cool until no longer warm.

Set the *bombales* on a rack with a sheet of foil beneath it (to catch the dripping glaze). Pour the glaze over the *bombales*. Lift the rack and tap it on the counter to even out and thin the glaze. Using a small angled metal spatula or pancake turner, lift the *bombales* from the rack and place them on wax paper or foil or a serving plate.

KEEPS Airtight, refrigerated, up to 3 days.

A PASSION FOR CHOCOLATE

LES GRECS

SMALL CHIMNEYS OF
CHOCOLATE CONTAINING TENDER DISCS OF
BISCUIT AND YOUR CHOICE
OF GANACHE

MAKES ABOUT 15 CAKES

COMPONENTS
Ganache (any one of your choice, pages 334–44)
• Biscuit

DECORATION
Bittersweet Chocolate Chimneys
(6 ounces/170 grams bittersweet chocolate)

INGREDIENTS	MEASURE	WEIGHT	
	VOLUME	OUNCES	GRAMS
6 large eggs, separated			
yolks	3.5 fluid ounces	4 ounces	112 grams
whites	¾ liquid cup	6.25 ounces	180 grams
superfine sugar	¾ cup	5.25 ounces	150 grams
vanilla	2½ teaspoons		10 grams
honey	1 tablespoon	0.75 ounce	21 grams
sifted cake flour	1½ cups	5.25 ounces	150 grams
cream of tartar	¾ teaspoon		

Two large baking sheets, buttered and floured or lined with parchment or foil.

Preheat the oven to 400°F.

In a large mixing bowl, beat the yolks and ½ cup of the sugar on high speed for 5 minutes, or until the mixture is very thick and forms ribbons when dropped from the beater. Lower the speed and beat in the vanilla and honey. Increase to high speed and beat for 30 seconds or until thick again. Sift the flour over the yolk mixture without mixing it in, and set aside.

In another large mixing bowl beat the whites until foamy. Add the cream of tartar and beat until soft peaks form when the beater is raised. Gradually beat in the remaining ¼ cup sugar, beating until very stiff peaks form when the beater is raised slowly. Add one third of the whites to the yolk mixture, and with a large rubber spatula fold until all the flour is incorporated. Gently fold in the remaining whites. Working quickly so that the batter does not lose volume, scoop the batter into a pastry bag fitted with a number 6 (½-inch) round tip and pipe about thirty 2-inch discs. Space them at least 1 inch apart, as they will spread slightly.

Bake 10 to 15 minutes, or until light golden brown and springy to the touch. Cool for a few minutes on the baking sheets, on wire racks. Remove from the baking sheets and finish cooling on the wire racks. Store airtight for 1 day or freeze until ready to fill.

NOTE FROM ROSE

The Bernachons pipe this batter onto ⅛-inch-thich heavy-duty cardboard. Jean-Jacques explained that cardboard does not absorb heat the way metal does, so the biscuit cooks from the top only and remains moister. Using baking sheets manufactured with double thickness and a layer of air between also works well. Or use two baking sheets—one on top of another—as insulation.

ASSEMBLING THE CAKES

Using a sharp melon baller or knife, without cutting through to the other side, carefully scoop out a 1-inch-wide depression in the center of half the disc. Using a small spoon or a pastry bag fitted with a round tip, fill these cavities with ganache.

Spread a thin coat of ganache over the bottom of the other half of the disc, and attach the discs in pairs (filled side against bottom). To obtain perfect circles, invert a small form or glass over each set of discs, and trim any excess with a sharp knife. Spread a smooth, thin coat of ganache around the sides, and set aside.

THE CHOCOLATE CHIMNEYS

Break the chocolate into squares and place them in the top of a double boiler set over very hot water (but no hotter than 160°F.). The water must not simmer or touch the bottom of the double boiler insert.

Stir until the chocolate begins to melt. Return the pan to low heat if the water cools, but be careful that it does not get too hot. Stir occasionally, until the chocolate is almost melted. Remove the upper container from the water and stir until the chocolate is cool to the touch (a dab placed on the upper lip should feel barely warm). (The chocolate may be melted in a microwave oven if stirred every 15 seconds.) Using either method, remove it from the heat source before it is fully melted and stir, using residual heat to complete the melting. Return the chocolate briefly to the hot water, stirring constantly, if it becomes too thick.

LITTLE CAKES AND COOKIES

Cut out fifteen bands of wax paper measuring 1½ by 6½ inches.

Using a small metal spatula (preferably an offset one), spread a fine even coat of chocolate on one side of each strip. As each strip is completed, lift it from the surface, leaving the excess chocolate behind, and transfer it to a clean surface. In a few minutes, when the chocolate begins to dull and set but is still flexible, wrap the strips, chocolate side against the cake, around the cakes. Do not overlap the chocolate.

Refrigerate the cakes for a few minutes, until the chocolate has hardened and the wax paper strips can be removed easily.

Decorate the center of each chimney with a rosette of the remaining ganache, piped with a number 12 star tip.

KEEPS These little cakes are at their most perfect when eaten the same day they are made. They will still be delicious the next day, but to keep the chocolate shiny, they should not be refrigerated.

NOTE FROM ROSE This is a fine dessert for a fancy tea or even after an elegant multi-course dinner. The softness of the biscuit, creaminess of the ganache, and crispness of the chocolate outer case are a delightful experience in both texture and flavor.

To pipe rosettes: Hold the pastry bag upright at a 90° angle, with the tube ¼ inch above the surface. As you squeeze out the buttercream, move the tube in a tight arc from the 9:00 position around to the 6:00 position. Release the pressure, but do not lift the tube until you have followed the circular motion all the way around to the 9:00 position.

A PASSION FOR CHOCOLATE

LES MADELEINES
AU CHOCOLAT

LITTLE CHOCOLATE SPONGE
CAKES SHAPED LIKE SHELLS

MAKES 36 CAKES

These dense, fine-textured, chocolatey little cakes, shaped in the traditional shell molds, have a slightly dry edge that is just perfect for a very French custom—dunking in coffee, tea (made famous by Proust), or perhaps even Cognac.

INGREDIENTS	MEASURE	WEIGHT	
	VOLUME	OUNCES	GRAMS
7 large eggs	1½ liquid cups	14 ounces	400 grams
		(weighed in the shells)	
sugar	1¼ cups	8.75 ounces	250 grams
sifted all-purpose flour	2 cups + 3 tablespoons	8.75 ounces	250 grams
unsalted butter, softened and creamed	1 cup + 1½ tablespoons	8.75 ounces	250 grams
unsweetened cocoa	¾ cup + 2 tablespoons (lightly spooned)	2.75 ounces	80 grams

Madeleine molds, well buttered.

Preheat the oven to 400°F.

In a large mixing bowl, set over simmering water, heat the eggs and sugar until just lukewarm, whisking constantly to prevent curdling. (The eggs may also be heated by placing them *still in their shells* in a large mixing bowl in an oven with a pilot light for 3 hours or up to overnight.) Using the whisk attachment, beat the mixture on high speed for 5 minutes or until tripled in volume. (A hand beater may be used, but it will be necessary to beat for at least 10 minutes.)

Sift the flour over the egg mixture, then fold it in with a large rubber spatula. Remove about 2 cups of the batter and whisk it with the butter until smooth. Then fold this mixture into the batter. Sift the cocoa over the mixture and fold it in.

Spoon the mixture into the madeleine molds. Bake 12 minutes or until they spring back when pressed lightly and can be dislodged from the mold. Unmold immediately, using the tip of a sharp knife if necessary, and cool on a rack.

NOTE Chocolate madeleines are moist and most chocolatey when they are warm from the oven. To store, however, let them cool completely before placing them in an airtight container for up to 2 days or frozen for 1 month.

LES ÉCLAIRS
AU CHOCOLAT

CHOCOLATE ÉCLAIRS

MAKES 12 ÉCLAIRS

Éclairs are a favorite dessert in America as well as in France. Although they are usually filled with a vanilla whipped cream or pastry cream filling, the Bernachons' recipe, happily, features a chocolate pastry cream.

COMPONENTS
*Cream-Puff Pastry • Chocolate Pastry Cream
• Glaze of bittersweet chocolate
(6 ounces/170 grams)*

INGREDIENTS	MEASURE	WEIGHT	
	VOLUME	OUNCES	GRAMS
milk	⅔ cup	5.5 ounces	160 grams
unsalted butter	5 tablespoons	2.5 ounces	71 grams
sugar	1½ teaspoons		7 grams
salt	½ teaspoon		
all-purpose flour	1 cup (lightly spooned)	4.25 ounces	121 grams
5 large eggs	1 liquid cup	10 ounces	284 grams (weighed in the shells)

Two 11 by 17-inch baking sheets, lined with parchment or greased.

Preheat the oven to 400°F.

In a medium saucepan, combine the milk, butter, sugar, and salt and bring the mixture to a full rolling boil. Remove immediately from the heat, and add the flour all at once. Stir with a wooden spoon until the mixture forms a ball, leaves the sides of the the pan, and clings slightly to the spoon. Return to low heat and cook, stirring and mashing continuously, for about 3 minutes (to cook the flour). Without scraping the pan, transfer the mixture to the bowl of a food processor fitted with the metal blade. Process 15 seconds with the feed tube open (to allow steam to escape). With the motor running, pour in the eggs and continue processing for 30 seconds. The mixture should be smooth, shiny, and too soft to hold peaks. (If you are using an electric mixer, allow the flour mixture to cool for 5 minutes in the bowl. Then beat in the eggs, one at a time, beating after each addition until incorporated.)

If you are using parchment, place a small dot of dough at each corner to attach it to the baking sheet. Form the batter into 4 by 1½-inch lengths, using a spoon or a pastry bag (or a heavy-duty zip-seal bag with one corner cut off) fitted with a number 6 (½-inch) tip. Space them 3 inches apart on the baking sheets. If you are using a spoon rather than a pastry bag use a damp

162

metal spatula to spread them into shape. The ends should be slightly wider than the centers. Bake for 20 to 30 minutes, or until the éclairs are golden brown and do not yield to pressure when squeezed gently. Leave the éclairs in the turned-off oven for 1 hour, using a wooden spoon to prop the oven door slightly ajar. Then remove the éclairs to a rack and cool completely.

Store in an airtight plastic bag up to 1 week refrigerated, 6 months frozen. Recrisp by placing the éclairs on racks in a 300°F. oven for 5 to 10 minutes and cool on racks before filling and serving.

NOTE To prevent the pastry from deflating, do not open the oven door until shortly before the end of baking time.

CHOCOLATE PASTRY CREAM

INGREDIENTS MEASURE		WEIGHT	
	VOLUME	POUNDS/OUNCES	GRAMS
milk	*2½ cups*	*1 pound 5.25 ounces*	*605 grams*
*1 vanilla bean**			
salt	*¾ teaspoon*		*5 grams*
5 large egg yolks	*3 fluid ounces*	*3.25 ounces*	*93 grams*
superfine sugar	*¾ cup*	*5.25 ounces*	*150 grams*
all-purpose flour	*⅓ cup (dip and sweep)*	*1.75 ounces*	*50 grams*
bittersweet chocolate, chopped	*½ (3-ounce) bar*	*1.5 ounces*	*43 grams*

*You may substitute 1 teaspoon vanilla extract for the vanilla bean, but the bean offers a fuller, more aromatic flavor. If you are using extract, add it after the pastry cream has cooled. If using a Tahitian bean, use only ½ bean.

In a saucepan, place 2 cups of the milk, the vanilla bean, and the salt. Bring it to a full boil, and remove it from the heat.

In a medium bowl, whisk together the egg yolks and sugar until thoroughly combined. Whisk in the flour, and then the remaining ½ cup of cold milk (to

prevent curdling). Whisking constantly, gradually add the hot milk.

Return the mixture to the saucepan and bring it to a boil, whisking constantly. Simmer for 3 minutes, whisking constantly. Remove from the heat and add the chocolate. Stir gently until completely melted and smooth.

Transfer the mixture to a bowl, press plastic wrap directly onto the surface (to prevent a skin from forming), and cool. Store airtight, refrigerated, up to 5 days. Remove the vanilla bean before using the pastry cream to fill the éclairs.

ASSEMBLING THE ÉCLAIRS Using a serrated knife, split the éclairs in half horizontally. Remove some of the soft dough from the inside. Using a teaspoon or a pastry bag fitted with a number 6 (½-inch) tube, fill the éclairs with pastry cream, a scant ¼ cup for each one.

TO GLAZE Break the chocolate into squares and place them in the top of a double boiler set over very hot water (but no hotter than 160°F.). The water must not simmer or touch the bottom of the double boiler insert.

Stir until the chocolate begins to melt. Return it to low heat if the water cools, but be careful that it does not get too hot. (The chocolate may be melted in a microwave oven if stirred every 15 seconds.) Using either method, remove it from the heat source before fully melted and stir, using the residual heat to complete the melting. Allow to cool just until no longer warm. Then use a small metal spatula to spread the melted chocolate over the tops of the éclairs.

NOTE FROM ROSE Éclairs are especially delicious if eaten within 3 hours of preparation, while the pastry is still crisp. They are also delicious after the pastry softens, and can be refrigerated for 2 days.

A PASSION FOR CHOCOLATE

PROFITEROLES AU CHOCOLAT

MINIATURE CREAM PUFFS FILLED WITH CHOCOLATE PASTRY CREAM AND FROSTED WITH BITTERSWEET CHOCOLATE

MAKES ABOUT 32 PUFFS

Profiteroles, often called cream puffs, are simply smaller, round versions of éclairs. For an interesting variation, they are also delicious filled with ice cream instead of pastry cream.

COMPONENTS
Cream Puffs • *Chocolate Pastry Cream*

DECORATION
Glaze of bittersweet chocolate
(6 ounces/170 grams)

CREAM PUFFS

INGREDIENTS	MEASURE	WEIGHT	
	VOLUME	OUNCES	GRAMS
milk	⅔ cup	5.5 ounces	160 grams
unsalted butter	5 tablespoons	2.5 ounces	71 grams
sugar	1½ teaspoons		7 grams
salt	½ teaspoon		
all-purpose flour	1 cup (lightly spooned)	4.25 ounces	121 grams
5 large eggs	1 liquid cup	10 ounces (weighed in the shells)	284 grams

Two 11 by 17-inch baking sheets, lined with parchment or buttered.

Preheat the oven to 400°F.

In a medium saucepan, combine the milk, butter, sugar, and salt and bring the mixture to a full rolling boil. Remove immediately from the heat, and add the flour all at once. Stir with a wooden spoon until the mixture forms a ball, leaves the sides of the pan, and clings slightly to the spoon. Return to low heat and cook, stirring and mashing continuously, for about 3 minutes (to cook the flour). Without scraping the pan, transfer the mixture to the bowl of a food processor fitted with the metal blade.

Process 15 seconds with the feed tube open (to allow steam to escape). With the motor running, pour in the eggs and continue processing for 30 seconds. The mixture should be smooth, shiny, and too soft to hold peaks. (If you are using an electric mixer, allow the flour mixture to cool for 5 minutes in the bowl. Then beat in the eggs, one at a time, beating after each addition until incorporated.)

If you are using parchment, place a small dot of dough at each corner to attach it to the baking sheet. Place 1½-inch-wide mounds of batter at least 1 inch apart on the prepared baking sheets, using a spoon or a pastry bag (or a 1-gallon zip-seal bag with one corner cut off) fitted with a number 6 (½-inch) tip. Bake 20 minutes, or until the puffs are golden brown and do not yield to pressure when squeezed gently. Transfer the puffs to cooling racks, and make a small hole in the bottom of each (to release steam and to use later for filling). Return the puffs, on the cooling racks, to the oven. Leave them in the turned-off oven for 1 hour, using a wooden spoon to prop the oven door slightly ajar.

Remove the puffs and cool completely on the racks. Store them in an airtight plastic bag up to 1 week refrigerated, 6 months frozen. Recrisp by placing the puffs on racks in a 300°F. oven for 5 to 10 minutes and then cool on racks before filling and serving.

Note: To prevent the pastry from collapsing, do not open the oven door until shortly before the end of the baking time.

CHOCOLATE PASTRY CREAM

INGREDIENTS MEASURE		WEIGHT	
	VOLUME	POUNDS/OUNCES	GRAMS
milk	*2 ½ cups*	*1 pound 5.25 ounces*	*605 grams*
*1 vanilla bean, split**			
salt	*¾ teaspoon*		*5 grams*
5 large egg yolks	*3 fluid ounces*	*3.25 ounces*	*93 grams*
superfine sugar	*¾ cup*	*5.25 ounces*	*150 grams*
all-purpose flour	*⅓ cup (dip and sweep)*	*1.75 ounces*	*50 grams*
bittersweet chocolate, chopped	*½ (3-ounce) bar*	*1.5 ounces*	*43 grams*

*You may substitute 1 teaspoon vanilla extract for the vanilla bean, but the bean offers a fuller, more aromatic flavor. If you are using extract, add it after the pastry cream has cooled. If using a Tahitian bean, use only ½ bean.

In a saucepan, place 2 cups of the milk, the vanilla bean, and the salt. Bring it to a full boil, and remove from the heat.

In a medium bowl, whisk together the egg yolks and sugar until thoroughly combined. Whisk in the flour, and then the remaining ½ cup of cold milk (to

prevent curdling). Whisking constantly, gradually add the hot milk.

Return the mixture to the saucepan and bring it to a boil, whisking constantly. Simmer for 3 minutes, whisking constantly. Remove from the heat and add the chocolate. Stir gently until completely melted and smooth.

Transfer the mixture to a bowl, press plastic wrap directly onto the surface (to prevent a skin from forming), and cool. Store refrigerated. Remove the vanilla bean before using to fill the puffs.

ASSEMBLING THE PROFITEROLES Using a pastry bag fitted with a long "Bismarck" filler tube or a ¼-inch round plain tube, fill each puff with pastry cream. The puffs will stay crisper if they are filled no more than 3 hours before serving.

TO GLAZE Break the chocolate into squares and place them in the top of a double boiler set over very hot water (but no hotter than 160°F.). The water must not simmer or touch the bottom of the double boiler insert.

Stir until the chocolate begins to melt. Return the pan to low heat if the water cools, but be careful that it does not get too hot. (The chocolate may be melted in a microwave oven if stirred every 15 seconds.) Using either method, remove it from the heat source before it is fully melted and stir, using the residual heat to complete the melting. Allow it to cool just until no longer warm. Then place the profiteroles in small dessert bowls and drizzle the chocolate over them. Serve at once.

NOTE Profiteroles are also delicious filled with ice cream. Use a serrated knife to split them in half horizontally, spoon in the ice cream, and freeze until serving time.

NOTE FROM ROSE If you are filling the puffs with ice cream, do not allow the chocolate to cool before pouring it on top. In this case, in fact, heated ganache (page 334) or chocolate sauce (page 346) is even better, as neither becomes as hard when encountering the cold puffs. Serve at once.

LES RELIGIEUSES
AU CHOCOLAT

BABY TOWERS OF
CHOCOLATE-FILLED, CHOCOLATE-GLAZED
CREAM PUFFS

MAKES ABOUT 15 PUFFS

This is yet another fanciful shape for the ever-popular cream puff: *religieuse* means "nun," and these cream puffs are said to resemble a nun's habit. They are easily prepared, simply by placing smaller cream puffs atop larger ones.

COMPONENTS
Cream-Puff Pastry • *Chocolate Pastry Cream* •
Melted bittersweet chocolate
(4 ounces/113 grams)

INGREDIENTS	MEASURE	WEIGHT	
	VOLUME	OUNCES	GRAMS
milk	⅔ *cup*	5.5 *ounces*	160 *grams*
unsalted butter	5 *tablespoons*	2.5 *ounces*	71 *grams*
sugar	1½ *teaspoons*		7 *grams*
salt	½ *teaspoon*		
all-purpose flour	1 *cup (lightly spooned)*	4.25 *ounces*	121 *grams*
5 large eggs	1 *liquid cup*	10 *ounces*	284 *grams*
		(weighed in the shells)	

Two 11 by 17-inch baking sheets, lined with parchment or buttered.

Preheat the oven to 400°F.

In a medium saucepan, combine the milk, butter, sugar, and salt and bring the mixture to a full rolling boil. Remove immediately from the heat, and add the flour all at once. Stir with a wooden spoon until the mixture forms a ball, leaves the sides of the pan, and clings slightly to the spoon. Return to low heat and cook, stirring and mashing continuously, for about 3 minutes (to cook the flour). Without scraping the pan, transfer the mixture to the bowl of a food processor fitted with the metal blade.

Process 15 seconds with the feed tube open (to allow steam to escape). With the motor running, pour in the eggs and continue processing for 30 seconds. The mixture should be smooth, shiny, and too soft to hold peaks. (If you are using an electric mixer, allow the flour mixture to cool for 5 minutes in the bowl. Then beat in the eggs, one at a time, beating after each addition until incorporated.)

If you are using parchment, place a small dot of dough at each corner to attach it to the baking sheets. Using a spoon or a pastry bag (or a 1-gallon zip-seal bag with one corner cut off) fitted with a number 6 (½-inch) tip, place mounds of the batter on the prepared baking sheets: use one third of the batter to form 1-inch-wide mounds on one sheet, and two thirds of the batter to form 2-inch mounds on the other sheet. (The different sizes should be on different baking sheets because the larger ones will take a little longer to bake.) Use your fingertip, dipped in water, to smooth the tops of the 2-inch mounds. Bake about 20 minutes, or until the puffs are golden brown and do not yield to pressure when squeezed gently. Remove the puffs to cooling racks, and make a small hole in the bottom of each to release steam and to use later for filling. Return the puffs, on the cooling racks, to the oven. Leave them in the turned-off oven for 1 hour, using a wooden spoon to prop the oven door slightly ajar.

Remove the puffs and cool completely on the racks. Store in an airtight plastic bag up to 1 week refrigerated, 6 months frozen. Recrisp by placing the puffs on racks in a 300°F. oven for 5 to 10 minutes and then cool before filling and serving.

Note: Do not open the oven door until toward the end of the baking time, or the puffs may deflate.

CHOCOLATE PASTRY CREAM

INGREDIENTS	MEASURE	WEIGHT	
	VOLUME	POUNDS/OUNCES	GRAMS
milk	2 ½ cups	1 pound 5.25 ounces	605 grams
1 vanilla bean*			
salt	¾ teaspoon		5 grams
5 large egg yolks	3 fluid ounces	3.25 ounces	93 grams
superfine sugar	¾ cup	5.25 ounces	150 grams
all-purpose flour	⅓ cup (dip and sweep)	1.75 ounces	50 grams
bittersweet chocolate, chopped	½ (3-ounce) bar	1.5 ounces	43 grams

*You may substitute 1 teaspoon vanilla extract for the vanilla bean, but the bean offers a fuller, more aromatic flavor. If you are using extract, add it after the pastry cream has cooled. If using a Tahitian bean, use only ½ bean.

In a saucepan, place 2 cups of the milk, the vanilla bean, and the salt. Bring it to a full boil.

In a medium bowl, whisk together the egg yolks and sugar until thoroughly combined. Whisk in the flour, and then the remaining ½ cup of cold milk (to prevent curdling). Whisking constantly, gradually add the hot milk.

Return the mixture to the saucepan and bring to a boil, whisking constantly. Simmer for 3 minutes, whisking constantly. Remove from the heat and add the chocolate. Stir gently until completely melted and smooth.

Transfer the mixture to a bowl, press plastic wrap directly onto the surface (to prevent a skin from forming) and cool. Store refrigerated, airtight, up to 5 days. Remove the vanilla bean before using the pastry cream to fill the puffs.

ASSEMBLING THE RELIGIEUSES

Using a pastry bag fitted with a long "Bismarck" filler tube or with a ¼-inch round plain tube, fill each puff with pastry cream. The puffs will stay crisper if they are filled no more than 3 hours before serving; however, they are still delicious even when they soften.

To melt the chocolate, break it into squares and place them in the top of a double boiler set over very hot water (but no hotter than 160°F.). The water must not simmer or touch the bottom of the double boiler insert.

Stir until the chocolate begins to melt. Return the pan to low heat if the water cools, but be careful that it does not get too hot. (The chocolate may be melted in a microwave oven if stirred every 15 seconds.) Using either method, remove it from the heat source before it is fully melted and stir, using the residual heat to complete the melting. Allow to cool just until no longer warm. Then, using a small metal spatula or your fingertip, spread a little of the melted chocolate on the underside of a smaller puff and attach it to a larger puff, pressing it gently into place. Continue with the remaining puffs in the same way.

A PASSION FOR CHOCOLATE

LES ÉVENTAILS

FAN-SHAPED NUT MERINGUES
FILLED WITH GANACHE

MAKES 8 PIECES

This cake is named for the fan-shaped form of its serving pieces. It is easy to make and very delicious to eat. Make this cake to serve after an Oriental-style dinner. The lightness of texture and fan motif couldn't be more appropriate.

COMPONENTS
Ganache • *Succès*

DECORATION
Powdered sugar

GANACHE

INGREDIENTS	MEASURE	WEIGHT	
	VOLUME	OUNCES	GRAMS
bittersweet chocolate	4 (3-ounce) bars	12 ounces	340 grams
crème fraîche (page 348) or heavy cream	1¼ cups	10 ounces	290 grams

Break the chocolate into pieces and process in a food processor until very fine.

Heat the crème fraîche to the boiling point, and with the motor running, pour it through the feed tube in a steady stream. Process a few seconds until smooth. Transfer to a bowl and cool for several hours, until frosting consistency. In cool weather ganache can remain unrefrigerated for at least 3 days or as long as 2 weeks. At room temperature it remains spreadable.

SUCCÈS

INGREDIENTS	MEASURE	WEIGHT	
	VOLUME	OUNCES	GRAMS
blanched sliced almonds	2 cups	6.25 ounces	180 grams
superfine sugar	¾ cup + 2 tablespoons	6.25 ounces	180 grams
7 large egg whites, room temperature	7 fluid ounces	7.25 ounces	210 grams
cream of tartar	1 teaspoon		3 grams

Two baking sheets, buttered and floured or lined with parchment, marked with three 8-inch circles.

Preheat the oven to 350°F.

In a food processor, place the almonds and ¾ cup sugar and process until the almonds are finely grated.

In a mixing bowl, beat the egg whites until foamy, add the cream of tartar, and beat until soft peaks form when the beater is raised slowly. Gradually add the remaining 2 tablespoons sugar, beating until stiff peaks form when the beater is raised slowly. Fold in the grated almond mixture.

Using a 1-gallon zip-seal bag with one corner cut off, or a pastry bag, fitted with a large plain number 6 (½-inch) tip, pipe the batter onto the prepared baking sheets to form three 8-inch circles, starting at the outer perimeter and spiraling inward toward the center. Using a small metal spatula, fill in any gaps with leftover batter and to smooth the surface. Bake for 15 to 20 minutes, or just until the discs begin to brown. Remove baking sheets to a rack. Loosen the succès from the sheets and allow them to cool on the sheets completely before transferring to a work surface or serving plate. They will have expanded to about 9 inches.

To obtain a perfect circle, invert a cake pan over the succès and trim any excess with a sharp knife.

NOTES FROM ROSE

Use superfine sugar for the best texture. It is not actually necessary to use flour on the baking sheets to keep it from sticking; however, the flour does keep the succès from spreading.

(Recipe makes three discs. Freeze one for future use.)

ASSEMBLING THE "FANS"

Place one disc of succès on a cardboard round or baking sheet. Spread the ganache on top, mounding it in the center. In order to achieve a good cone shape, the ganache must be firm. If necessary, refrigerate it before placing the second succès disc on top.

Place the second disc on top, flat side up, pressing it gently in place to retain the mounded cone shape. Refrigerate for at least 1 hour.

Dust the succès with powdered sugar, and cut it into eight wedges to form the "fans."

KEEPS

Airtight, refrigerated, up to 5 days.

LES ROULÉS
AU CHOCOLAT

NUTTY MERINGUE SPIRALS, EXTERIORS COVERED WITH DARK CHOCOLATE

LES ROULÉS AUX MARRONS
CHESTNUT ROLLS

MAKES ABOUT 16 SLICES

Soft, tender, nutty succès is used as a cake roll, filled with silken chocolate pastry cream and lush ganache. The slices form attractive spirals of white meringue, pale chocolate, and dark chocolate, encased in a dark chocolate glaze.

COMPONENTS
Chocolate Pastry Cream • Succès • Ganache of your choice (pages 334–44)

DECORATION
Glaze of bittersweet chocolate
(6 ounces/170 grams)

CHOCOLATE PASTRY CREAM

INGREDIENTS MEASURE		WEIGHT	
	VOLUME	POUNDS/OUNCES	GRAMS
milk	*2½ cups*	*1 pound 5.25 ounces*	*605 grams*
*1 vanilla bean, split**			
salt	*¾ teaspoon*		*5 grams*
5 large egg yolks	*3 liquid ounces*	*3.25 ounces*	*92 grams*
superfine sugar	*¾ cup*	*5.25 ounces*	*150 grams*
all-purpose flour	*⅓ cup (dip and sweep)*	*1.75 ounces*	*50 grams*
bittersweet chocolate, coarsely chopped	*½ (3 ounce) bar*	*1.5 ounces*	*43 grams*

*You may substitute 1 teaspoon vanilla extract for the vanilla bean, but the bean offers a fuller, more aromatic flavor. If you are using extract, add it after the pastry cream has cooled. If using a Tahitian bean, use only ½ bean.

In a saucepan, place 2 cups of the milk, the vanilla bean, and the salt. Bring it to a full boil, and remove from the heat.

In a medium bowl, whisk together the egg yolks and sugar until thoroughly combined. Whisk in the flour, and then the remaining ½ cup of cold milk (to prevent curdling). Whisking constantly, gradually add the hot milk.

Return the mixture to the saucepan and bring it to a boil, whisking constantly. Simmer for 3 minutes, whisking constantly. Remove the pan from the heat and add the chocolate. Stir gently until completely melted and smooth.

Transfer the mixture to a bowl, press plastic wrap directly onto the surface (to prevent a skin from forming), and cool. Remove the vanilla bean and return plastic to the surface. Store airtight, refrigerated, up to 5 days.

INGREDIENTS	MEASURE	WEIGHT	
	VOLUME	OUNCES	GRAMS
blanched sliced almonds	2 cups	6.25 ounces	180 grams
superfine sugar	¾ cup + 2 tablespoons	6.25 ounces	180 grams
7 large egg whites, room temperature	7 fluid ounces	7.25 ounces	210 grams
cream of tartar	1 teaspoon		3 grams

One 17 by 12-inch jelly-roll pan, greased, bottom lined with parchment or foil (extending slightly over the long sides), and then greased again and floured.

Preheat the oven to 350°F.

In a food processor, place the almonds and ¾ cup sugar and process until the almonds are finely grated.

In a mixing bowl, beat the egg whites until foamy, add the cream of tartar, and beat until soft peaks form when the beater is raised slowly. Gradually add the remaining 2 tablespoons sugar, beating until stiff peaks form when the beater is raised slowly. Fold in the grated almond mixture.

Spread the mixture evenly in the prepared pan, and bake 15 to 20 minutes or until just beginning to brown. Cool completely in the pan.

Use a sharp knife to dislodge the succès from the short sides of the pan, and grasping the parchment or foil, slide the succès out of the pan and onto a work surface. Flip it over onto a clean dish towel lightly sprinkled with powdered sugar. Carefully remove the parchment.

ASSEMBLING THE "ROLLS" Spread the cake evenly with the pastry cream, and refrigerate, covered with lightly greased plastic wrap, for 30 minutes to firm. Then spread the ganache (softened if necessary) evenly over the cream and roll it tightly from the long end, using the towel to help begin the roll. Place the roll on a baking sheet.

If possible, bake the succès a day ahead and cover it tightly with plastic wrap. This softens it and makes it even more flexible for rolling.

NOTE FROM ROSE

Break the chocolate into squares and place them in the top of a double boiler set over very hot water (but no hotter than 160°F.). The water must not simmer or touch the bottom of the double boiler insert.

TO GLAZE

Stir until the chocolate begins to melt. Return the pan to low heat if the water cools, but be careful that it does not get too hot. (The chocolate may be melted in a microwave oven if stirred every 15 seconds.) Using either method, remove it from the heat source before it is fully melted and stir, using residual heat to complete the melting. Allow it to cool until tepid, and pour at once over the roll, spreading it evenly with a long metal spatula. Using two pancake turners, lift the roll onto a clean flat surface. (The roll can also be left on the rack for cutting.)

Refrigerate for at least 1 hour or up to 1 week to set the pastry cream.

Use a heated knife to score the surface of the chocolate glaze (this will keep it from cracking). The knife can be heated by running it under hot water. Cut the roll into 1-inch-thick slices.

TO SERVE

Ganache Antillaise, with its rum flavoring, is an excellent choice for this cake; chestnut and rum are particularly harmonious flavors. After spreading the pastry cream and ganache over the cake, scatter 8 large (7 ounces/200 grams) coarsely chopped marrons glacés (candied chestnuts—available in specialty stores) over the ganache and roll it up.

VARIATION:
Les Roulés
Aux Marrons
(Chestnut Rolls)

LES BAISERS DE NÈGRE

MERINGUE SANDWICHES
FILLED WITH GANACHE

MAKES ABOUT 40 CAKES

These crunchy white meringues sandwiching a dark creamy ganache are sometimes called "chocolate kisses." Actually, they resemble little yo-yos!

COMPONENTS
Meringue • *Ganache*

A PASSION FOR CHOCOLATE

GANACHE

INGREDIENTS	MEASURE	WEIGHT	
	VOLUME	OUNCES	GRAMS
bittersweet chocolate	*2 (3-ounce) bars*	*6 ounces*	*170 grams*
crème fraîche (page 348) or heavy cream	*⅔ cup*	*5.25 ounces*	*150 grams*

Break the chocolate into pieces and process in a food processor until very fine.

Heat the crème fraîche to the boiling point, and with the motor running, pour it through the feed tube in a steady stream. Process a few seconds until smooth. Transfer to a bowl and cool for several hours, until frosting consistency. In cool weather ganache can remain unrefrigerated for 3 days or as long as 2 weeks. At room temperature it remains spreadable.

MERINGUE

INGREDIENTS	MEASURE	WEIGHT	
	VOLUME	POUNDS/OUNCES	GRAMS
7 large egg whites, room temperature	*7 fluid ounces*	*7.25 ounces*	*210 grams*
cream of tartar	*1 teaspoon*		*3 grams*
superfine sugar	*2½ cups + 1½ tablespoons*	*1 pound 2.25 ounces*	*520 grams*

Two baking sheets, buttered and floured or lined with parchment.

Preheat the oven to 300°F.

In a mixing bowl, beat the whites until frothy. Add the cream of tartar, and beat at medium speed while gradually adding the 1½ tablespoons of sugar. Continue beating until stiff peaks form when the beater is raised slowly.

With a large rubber spatula, gently fold in the remaining 2½ cups of sugar, in two batches.

Using a teaspoon or a pastry bag (or a 1-gallon zip-seal bag with one corner cut off) fitted with a large plain number 6 (½-inch) tip, pipe the batter into about eighty rounds the size of Ping-Pong balls, leaving about 1 inch in between. Bake for 20 to 25 minutes, or until firm enough to remove from the sheets without crushing. Cool the meringues on wire racks. With a small metal spatula, spread some ganache on the bottom of one of the meringues and attach a second one to it, also by its base. Continue with the remaining meringues.

NOTES FROM ROSE

Stored airtight, these meringues will keep for months. Once spread with ganache, they are best eaten within 2 days; any longer and they will begin to soften and lose their appealing crunch.

The Bernachons sometimes glaze their chocolate kisses with melted bittersweet chocolate, first glazing one rounded end, and when it is set, inverting it and glazing the other one.

A PASSION FOR CHOCOLATE

LES BATONS DE ROTHSCHILD

CRUNCHY MERINGUE COOKIES GLAZED WITH CHOCOLATE AND ALMONDS

MAKES ABOUT 50 BARS

These batons of tender, nutty succès have a crunchy exterior of browned chopped almonds and chocolate glaze.

COMPONENTS

Succès • *Bittersweet chocolate glaze (12 ounces/340 grams)*

INGREDIENTS	MEASURE	WEIGHT	
	VOLUME	OUNCES	GRAMS
blanched sliced (or slivered) almonds	2 cups	6.25 ounces	180 grams
sugar	¾ cup + 2 tablespoons	6.25 ounces	180 grams
7 large egg whites, room temperature	7 fluid ounces	7.25 ounces	210 grams
cream of tartar	1 teaspoon		3 grams
slivered almonds, coarsely chopped	½ cup + 1 ½ tablespoons	1.75 ounces	50 grams
powdered sugar	¼ cup	1 ounce	28 grams

One 17 by 12-inch jelly-roll pan, greased, bottom lined with parchment or foil.

Preheat the oven to 350°F.

In a food processor, place the sliced almonds and ¾ cup sugar and process until the almonds are finely grated.

In a mixing bowl, beat the egg whites until foamy, add the cream of tartar, and beat until soft peaks form when the beater is raised slowly. Gradually add the remaining 2 tablespoons sugar, beating until stiff peaks form when the beater is raised slowly. Fold in the grated almond mixture.

Using a pastry bag (or a 1-gallon zip-seal bag with one corner cut off) fitted with a large plain number 6 (½-inch) tip, or a teaspoon, pipe the batter onto the prepared pan in 3-inch lengths. Sprinkle each bar with coarsely chopped almonds, and sift the powdered sugar on top.

Bake 10 to 12 minutes or until lightly browned.

TO GLAZE Break the chocolate into squares and place them in the top of a double boiler set over very hot water (but no hotter than 160°F.). The water must not simmer or touch the bottom of the double boiler insert.

Stir until the chocolate begins to melt. Return the pan to low heat if the water cools, but be careful that it does not get too hot. (The chocolate may be melted in a microwave oven if stirred every 15 seconds.) Using either method, remove it from the heat source before it is fully melted and stir, using residual heat to complete the melting. Dip the rounded side of each baton in melted chocolate, then place it flat side down on a counter or cookie sheet to set. Alternatively, drizzle the chocolate glaze over the tops.

KEEPS Several days in an airtight container, several months refrigerated or frozen.

NOTE FROM ROSE Sliced almonds are preferable for grating because they release less oil and grate more evenly.

LES BIARRITZ

CRISP AND CHEWY
BUTTER NUT–MERINGUE COOKIES

MAKES ABOUT 100 COOKIES

These cookies are crisp yet slightly chewy, and deliciously fragrant with hazelnuts. They freeze well so that it is well worth making the whole batch!

INGREDIENTS	MEASURE	WEIGHT	
	VOLUME	OUNCES	GRAMS
hazelnuts	1 ¾ cups	8.75 ounces	250 grams
baking soda	¼ cup	2 ounces	60 grams
sifted all-purpose flour	1 ¾ cups	7 ounces	200 grams
superfine sugar	1 ¼ cups	8.75 ounces	250 grams
salt	pinch		
milk	1 liquid cup	8.5 ounces	242 grams
vanilla	1 teaspoon		
unsalted butter, softened	10 ½ table-spoons	5.25 ounces	150 grams
5 large egg whites, room temperature	5 fluid ounces	5.25 ounces	150 grams
cream of tartar	½ teaspoon		
bittersweet chocolate	4 (3-ounce) bars	12 ounces	340 grams

Baking sheets, lightly buttered.

Preheat the oven to 350°F.

BLANCH THE HAZELNUTS In a medium saucepan, place 3 cups of water and bring it to a boil. Add the nuts and the baking soda, and boil for 3 minutes. Test a nut by running it under cold water. If the skin is not easy to remove with slight pressure from the fingers, return to the heat for a minute or so more. Drain. Peel.

Toast the hazelnuts in the oven for 10 to 15 minutes, or until golden brown. Allow them to cool.

Place the hazelnuts in the container of a food processor together with the flour, 1 cup of the sugar, and the salt. Process until the nuts are finely chopped. Add the milk and vanilla, and process to combine. Add the butter, and pulse to combine. Transfer the mixture to a large bowl.

In a mixing bowl, beat the egg whites until foamy, add the cream of tartar, and beat until soft peaks form when the beater is raised slowly. Gradually beat in the

LITTLE CAKES AND COOKIES

remaining ¼ cup of sugar until stiff peaks form when the beater is raised slowly. Using a large rubber spatula, fold the whites into the nut mixture.

Using a teaspoon or a pastry bag (or a heavy duty quart zip-seal bag with a coupler) fitted with a number 12 round decorating tube, form 1-inch rounds about 2 inches apart on the prepared baking sheets. Tap the baking sheets against the counter to spread and flatten the batter.

Bake 8 to 10 minutes, or until the cookies begin to brown around the edges. Allow them to cool for a few minutes on the baking sheets before transferring them to wire racks to finish cooling.

Break the chocolate into squares and place them in the top of a double boiler set over very hot water (but no hotter than 160°F.). The water must not simmer or touch the bottom of the double boiler insert.

Stir until the chocolate begins to melt. Return the pan to low heat if the water cools, but be careful that it does not get too hot. (The chocolate may be melted in a microwave oven if stirred every 15 seconds.) Using either method, remove it from the heat source before it is fully melted and stir, using residual heat to complete the melting. Keep warm over a bowl of warm water (water must not exceed 120°F.).

Using a small metal spatula, spread melted chocolate on the underside of each cookie. If desired, use a cake-decorating triangular comb or a fork to make wavy lines on the chocolate.

NOTE FROM ROSE If you are making many lines in the chocolate, for a more uniform effect it helps to use a second coat of chocolate. Be sure to melt about 6 ounces of extra chocolate.

KEEPS Several days in an airtight container or for several months frozen.

LES MACARONS
AU CHOCOLAT

FLAT CHOCOLATE MACAROONS
WITH CHEWY CENTERS

MAKES ABOUT 50 COOKIES

The Bernachon macaroons are different from the traditional little puffs found in most French bakeries. Their flat shape gives them an especially crisp outer shell with a soft chewy interior.

INGREDIENTS	MEASURE	WEIGHT	
	VOLUME	OUNCES	GRAMS
unblanched almonds, sliced	2⅓ cups	7 ounces	200 grams
sugar	2 cups	14 ounces	400 grams
unsweetened cocoa	½ cup (lightly spooned)	1.75 ounces	50 grams
5 large egg whites, room temperature	5 fluid ounces	5.25 ounces	150 grams

Baking sheets covered with parchment.

The night before (or 8 to 10 hours before): In a food processor, combine the almonds, sugar, and cocoa and process until the almonds are very finely ground.

Transfer the mixture to a mixing bowl, and beat in the egg whites until smooth. Place a layer of plastic wrap (preferably Saran Wrap which is airtight) directly on the surface of the batter (to keep a skin from forming on the surface). Place the bowl in a cool spot such as by an open window.

When you are ready to bake: Preheat the oven to 325°F.

Using a pastry bag (or a heavy-duty quart zip-seal bag with a coupler) fitted with a number 12 plain round tube, or a teaspoon, pipe little 1-inch balls of the batter onto the prepared baking sheets, leaving about 2 inches between them. Use a pastry brush dipped in water to flatten the balls to about 2 inches in diameter.

Bake the macaroons for 5 minutes. Then raise the oven temperature to 425°F. and continue baking for 5 to 7 minutes, or until the macaroons are set. Cool the macaroons on the baking sheets.

To remove the macaroons, invert the parchment and brush the back of it with water. Reinvert the parchment, and the macaroons will lift off easily with your fingers.

Macaroons will keep for several days in an airtight container, or for several months frozen. **KEEPS**

The batter is allowed to rest so that the cocoa evenly absorbs the moisture and thickens the batter. **NOTES FROM ROSE**

The Bernachons often sandwich two macaroons with ganache—a lovely textural treat of creamy chocolate against the crunchy, chewy macaroon. This is one of my favorite Bernachon cookies.

LES MASSEPAINS AU CHOCOLAT

ALMOND-COCOA MERINGUES FILLED WITH GANACHE

MAKES ABOUT 40 COOKIES

Delicious, nutty cocoa meringues. The contrast of crisp chewy meringue and creamy chocolatey ganache is superb!

GANACHE

INGREDIENTS	MEASURE	WEIGHT	
	VOLUME	OUNCES	GRAMS
bittersweet chocolate	*2 (3-ounce) bars*	*6 ounces*	*170 grams*
crème fraîche (page 348) or heavy cream	*⅔ cup*	*5.25 ounces*	*150 grams*

Break the chocolate into pieces and process in a food processor until very fine.

Heat the crème fraîche to the boiling point, and with the motor running, pour it through the feed tube in a steady stream. Process a few seconds until smooth. Transfer to a bowl and cool for several hours, until frosting consistency. In cool weather ganache can remain unrefrigerated for at least 3 days and as long as 2 weeks. At room temperature it remains spreadable.

COOKIE BATTER

INGREDIENTS	MEASURE	WEIGHT	
	VOLUME	OUNCES	GRAMS
unblanched almonds, sliced	*1¼ cups*	*3.5 ounces*	*100 grams*
superfine sugar	*1 cup*	*7 ounces*	*200 grams*
unsweetened cocoa	*3 tablespoons*	*0.75 ounce*	*20 grams*
5 large egg whites	*5 fluid ounces*	*5.25 ounces*	*150 grams*
cream of tartar	*½ teaspoon*		
sifted powdered sugar	*½ cup*	*1.75 ounces*	*50 grams*

Baking sheets lined with parchment or foil.

Preheat the oven to 300°F.

In the bowl of a food processor, place the almonds, sugar, and cocoa and process until the almonds are very finely ground.

In a mixing bowl, beat the egg whites until foamy. Add the cream of tartar and beat until soft peaks form when the beater is raised slowly. Gradually beat in the powdered sugar until stiff peaks form when the beater is raised slowly. Using a large rubber spatula, fold the whites into the nut mixture.

Using a pastry bag (or a 1-gallon zip-seal bag with one corner cut off) fitted with a number 6 round pastry tube (½ inch), pipe small balls of the mixture about 2 inches apart on the prepared baking sheets. (A teaspoon can also be used.) Bake about 25 to 30 minutes. Using the handle of a wooden spoon to prop the oven door ajar. Use a small metal spatula to dislodge one cookie. If it crushes from the pressure, bake a little longer. Remove the cookies from the oven and allow them to cool on the baking sheets.

To remove the cookies easily, lift the parchment off the baking sheet, carefully turn it upside-down, and brush the back with water. Reinvert the parchment and remove the cookies with your fingers.

With a small metal spatula, spread some ganache on the bottom of one of the cookies and attach a second one to it. Continue in this way with all the cookies.

NOTE FROM ROSE Use dots of the raw batter in all four corners of the baking sheet to attach the parchment.

KEEPS Stored airtight, these cookies will keep for months. Once spread with ganache, however, they are best eaten within 2 days, as they begin to soften and lose their appealing crunch.

LES ROCHERS CONGOLAIS

CHOCOLATE COCONUT MERINGUES

LES ROCHERS SAN ANTONIO
CHOCOLATE ALMOND MERINGUES

MAKES ABOUT 80 COOKIES

These crunchy little meringues are shaped like rocky mountain peaks. They are great served with ice cream.

INGREDIENTS MEASURE		WEIGHT	
	VOLUME	POUNDS/OUNCES	GRAMS
unsweetened cocoa	1 cup (lightly spooned)	3.5 ounces	100 grams
grated coconut, preferably unsweetened	2/3 cup	1.75 ounces	50 grams
superfine sugar	3 cups	1 pound 5 ounces	600 grams
1 vanilla bean, split*			
10 large egg whites, room temperature	1 1/4 liquid cups	10.5 ounces	300 grams

*You may substitute 1 teaspoon vanilla extract for the vanilla bean, but the bean offers a fuller, more aromatic flavor. If you are using extract, add it at the very end. If using a Tahitian bean, use only 1/2 bean.

Baking sheets lined with parchment or foil, or lightly greased and floured.

Preheat the oven to 300°F.

In a small bowl, stir together the cocoa and coconut.

In a large mixing bowl, combine the sugar, vanilla bean, and egg whites and place over a large pan of simmering water. (The bottom of the bowl should not touch the water.) Stir constantly with a whisk until the mixture is warm. Then beat, preferably with the whisk attachment, until the meringue is stiff and shiny. Remove the vanilla bean.

With a large rubber spatula, gently and quickly fold in the cocoa mixture just until evenly incorporated.

Using a pastry bag (or a 1-gallon zip-seal bag with one corner cut off) fitted with a large plain number 6 (1/2-inch) tip, or a teaspoon, pipe the meringue into rounds about the size of Ping-Pong balls on the prepared baking sheets, leaving about 1 inch in between. Use a small metal spatula, dipped in water, to shape the mounds into conical peaks.

Bake 25 to 30 minutes, or until the meringues are firm enough to be removed from the sheets without crushing. If desired, dust the meringues with unsweetened cocoa. Cool the meringues on wire racks.

Vanilla bean can be rinsed, dried in a warm oven, and reused.

NOTES FROM ROSE

When separating the eggs, break them over two custard cups before adding each white to the mixing bowl. Even a speck of yolk will keep the whites from beating. If any yolk gets mixed in, fish it out with half an eggshell.

Replace the cocoa and coconut mixture with ½ cup (1.75 ounces/50 grams) unsweetened cocoa and 3 cups (8.75 ounces/250 grams) sliced almonds, toasted and finely ground.

VARIATION: Les Rochers San Antonio (Chocolate Almond Meringues)

Use a large plain number 10 (½-inch) tip or a large plain number 6 (½-inch) tip or a large star tip (such as a number 8) to pipe peak shapes 1 ½ inches in diameter at the base. Hold the pastry bag so that the tip is straight up, and continue squeezing slightly as you lift it up to form the peaks.

Bake about 30 minutes, or until they are firm enough to be removed from the sheets without crushing.

For an attractive look, when they are cool, dip the tips in melted bittersweet chocolate.

Airtight at room temperature for several months.

KEEPS

LES PIQUE-NIQUES

FLAKY COCOA-CINNAMON COOKIES

MAKES ABOUT 20 COOKIES

This delicious cookie is actually a pie dough (*pâte sucrée*), with the happy addition of cocoa and just a hint of cinnamon for those who adore its taste. It is very crisp and pleasantly chocolatey. If you really love cinnamon, make the Cinghalaise version of the ganache (page 338). The cookies are called *pique-niques* because their excellent keeping quality makes them suitable for taking on a picnic.

COMPONENTS
Ganache • *Pâte à Pique-Nique*

GANACHE

INGREDIENTS	MEASURE	WEIGHT	
	VOLUME	OUNCES	GRAMS
bittersweet chocolate	*4 (3-ounce) bars*	*12 ounces*	*340 grams*
crème fraîche (page 348) or heavy cream	*1 ¼ cups*	*10 ounces*	*290 grams*

Break the chocolate into pieces and process in a food processor until very fine.

Heat the crème fraîche to the boiling point, and with the motor running, pour it through the feed tube in a steady stream. Process a few seconds until smooth. Transfer to a bowl and cool for several hours, until frosting consistency. In cool weather ganache can remain unrefrigerated for at least 3 days or as long as 2 weeks. At room temperature it remains spreadable.

PÂTE À PIQUE-NIQUE

INGREDIENTS	MEASURE	WEIGHT	
ROOM TEMPERATURE	VOLUME	OUNCES	GRAMS
1 extra-large egg			
milk	*1 tablespoon*		
unsalted butter, softened	*9 tablespoons*	*4.5 ounces*	*125 grams*
superfine sugar	*1 cup*	*7 ounces*	*200 grams*
salt	*¼ teaspoon*		
sifted all-purpose flour	*2 ¼ cups*	*8.75 ounces*	*250 grams*
unsweetened cocoa	*¼ cup (lightly spooned)*	*1 ounce*	*25 grams*
unblanched almonds, sliced, chopped fine	*½ cup + 1 ½ tablespoons*	*1.75 ounces*	*50 grams*
cinnamon (optional)	*½ teaspoon*		

Two 11 by 17-inch baking sheets, lightly buttered.

Preheat the oven to 350°F.

In a small bowl, mix together the egg and the milk. Set aside.

199

In a large mixing bowl, beat the butter with the sugar and salt for about 30 seconds. Add the flour and mix for a few seconds. Continue to mix the dough by rubbing it together with the palms of your hands until the dough looks like coarse grains. Do not overdo this or the dough can become too tender and fragile.

Make a well in the center of the dough and add the egg and milk mixture, stirring with a fork until the dough is moistened and begins to form a ball. Dump the dough onto a sheet of plastic wrap.

Stir together the cocoa, almonds, and cinnamon and sprinkle this mixture over the dough. Use the plastic wrap to knead it into the dough until evenly incorporated.

Flatten the dough into a disc, wrap in the plastic, and refrigerate it for at least 1 hour or up to overnight.

Roll out the dough between sheets of plastic wrap to about ⅛-inch thickness. Using a drinking glass with about a 2½-inch-diameter rim, stamp out rounds of dough. Knead together any scraps and reroll, refrigerating briefly if the dough softens.

Use a pancake turner to lift the rounds onto the prepared baking sheets. Bake about 10 minutes or until set. Cool on the baking sheets, on wire racks.

Attach the cookies in pairs with a thin layer of ganache.

KEEPS   *Pique-niques* are most perfect eaten within days of baking. But they will still be delicious up to 1 week if stored in an airtight container, but they should not be refrigerated.

NOTE
FROM ROSE   It is easiest to chop almonds if you start with ones already sliced. If you are using whole almonds, grate them first with the shredding disc of the food processor and then pulse with the metal blade until fine. You may also add the cocoa and cinnamon before pulsing.

LES CIGARETTES AU CHOCOLAT

ROLLED BUTTER THINS
FILLED WITH GANACHE

MAKES ABOUT 45 COOKIES

These crisp little cookies provide a perfect container for delectable ganache fillings. The Bernachons often dip the ganache-filled "cigarettes" into melted bittersweet chocolate to form a thin, crisp encasement.

GANACHE

INGREDIENTS	MEASURE	WEIGHT	
	VOLUME	OUNCES	GRAMS
bittersweet chocolate	4 (3-ounce) bars	12 ounces	340 grams
crème fraîche (page 348) or heavy cream	1 ¼ cups	10 ounces	290 grams

Break the chocolate into pieces and process in a food processor until very fine.

Heat the crème fraîche to the boiling point, and with the motor running, pour it through the feed tube in a steady stream. Process a few seconds until smooth. Transfer to a bowl and cool for several hours, until frosting consistency.

COOKIE BATTER

INGREDIENTS	MEASURE	WEIGHT	
	VOLUME	OUNCES	GRAMS
unsalted butter	1 cup + 1 ½ tablespoons	8.75 ounces	250 grams
sifted all-purpose flour	1 ⅔ cups	6.75 ounces	190 grams
powdered sugar	2 cups (lightly spooned)	8 ounces	225 grams
salt	pinch		
6 large egg whites, room temperature	¾ liquid cup	6.25 ounces	180 grams
vanilla	1 teaspoon		

Baking sheets, buttered.

Three to 24 hours ahead: Prepare the batter.

In a small saucepan over very low heat, melt the butter. Set it aside to cool to room temperature.

In a large mixing bowl, mix together the flour, sugar, and salt. Mix in the melted butter and then the egg whites and the vanilla just until incorporated. Allow the batter to rest.

When you are ready to bake: Preheat the oven to 400°F.

Using a pastry bag (or a heavy-duty quart zip-seal bag with a coupler) fitted with a number 12 round decorating tube, pipe rounds of batter on the prepared baking sheets, about 2 inches in diameter and at least 2 inches apart, as the batter will spread considerably. Bake for about 10 minutes, or until beginning to brown around the edges.

Remove the cookies from the oven and roll them while they are still hot and flexible (if they become too firm, return them briefly to the oven): Lift one edge of a cookie with a small offset metal spatula and roll it around a pencil or narrow dowel. Press down lightly along the edge to seal it. Repeat with all the cookies. When cool, the "cigarettes" will keep their shape.

Use a pastry bag (or a heavy-duty quart zip-seal bag with a coupler) fitted with a number 12 round decorating tube to fill the cigarettes with the ganache.

NOTE It is important to allow the batter to rest and thicken, or it will spread more when piped.

LES FLORENTINS

THIN ORANGE-AND-CITRON–INFUSED BUTTER COOKIES COATED WITH BITTERSWEET CHOCOLATE

MAKES ABOUT 50 COOKIES

These thin, crisp, nutty cookies are accented with a light touch of orange and citron. This Bernachon version of a classic is less lacy and more substantial than candied fruit. The citrus flavors blend perfectly with the thin coating of bittersweet chocolate.

| INGREDIENTS | MEASURE | | WEIGHT | |
	VOLUME		OUNCES	GRAMS
slivered almonds	2 cups		8.75 ounces	250 grams
sugar	1¼ cups		8.75 ounces	250 grams
sifted all-purpose flour	¾ cup + 2 tablespoons		3.5 ounces	100 grams
salt	pinch			
6 large egg whites, room temperature	¾ liquid cup		6.25 ounces	180 grams
vanilla	1 teaspoon			
candied orange peel (page 248)	2 tablespoons		2 ounces	60 grams
candied citron	2½ teaspoons		1 ounce	25 grams
unsalted butter	4½ tablespoons		2.25 ounces	65 grams
bittersweet chocolate	2 (3-ounce) bars		6 ounces	170 grams

Baking sheets, well buttered.

Three to 24 hours ahead: In a food processor, combine the almonds, sugar, flour, and salt and process until the almonds are finely chopped. Transfer this mixture to a large mixing bowl. Beat in 3 of the egg whites, and when they are incorporated, beat in the remaining 3 until well incorporated. Beat in the vanilla.

Finely chop the candied orange peel, and cut the citron into tiny dice.

Melt the butter and allow it to cool until just warm. Then, beating constantly, gradually add the butter to the batter. Beat in the orange peel and citron. Cover tightly, and leave at cool room temperature for up to 24 hours.

When you are ready to bake: Preheat the oven to 350°F.

Using a measuring teaspoon, measure out level teaspoons of batter at least 2 inches apart on the prepared baking sheets. If the batter does not flatten by itself, flatten each mound, as thin as possible, with the back of a spoon dipped in water. Bake about 12 to 15 minutes or until golden and browned around the edges. Cool on baking sheets until firm. Transfer to wire racks to finish cooling.

Break the chocolate into squares and place them in the top of a double boiler set over very hot water (but no hotter than 160°F.). The water must not simmer or touch the bottom of the double boiler insert.

Stir until the chocolate begins to melt. Return the pan to low heat if the water cools, but be careful that it does not get too hot. (The chocolate may be melted in a microwave oven if stirred every 15 seconds.) Using either method, remove it from the heat source before it is fully melted and stir, using residual heat to complete the melting. Keep warm over a bowl of warm water (water must not exceed 120°F.).

Using a small metal spatula, spread melted chocolate on the underside of the cookies. If desired, use a cake decorating triangular comb or a fork to make wavy lines on the chocolate. Store airtight at room temperature up to 5 days.

NOTE FROM ROSE If you can, prepare the batter the night before, so that it will have more body for piping.

If you are making wavy lines on the chocolate, for a more uniform effect it helps to use a second coat of chocolate. Be sure to melt about 3 ounces of extra chocolate.

LES TUILES
AU CHOCOLAT

THIN ORANGE-CHOCOLATE
BUTTER COOKIES IN THE SHAPE
OF ROOF TILES

MAKES ABOUT 50 COOKIES

These "tiles" are prepared with the same nutty, faintly orange-flavored batter as for Florentins, but without the citron. Their shape, however, is gently curved instead of flat. In my experience, this batter is the most foolproof. These are the cookies so often served with coffee in three-star French restaurants.

INGREDIENTS	MEASURE	WEIGHT	
	VOLUME	OUNCES	GRAMS
almonds, slivered	2 cups	8.75 ounces	250 grams
sugar	1¼ cups	8.75 ounces	250 grams
sifted all-purpose flour	¾ cup + 2 tablespoons	3.5 ounces	100 grams
salt	pinch		
6 large egg whites, room temperature	¾ liquid cup	6.25 ounces	180 grams
vanilla	1 teaspoon		
candied orange peel (page 248)	2 tablespoons	2 ounces	60 grams
unsalted butter	4½ table-spoons	2.25 ounces	65 grams
bittersweet chocolate	2 (3-ounce) bars	6 ounces	170 grams

Baking sheets, well buttered.
Lightly greased baguette pan or greased rolling pin.

Three to 24 hours ahead: In a food processor, combine the almonds, sugar, flour, and salt and process until the almonds are finely chopped. Transfer this mixture to a large mixing bowl. Beat in 3 of the egg whites, and when they are incorporated, beat in the remaining 3 until well incorporated. Beat in the vanilla.

Finely chop the candied orange peel.

Melt the butter and allow it to cool until just warm. Then, beating constantly, gradually add the butter to the batter. Beat in the orange peel. Cover tightly, and leave at cool room temperature for up to 24 hours.

When you are ready to bake: Preheat the oven to 350°F.

Using a measuring teaspoon, measure out level teaspoons of batter at least 2 inches apart on the prepared baking sheets. If the batter does not flatten by itself, flatten each mound, as thin as possible, with the back of a spoon dipped in water. Bake about 12 to 15 minutes or until golden and browned around the edges.

A PASSION FOR CHOCOLATE

Working quickly, using a pancake turner, remove the cookies one at a time and place them, top side up, in the prepared baguette pan, or over the rolling pin, top side down. (The smooth side of the cookie must end up on the curved outside in order to be able to apply an even coat of chocolate.)

TO GLAZE

Break the chocolate into squares and place them in the top of a double boiler set over very hot water (but no hotter than 160°F.). The water must not simmer or touch the bottom of the double boiler insert.

Stir until the chocolate begins to melt. Return the pan to low heat if the water cools, but be careful that it does not get too hot. (The chocolate may be melted in a microwave oven if stirred every 15 seconds.) Using either method, remove it from the heat source before it is fully melted and stir, using residual heat to complete the melting. Keep it warm over a bowl of warm water (water must not exceed 120°F.).

Using a small metal spatula, spread the melted chocolate on the curved outer side of the cookie. If desired, use a cake-decorating triangular comb or a fork to make wavy lines on the chocolate. Alternatively, create a lacy pattern by drizzling the melted chocolate over the cookies. A small zip-seal bag with one corner cut off is ideal for this. A fork also works well. Store airtight at room temperature up to 5 days.

NOTES FROM ROSE

If you can, prepare the batter the night before, so as to give it more body for piping. The cookies will also be less fragile and easier to mold.

If the cookies start to cool and stick to the pan or become too rigid to flex, simply return them briefly to the oven.

Les Marthas

Little Chocolate Cups
Filled with Leftover Cakes and Creams

Makes About 50 Containers

These elegant little chocolate containers are paper-thin and wondrously melting and not all that difficult to prepare. They are, however, quite time-consuming! The Bernachons fill the hollow centers with bits of liqueur-moistened génoise or biscuit, and top them with little swirls of ganache or buttercream. These cakes are an ingenious way to use bits of "leftovers" such as buttercream and ganache from larger cakes.

INGREDIENTS	MEASURE		WEIGHT	
	VOLUME		POUNDS	GRAMS
*bittersweet chocolate**			**1 pound**	**450 grams**

*For the finest coating of chocolate, use couverture, available in specialty stores (page 382).

Fifty 4-inch squares of tissue paper or aluminum foil.
A wooden dowel about 1 inch in diameter.

Break the chocolate into squares and place them in the top of a double boiler set over very hot water (but no hotter than 160°F.). The water must not simmer or touch the bottom of the double boiler insert.

Stir until the chocolate begins to melt. Return the pan to low heat if the water cools, but be careful that it does not get too hot. (The chocolate may be melted in a microwave oven if stirred every 15 seconds.) Using either method, remove it from the heat source before it is fully melted and stir constantly, using the residual heat to complete the melting and to cool the chocolate to 89° to 91°F. (If you are not using a thermometer, dab a small amount on your upper lip. It should feel cool. If it is still warm, stir in a few extra squares of chocolate and remove any unmelted chocolate when the mixture reaches the correct temperature.)

Place the wooden dowel in the center of the paper or foil square, and using your fingers, smooth the sides against the dowel. Allow the paper or foil to fold and pleat to conform to the shape of the dowel.

Dip the covered dowel into the chocolate so that it comes about 3/4 inch up the sides. Set it on a sheet of parchment or foil, and carefully remove the dowel. (An attractive little "base" will form at the bottom if you allow it to fall slightly from the dowel instead of setting the dowel on the surface.) Continue with the rest of the chocolate, returning it very briefly to the heat, stirring constantly, if it begins to cool and thicken.

Refrigerate the chocolate forms for 1 hour before removing the paper or foil. If the chocolate is not cool enough, it will show marks such as fingerprints. Feel it with the *backs* of your fingers. It should feel cool.

To remove the paper, carefully draw it toward the center, and lift it out using a twisting motion.

NOTE FROM ROSE If you prefer sturdier, less fragile chocolate containers, they may be dipped a second time for another coat.

SUGGESTED FILLINGS

- Sprinkle little génoise or biscuit cubes with dark rum. Fill the chocolate molds two thirds full. Pipe in chestnut buttercream ruffles or rosettes, using a number 2 D drop flower or 22 star tip. Decorate the tops with little bits of candied chestnut.
- Sprinkle little génoise or biscuit cubes with Grand Marnier. Fill the chocolate molds two thirds full. Pipe in ganache ruffles or rosettes, using a number 2 D drop flower or 22 star tip.
- Sprinkle little génoise or biscuit cubes with Cherry Marnier or cherry liqueur. Fill the chocolate molds two thirds full. Pipe in Président Ganache ruffles or rosettes, using a number 2 D drop flower or 22 star tip. Decorate with little bits of candied violet.
- Sprinkle little génoise or biscuit cubes with dark rum. Fill the chocolate molds two thirds full. Pipe in mocha ganache ruffles or rosettes, using a number 2 D drop flower or 22 star tip. Decorate the tops with a chocolate coffee bean.
- Sprinkle little génoise or biscuit cubes with kirsch. Fill the chocolate molds two thirds full. Pipe in pistachio buttercream ruffles or rosettes, using a number 2 D drop flower or 22 star tip. Decorate the top with bits of toasted almonds, pralines, or blanched pistachios.

KEEPS Airtight, refrigerated, up to 5 days. Containers alone will keep for months, airtight, at cool room temperature.

NOTES FROM ROSE *To pipe rosettes:* Hold the pastry bag upright at a 90° angle, with the tube ¼ inch above the surface. As you squeeze out the buttercream, move the tube in a tight arc from the 9:00 position around to the 6:00 position. Release the pressure, but do not lift the tube until you have followed the circular motion all the way around to the 9:00 position. To pipe ruffles, simply use a number 2 D drop flower (the little teeth are curved inward) and pipe with the bag in a upright position.

A Portuguese woman who has been dipping chocolate at Bernachon for many years told me to feel chocolate with the backs of the fingers because they are much more sensitive to temperature than the fingertips.

A PASSION FOR CHOCOLATE

DESSERTS: MOUSSES, ICE CREAMS, SOUFFLÉS

LA MOUSSE AUX AMANDES

BITTERSWEET CHOCOLATE ALMOND-FLECKED MOUSSE

SERVES 10

This incredibly rich chocolate mousse is really a ganache—made richer and silkier with the addition of egg yolks and lighter with the addition of beaten egg whites.

| INGREDIENTS | MEASURE | WEIGHT | |
	VOLUME	OUNCES	GRAMS
bittersweet chocolate	2 (3-ounce) bars	6 ounces	170 grams
almonds, slivered	1¼ cups	5.5 ounces	150 grams
crème fraîche (page 348) or heavy cream	1 liquid cup	8 ounces	232 grams
7 large eggs, separated			
yolks	½ liquid cups	4.5 ounces	130 grams
whites	7 fluid ounces	7.25 ounces	210 grams

Ten ramekins or long-stemmed wine goblets.

Break the chocolate into pieces and process, with the almonds, in a food processor until the almonds are ground very fine. Heat the crème fraîche to the boiling point, and with the motor running, pour it through the feed tube in a steady stream. Process a few seconds until smooth.

Separate the eggs. Add the egg yolks to the hot chocolate mixture and process for a few seconds to incorporate. Transfer to a large bowl and cool completely.

In a large mixing bowl, beat the egg whites until stiff but not dry. The *"bec d'oiseau"* stage—when the whites will hold a peak that is slightly curved, like a "bird's beak"—is just right. Scoop about one quarter of the beaten whites onto the chocolate mixture, and using a large rubber spatula, stir them into the mixture. Gently and quickly fold in the remaining whites.

Pour the mousse into the serving dishes, cover tightly with plastic wrap, and refrigerate for at least 4 and up to 12 hours.

NOTES FROM ROSE For a more intense almond flavor, toast the slivered almonds in a 350°F. oven for about 10 minutes, or until golden brown, before grinding them with the chocolate.

Adding the yolks to the hot chocolate mixture

A PASSION FOR CHOCOLATE

cooks them slightly and gives a creamier texture to the mousse.

Chocolate mousse has its best texture the day it is prepared, after which it begins to break down.

The mousse can be decorated with chocolate curls or sliced honeyed almonds (page 245).

LA MOUSSE CHOCOLATÉE À LA CANNELLE

RICH CINNAMON-INFUSED CHOCOLATE MOUSSE

SERVES 6

The subtle cinnamon flavor in this mousse greatly enhances the bittersweet chocolate.

INGREDIENTS	MEASURE	WEIGHT	
	VOLUME	OUNCES	GRAMS
bittersweet chocolate	2 ⅓ *(3-ounce) bars*	7 ounces	200 grams
cinnamon	¼ *teaspoon*		
heavy cream	1 *liquid cup*	8 ounces	232 grams
3 extra-large eggs, separated			
yolks	2 *full fluid ounces*	2.5 ounces	72 grams
whites	4 *scant fluid ounces*	4 ounces	114 grams

Six ramekins or long-stemmed wine goblets.

Break the chocolate into pieces and process, with the cinnamon, in a food processor until ground very fine.

Heat the cream to the boiling point, and with the motor running, pour it through the feed tube in a steady stream. Process a few seconds until smooth.

Separate the eggs. Add the egg yolks to the hot chocolate mixture, and process for a few seconds to incorporate. Transfer to a large bowl and cool completely.

In a large mixing bowl, beat the egg whites until stiff but not dry. The *"bec d'oiseau"* stage—when the whites will hold a peak that is slightly curved, like a "bird's beak"—is just right. Scoop about one quarter of the beaten whites onto the chocolate mixture, and using a large rubber spatula, stir them into the mixture. Gently and quickly fold in the remaining whites.

Pour the mousse into the serving dishes, cover tightly with plastic wrap, and refrigerate for at least 4 and up to 12 hours.

NOTES FROM ROSE

Adding the yolks to the hot chocolate mixture cooks them slightly and gives a creamier texture to the mousse.

The mousse has its best texture the day it is prepared, after which it begins to break down.

The mousse can be decorated with chocolate curls or a small piece of cinnamon bark.

MOUSSES, ICE CREAMS, SOUFFLÉS

La Mousse
Chocolatée Créole

Rich Chocolate Mousse
Perfumed with Raisins
and Rum

SERVES 6

Raisins soaked in rum offer not only extra flavor but also an extra textural dimension that punctuates and complements the richness of this mousse.

| INGREDIENTS | MEASURE | | WEIGHT | |
	VOLUME	OUNCES	GRAMS	
dark raisins	¼ *cup*		*36 grams*	
dark rum	¼ *cup*	*2 ounces*	*55 grams*	
bittersweet chocolate	*2 ⅓ (3-ounce) bars*	*7 ounces*	*200 grams*	
crème fraîche (page 348) or heavy cream	*1 liquid cup*	*8 ounces*	*232 grams*	
3 extra-large eggs, separated				
yolks	*2 full fluid ounces*	*2.5 ounces*	*72 grams*	
whites	*4 scant fluid ounces*	*4 ounces*	*114 grams*	

Six ramekins or long-stemmed wine goblets.

Several hours (up to 24) ahead, combine the raisins and the rum in a small bowl, cover tightly with plastic wrap, and set aside to soak.

Break the chocolate into pieces and process in a food processor until ground very fine.

Heat the crème fraîche to the boiling point, and with the motor running, pour it through the feed tube in a steady stream. Process a few seconds until smooth.

Separate the eggs. Add the egg yolks to the hot chocolate mixture, and process for a few seconds to incorporate. Transfer to a large bowl, stir in the drained raisins, and cool completely.

In a large mixing bowl, beat the egg whites until stiff but not dry. Scoop about one quarter of the beaten whites onto the chocolate mixture, and using a large rubber spatula, stir them into the mixture. Gently and quickly fold in the remaining whites.

Pour the mousse into the serving dishes, cover tightly with plastic wrap, and refrigerate for at least 4 hours and as long as 12 hours.

Adding the yolks to the hot chocolate mixture cooks them slightly and gives a creamier texture to the mousse, which is best served the day it is prepared. Decorate with chocolate curls or extra rum-soaked raisins.

NOTES FROM ROSE

LA MOUSSE CHOCOLATÉE AU MOKA

RICH COFFEE-FLAVORED CHOCOLATE MOUSSE

SERVES 6

The aromatic coffee flavor is perfectly balanced by the rich bittersweetness of the chocolate and cream.

INGREDIENTS	MEASURE	WEIGHT	
	VOLUME	OUNCES	GRAMS
bittersweet chocolate	2⅓ (3-ounce) bars	7 ounces	200 grams
Medaglia d'Oro instant espresso powder	1 tablespoon		
crème fraîche* or heavy cream	1 liquid cup	8 ounces	232 grams
3 extra-large eggs, separated			
yolks	2 full fluid ounces	2.5 ounces	72 grams
whites	4 scant fluid ounces	4 ounces	114 grams

*Crème fraîche (page 348) adds a gentle tang that is surprisingly harmonious with the mocha flavor.

Six ramekins or long-stemmed wine goblets.

Break the chocolate into pieces and process, with the espresso powder, in a food processor until ground fine.

Heat the crème fraîche to the boiling point, and with the motor running, pour it steadily through the feed tube. Process a few seconds until smooth.

Separate the eggs. Add the yolks to the hot chocolate mixture and process a few seconds to incorporate. Transfer to a large bowl and cool completely.

In a large mixing bowl, beat the egg whites until stiff but not dry. The *"bec d'oiseau"* stage—when the whites will hold a peak that is slightly curved, like a "bird's beak"—is just right. Scoop about one quarter of the beaten whites onto the chocolate mixture, and using a large rubber spatula, stir them into the mixture. Gently and quickly fold in the remaining whites.

Pour the mousse into the serving dishes, cover tightly with plastic wrap, and refrigerate for at least 4 and up to 12 hours.

NOTES FROM ROSE

Adding the yolks to the hot chocolate mixture cooks them slightly and gives a creamier texture to the mousse, which is best served the day it is prepared. Decorate with chocolate curls or chocolate coffee beans.

LES POIRES
BELLE-HÉLÈNE

POACHED PEARS SURROUNDED
BY VANILLA ICE CREAM AND
CHOCOLATE SAUCE

SERVES 8

This classic French dessert combines translucent poached pears with creamy vanilla ice cream and dark bittersweet chocolate sauce. For a richer, creamier version see the note.

COMPONENTS
Poached Pears • *Vanilla Ice Cream* •
Chocolate Sauce

VANILLA ICE CREAM

INGREDIENTS MEASURE		WEIGHT	
	VOLUME	POUNDS/OUNCES	GRAMS
7 large egg yolks	½ liquid cup	4.5 ounces	128 grams
superfine sugar	1 cup	7 ounces	200 grams
salt	a pinch		
heavy cream	1 liquid cup	8 ounces	232 grams
milk	2¼ cups	1 pound 3 ounces	539 grams
2 vanilla beans, split*			

*You may substitute 2 teaspoons vanilla extract for the vanilla beans, but the beans offer a fuller, more aromatic flavor. If you are using extract, add it after the mixture has cooled. If using a Tahitian bean, use only 1 bean.

Place a fine strainer near the stove, suspended over a medium mixing bowl.

In a medium-size heavy noncorrodible saucepan, using a wooden spoon, stir together the yolks, sugar, and salt until well blended.

In a small saucepan (or heatproof glass measure if using a microwave on high power), heat the cream, milk, and vanilla beans to the boiling point. Stir a few tablespoons into the yolk mixture; then gradually add the remainder, stirring constantly.

Heat the mixture to just below the boiling point (170° to 180°F.). Steam will begin to appear and the mixture will be slightly thicker than heavy cream. It will leave a well-defined track when a finger is run across the back of a spoon that has been dipped in the mixture. Immediately remove the pan from the heat and pour the mixture into the strainer, scraping up any thickened cream that has settled on the bottom of the pan. Remove the vanilla beans and scrape the seeds into the cream. Stir until the seeds separate. Return the pod to the cream until ready to freeze, then remove it.

Cool the mixture in an ice-water bath or the refrigerator until cold. Freeze in an ice cream maker. Allow to ripen for 2 hours in the freezer before serving. Store up to 3 days.

NOTE FROM ROSE I find that a higher percentage of cream to milk results in a smoother ice cream. I recommend 2½ cups of cream and ¾ cup of milk. I also prefer to use only ¾ cup of sugar. Adding 1 tablespoon of vodka before freezing also helps to keep the ice cream creamy.

POACHED PEARS

INGREDIENTS MEASURE		WEIGHT	
	VOLUME	POUNDS/OUNCES	GRAMS
8 large ripe but firm pears, such as Bartlett or Bosc			
water	4 cups	2 pounds 1.25 ounces	944 grams
superfine sugar	2 cups	7 ounces	200 grams
½ vanilla bean, split			

Peel, halve, and core the pears just before poaching (so that they do not darken).

In a large casserole, combine the water, sugar, and vanilla bean and bring it to a boil, stirring to dissolve the sugar. Add the pears and simmer, tightly covered, for 8 to 10 minutes, or until a cake tester inserted in the thickest part of a pear enters easily. The pears should still be slightly firm.

Remove the pan from the heat and let the pears cool in it, covered. Refrigerate the pears in their liquid, covered, until ready to serve.

CHOCOLATE SAUCE

INGREDIENTS MEASURE		WEIGHT	
	VOLUME	POUNDS/OUNCES	GRAMS
bittersweet chocolate	2 (3-ounce) bars	6 ounces	170 grams
crème fraîche (page 348) or heavy cream	2 cups	1 pound	464 grams

Break the chocolate into small pieces.

In a small saucepan, bring the cream to a boil, stirring constantly. Remove it from the heat, add the chocolate, and stir until the chocolate is fully melted and the sauce is smooth. Use at once or reheat when ready to serve.

Place a scoop of ice cream on each plate and one or two pear halves, cored side down, next to it. Pour the chocolate sauce into a little pool on the plate. Serve immediately, and pass extra chocolate sauce in a pitcher. **ASSEMBLING THE *POIRES BELLE- HÉLÈNE***

LE SOUFFLÉ CHAUD
AU CHOCOLAT

CHOCOLATE SOUFFLÉ

SERVES 4

The Bernachons' very chocolatey version of everyone's favorite hot soufflé!

INGREDIENTS	MEASURE	WEIGHT	
	VOLUME	OUNCES	GRAMS
unsalted butter	*2 tablespoons*	*1 ounce*	*30 grams*
all-purpose flour	*3 tablespoons*	*1 ounce*	*30 grams*
bittersweet chocolate	*1 (3-ounce) bar*	*3 ounces*	*85 grams*
7 large eggs	*1½ liquid cups*	*14 ounces (weighed in the shells)*	*400 grams*
powdered sugar	*¾ cup (lightly spooned) + 2 tablespoons*	*3.5 ounces*	*100 grams*
cream of tartar	*1 teaspoon*		*3 grams*

One 6-cup soufflé dish, with a foil collar, buttered and sugared. One baking sheet.*

Preheat the oven to 400°F.

In a medium-size heavy saucepan, melt the butter. Add the flour and cook, stirring constantly, for about 3 minutes, or until the flour just begins to take on a golden color. Set aside.

Break the chocolate into pieces and place them in the top of a double boiler set over very hot water (but no hotter than 160°F.). The water must not simmer or touch the bottom of the double boiler insert.

Stir until the chocolate begins to melt. Return the pan to low heat if the water cools, but be careful that it does not get too hot. Stir 10 minutes or until smooth. (The chocolate may be melted in a microwave oven if stirred every 15 seconds.) Using either method, remove it from the heat source before fully melted and stir, using residual heat to complete the melting. Set aside.

Separate the eggs, placing the yolks in a medium mixing bowl and the whites in a large mixing bowl.

*To make a collar, fasten a band of aluminum foil around the soufflé dish with string or paper clips. The band should be 4 inches higher than the sides of the dish. Butter and sugar the soufflé dish and the inside of the band. Be sure to empty out any excess sugar that does not cling to the dish and band.

Beat the yolks with the sugar until they are light in color and fall in a thick ribbon when the beater is raised. Add the butter/flour mixture and the chocolate, and beat until combined.

Beat the whites until foamy. Add the cream of tartar and continue beating until stiff peaks form when the beater is raised slowly. Stir about one quarter of the beaten egg whites into the chocolate mixture, and then carefully fold in the remainder. Pour the mixture into the prepared soufflé dish, set it on the baking sheet in the oven, and bake for 40 minutes or until a knife inserted 2 inches from the center comes out clean. Serve at once. If desired, serve with lightly sweetened whipped cream (1 tablespoon of superfine sugar for 1 cup of heavy cream).

NOTE FROM ROSE The baking sheet "cushions" the heat, preventing the bottom of the soufflé from overcooking.

Le Dauphin
au Chocolat

Soft Cocoa-Flavored
Ice Cream

Serves 4 to 6

This dense, ice-cold chocolate cream has an incredibly smooth, voluptuous texture that results from whipping sugar, egg whites, and cocoa into a meringue and combining it with whipped cream. This dessert is quite sweet, but it is the large amount of sugar that makes it incapable of freezing solid or forming ice crystals. This type of dessert is sometimes called *semi-freddo*. It is similar to a soft ice cream and has the additional advantage of not requiring an ice cream freezer to prepare.

If you have an addictive personality, don't even try this one!

INGREDIENTS	MEASURE	WEIGHT	
	VOLUME	OUNCES	GRAMS
5 large egg whites	⅔ cup	5.25 ounces	150 grams
superfine sugar	1½ cups	10.5 ounces	300 grams
½ vanilla bean, split*			
unsweetened cocoa	½ cup + 2 tablespoons (lightly spooned into cup)	2.25 ounces	63 grams
heavy cream	1 liquid cup	8 ounces	232 grams

*You may substitute ½ teaspoon vanilla extract for the vanilla bean, but the bean offers a fuller, more aromatic flavor. If you are using extract, add it to the cream at the very end. If using a Tahitian bean, use only ¼ bean.

A 1-quart soufflé dish or 4 to 6 individual dessert cups.

At least 4 hours ahead, place the egg whites, sugar, and vanilla bean in a large mixing bowl, and place over a large pan of simmering water. (The bottom of the bowl should not touch the water.) Stir constantly with a whisk until the mixture is warm. Then beat, preferably with the whisk attachment, until the meringue is stiff and shiny. Remove the vanilla bean. Sift the cocoa over the meringue, and beat just a few seconds, until incorporated.

In a large chilled mixing bowl, beat the cream until it mounds softly when dropped from a spoon. Using a large balloon whisk or a rubber spatula, fold the meringue into the whipped cream. Pour the mixture into the soufflé dish or individual cups, cover tightly with plastic wrap (preferably Saran Wrap, which is airtight), and freeze for at least 4 hours, or up to 5 days, before serving.

To create cocoa designs or initials on the surface, make a template (or use a doily) and set it on top of the soufflé dish or cups so that it sits on the rim without touching the surface of the mixture. Place the cocoa in a small strainer and sift it over the top of the template. Lift off the template.

NOTE FROM ROSE The vanilla bean can be rinsed, dried in a warm oven, and reused.

A PASSION FOR CHOCOLATE

La Glace Caramel au Chocolat

Bittersweet Chocolate Ice Cream with Faint Caramel Undertones

Serves 4 to 6

A perfectly smooth and creamy ice cream, the chocolate flavor is enhanced by the caramel. For a richer, creamier version see the note.

INGREDIENTS	MEASURE	WEIGHT	
	VOLUME	OUNCES	GRAMS
sugar	1 cup	7 ounces	200 grams
water (hot)	⅔ cup	5.5 ounces	156 grams
7 large egg yolks	½ liquid cup	4.5 ounces	128 grams
milk	2 cups	1 pound 1 ounce	484 grams
heavy cream	1 liquid cup	8 ounces	232 grams
bittersweet chocolate, coarsely chopped	1 (3-ounce) bar	3 ounces	85 grams

Place a fine strainer near the stove, suspended over a medium mixing bowl.

In a small heavy saucepan, combine the sugar and ⅓ cup of the hot water and cook over medium-low heat, stirring constantly, to dissolve the sugar. Increase the heat and boil without stirring until deep amber (360°F.). Remove from the heat and slowly pour in the remaining ⅓ cup hot water. Return to low heat and cook, stirring, until the caramel is totally dissolved. Set aside to cool.

When the caramel has cooled to lukewarm, whisk in the yolks.

In a medium saucepan (or heat-proof glass measure if using a microwave on high power), bring the milk and cream to a boil. Remove it from the heat and add the chocolate. Stir until the chocolate is melted. Then add this mixture to the egg yolk mixture, whisking constantly. Strain.

Allow the mixture to cool, stirring occasionally to prevent a skin from forming. (Placing the bowl in a larger bowl full of salted ice water helps to speed the process.)

Freeze in an ice cream maker. Allow the ice cream to ripen for 2 hours in the freezer before serving. Store up to 3 days.

I find that a higher percentage of cream to milk results in a smoother ice cream. I recommend 2 cups of cream and 1 cup of milk. I also prefer to use only ¾ cup of sugar for extra bittersweetness. Adding 1 tablespoon of vodka before freezing helps to keep the ice cream creamy.

The exact temperature of the egg mixture is not important when chocolate is used, as it adequately thickens the mixture.

LA GLACE
AU CHOCOLAT

CHOCOLATE ICE CREAM

SERVES 4 TO 6

A truly bittersweet chocolate ice cream—the crème fraîche adds additional tang. For a richer, creamier version see the note.

INGREDIENTS MEASURE		WEIGHT	
	VOLUME	POUNDS/OUNCES	GRAMS
milk	2¼ cups	1 pound 3 ounces	539 grams
crème fraiche (page 348) or heavy cream	2 liquid cups	16.25 ounces	464 grams
7 large egg yolks	½ liquid cup	4.5 ounces	130 grams
superfine sugar	1 cup	7 ounces	200 grams
unsweetened cocoa	⅔ cup (lightly spooned)	2 ounces	60 grams

Place a fine strainer near the stove, suspended over a medium mixing bowl.

In a medium-size heavy saucepan (or heat-proof glass measure if using a microwave on high power), bring the milk and cream to a boil. Remove it from the heat.

In a medium-size, heavy, noncorrodible saucepan, whisk the egg yolks. Whisk in the sugar, then the cocoa, until well incorporated. Gradually add the hot milk and cream to the yolk mixture, stirring constantly. Heat to just below the boiling point (170° to 180°F.), stirring constantly. Steam will begin to appear and the mixture will be slightly thicker than heavy cream. It will leave a well-defined track when a finger is run across the back of a spoon that has been dipped in the mixture. Immediately remove the pan from the heat, and pour the mixture into the strainer, scraping up any thickened cream that has settled on the bottom.

Allow the mixture to cool, stirring occasionally to prevent a skin from forming. (Place the bowl in a larger bowl full of salted ice water to speed the process.)

Freeze in an ice cream maker and at least 2 hours in the freezer before serving. Store up to 3 days.

NOTE FROM ROSE

I find that a higher percentage of cream to milk results in a smoother ice cream. I recommend 2¾ cups of cream and 1½ cups of milk. Adding 2 tablespoons of Kahlúa before freezing helps to keep the ice cream creamy and adds a subtle coffee flavor.

LE SOUFFLÉ GLACÉ
AU CHOCOLAT

FROZEN CHOCOLATE
SOUFFLÉ

SERVES 8

Alight ganache enriched with egg yolks and lightened by egg whites. Richer than a mousse.

INGREDIENTS MEASURE		WEIGHT	
	VOLUME	POUNDS/OUNCES	GRAMS
bittersweet chocolate	*3 (3-ounce) bars*	*9 ounces*	*255 grams*
crème fraîche (page 348) or heavy cream	*2 cups*	*1 pound*	*454 grams*
4 large eggs	*6 full fluid*	*7 ounces (weighed in the shells)*	*200 grams*

One 6-cup soufflé dish, with a foil collar.*

Break the chocolate into pieces and process in a food processor until very fine.

Heat the crème fraîche to the boiling point, and with the motor running, pour it through the feed tube in a steady stream. Process a few seconds until smooth.

Separate the eggs, and add the yolks to the hot chocolate mixture. Process for a few seconds to incorporate. Then transfer the mixture to a bowl and allow it to cool until it has thickened to spreading consistency.

In a large mixing bowl, beat the egg whites until stiff peaks form when the beater is raised slowly. Stir about one quarter of the whites into the chocolate mixture, and then carefully fold in the remaining whites until uniform. Pour the mixture into the prepared soufflé dish, and freeze for at least 3 hours. Store up to 3 days.

When ready to serve, carefully remove the foil collar and serve at once.

*Fasten a band of aluminum foil around the soufflé dish with string or paper clips. The band should be 4 inches higher than the sides of the dish to create the illusion of a risen mousse.

LE PARFAIT
AU CHOCOLAT

CHOCOLATE PARFAIT

SERVES 4

This delicious frozen chocolate dessert is actually an egg yolk–enriched ganache with whipped cream folded into it.

INGREDIENTS	MEASURE		WEIGHT	
	VOLUME	OUNCES		GRAMS
bittersweet chocolate	*2 (3-ounce) bars*	*6 ounces*		*170 grams*
crème fraîche (page 348) or heavy cream	*⅔ cups*	*5.25 ounces*		*150 grams*
2 extra-large egg yolks	*3 tablespoons*	*1.75 ounces*		*50 grams*
heavy cream	*⅔ cup*	*5.25 ounces*		*150 grams*

One 3- to 4-cup soufflé dish or ice cream mold.

Break the chocolate into pieces and process in a food processor until very fine.

Heat the crème fraîche to the boiling point, and with the motor running, pour it through the feed tube in a steady stream. Process a few seconds until smooth. Add the egg yolks to the hot chocolate mixture, and process for a few seconds to incorporate. Transfer the mixture to a bowl, and allow it to cool until it has thickened to spreading consistency.

Whip the heavy cream until it mounds softly when dropped from a spoon. Gently fold it into the chocolate mixture until evenly incorporated. Pour the parfait into the soufflé dish or ice cream mold, and freeze for at least 3 hours. Store up to 3 days.

If desired, serve topped with whipped cream.

Two teaspoons of Kahlúa added to the whipped cream will keep the parfait softer when frozen.

NOTE FROM ROSE

CONFECTIONS: CHOCOLATE TRUFFLES AND CANDIES

LES AMANDINES

CHOCOLATE-COVERED
HONEYED ALMONDS

MAKES ABOUT 100 CANDIES

INGREDIENTS MEASURE		WEIGHT	
	VOLUME	POUNDS/OUNCES	GRAMS
water	4 cups	2 pounds 1.25 ounces	944 grams
sugar	3 ¾ cups	1 pound 10.25 ounces	750 grams
2 vanilla beans, split			
honey	2 table-spoons	1.5 ounces	42 grams
slivered almonds	3 ⅓ cups	14 ounces	400 grams
bittersweet or milk chocolate	2 ⅔ (3-ounce) bars	2 pounds 8 ounces	1 kilogram 134 grams

One large baking sheet, greased.
Several baking sheets lined with smooth aluminum foil or wax paper.

Preheat the oven to 400°F.

In a large saucepan, combine the water, sugar, vanilla beans, and honey. Bring it to a boil, stirring constantly. Add the almonds, and boil undisturbed for about 3 minutes.

Using a strainer, drain the almonds. Place them in one layer on the unlined, greased baking sheet and bake, gently stirring them occasionally to promote even browning, for 6 to 10 minutes, or until golden. Cool.

Break the chocolate into pieces and place all but about 4 ounces in the top of a double boiler set over very hot water (but no hotter than 160°F.). The water must not simmer or touch the bottom of the double boiler insert.

Stir until the chocolate is fully melted. Return the pan to low heat if the water cools, but be careful that it does not get too hot (the water must not start to simmer). (The chocolate may be melted in a microwave oven if stirred every 15 seconds.) Remove the double boiler insert from the base and add the reserved unmelted chocolate. Stir continuously until the temperature of the chocolate reaches 88° to 91°F. (84° to

A PASSION FOR CHOCOLATE

87°F. if milk chocolate). (If you are not using a thermometer, dab a small amount on your upper lip. It should feel cool.) Remove any unmelted chocolate when the mixture reaches the correct temperature.*

Stir in the toasted almonds. Drop spoonfuls of the mixture onto the lined baking sheets. Using a fork, flatten them so they are about 2½ inches wide. Allow them to cool until the chocolate dulls and they can be lifted from the sheets without sticking. Store airtight at room temperature for several weeks.

The almonds will be sticky when hot from the oven but they dry in cooling.

NOTE FROM ROSE

---

*To maintain this temperature, you can place the pan of chocolate on a heating pad set on "low." (Plastic wrap helps to keep it free of chocolate!) This method was created by Adrienne Welch.

CHOCOLATE TRUFFLES AND CANDIES

Les Écorces d'Oranges Confites Enrobées de Chocolat

Candied Orange Peel
Dipped in Chocolate

MAKES 1¼ CUPS CANDIED PEEL,
2¼ CUPS SYRUP

Orange and chocolate is a divine combination. It takes many days—but actually not much time—to make homemade candied orange peel. These succulent, bright orange candied peels are well worth the effort. They are elegant served with after-dinner espresso.

INGREDIENTS MEASURE		WEIGHT	
	VOLUME	POUNDS/OUNCES	GRAMS
4 large thick-skinned oranges		*2.25 pounds*	*1 kilo-gram*
water	*4 ¼ cups*	*2 pounds 3 ounces*	*1 kilo-gram*
sugar	*3 ¾ cups*	*1 pound 10.25 ounces*	*750 grams*
1 vanilla bean, split			
corn syrup	*2 tablespoons*	*1.5 ounces*	*41 grams*
*bittersweet or milk chocolate**		*1 pound*	*450 grams*

*Couverture, available in specialty stores (page 382), contains more cocoa butter and will create a thinner, glossier coating of chocolate.

A densimeter with a syrup density test tube (available at La Cuisine, page 382).
Baking sheets lined with smooth aluminum foil or wax paper.

Begin preparation at least 10 days ahead.

Score the peel of each orange into six vertical pieces, and remove the peel. (The fruit is not needed; use it for a fruit cup.) Scrape most of the white pith from the inside of the peel.†

Fill a large stainless steel, glass, or enamel saucepan or casserole with water and bring it to a boil. Add the peels and boil them for 5 minutes. Have ready a bowl of ice water.

Drain the peels and immediately plunge them into the ice water, then drain them again. (This sets their magnificent orange color.)

In the same large saucepan, bring the 4¼ cups of water, the sugar, and the vanilla bean to a boil, stirring constantly. Remove the pan from the heat and add the orange peels without stirring, swirling the pan slightly to incorporate them. Cover tightly and set aside at room temperature for 3 to 4 hours. Heat the mixture, uncovered, for about 5 minutes, or until a densimeter

†Jean-Jacques says leaving a small amount adds a pleasant bitterness.

CHOCOLATE TRUFFLES AND CANDIES

registers 1140.* Remove the pan from the heat, cover, and set aside until the next day.

Return the pan to the heat, uncovered. Bring it to a boil and bring the syrup to 1160 on the densimeter.

Continue in this way for nine more days, each day increasing the density by 20 gradations. This takes about 2 minutes after the syrup comes to a boil. On the sixth day, when the density of 1240 is reached, add the 2 tablespoons of corn syrup to prevent crystallization. On the ninth day, increase the density by 30 gradations, to 1310. Allow the peels to sit for at least 2 to 3 hours longer.

Drain the peels, reserving the syrup for another use. Then cut them into thin lengths (see color photograph) and allow them to dry for several hours. This prevents the chocolate from seizing (becoming stiff and unworkable).

NOTES FROM ROSE

Always use the densimeter when the syrup is hot, as the density increases when cool.*

Pour the syrup into the syrup density test tube and insert the densimeter. The denser the syrup, the higher the densimeter will float and the higher the reading will be.

TO COAT THE ORANGE PEELS IN CHOCOLATE

Break the chocolate into pieces and place all but about 4 ounces in the top of a double boiler set over very hot water (but no hotter than 160°F.). The water must not simmer or touch the bottom of the double boiler insert.

Stir until the chocolate begins to melt. Return the pan to low heat if the water cools, but be careful that it does not get too hot. The water must not start to simmer. (The chocolate may be melted in a microwave oven if stirred every 15 seconds.) Remove the double boiler insert from the base and add the reserved unmelted chocolate. Stir continuously until the temperature of the chocolate reaches 88° to 91°F. (84° to 87°F. if milk chocolate). (If you are not using a thermometer, dab a small amount on your upper lip. It

*To maintain this temperature, place the pan of chocolate on a heating pad set on "low." (Plastic wrap helps to keep it free of chocolate!)

A PASSION FOR CHOCOLATE

should feel cool.) Remove any unmelted chocolate when the mixture reaches the correct temperature.*

Add the peels, a few at a time, to the melted chocolate, and using a fork (preferably a dipping fork), lift them out one at a time, tapping the fork against the side of the pan to drain off any excess chocolate. Place the chocolate-covered peels on the prepared baking sheets. Allow them to cool until the chocolate dulls and they can be lifted from the sheets without sticking. Store airtight.

Several months, unrefrigerated, in an airtight container. (The undipped peels will keep for months stored in the same way. A fine layer of sugar crystals will form on the outside of the peels, which adds interest to the texture.) **KEEPS**

The syrup is delicious diluted with Grand Marnier and sprinkled on cake, adding extra moisture. **NOTES FROM ROSE**

The candied peels, chopped, are wonderful to use in Florentins (page 204), Tuiles (page 207), and Truffettes (page 268).

CHOCOLATE NOUGAT

MAKES 2¼ POUNDS/1 KILOGRAM
(100 PIECES)
*DO NOT PREPARE THIS
ON A HUMID DAY*

This nougat is so delicately fragrant with pistachio nuts and honey that many prefer it undipped. But the crisp, dark bittersweet chocolate coating does provide a beautiful contrast to the white sticky nougat within.

In Lyon, the Bernachons are still making nougat the artisanal way, which involves stirring a very stiff mass until one's arm feels like it's about to drop off. This easy method, adapted to a mixer, offers the same results with considerably less wear and tear!

INGREDIENTS MEASURE		WEIGHT	
	VOLUME	POUNDS/OUNCES	GRAMS
sugar	1½ *cups*	10.5 *ounces*	300 *grams*
honey	1¼ *liquid cups*	15 *ounces*	430 *grams*
⅔ *vanilla bean, split**			
2 *large egg whites*	½ *liquid cup*	2 *ounces*	60 *grams*
cream of tartar	¼ *teaspoon*		
slivered almonds	4 *cups*	1 *pound 1 ounce*	500 *grams*
pistachio nuts, chopped	1 *cup*	5 *ounces*	140 *grams*
powdered sugar	½ *cup*	2 *ounces*	58 *grams*
bittersweet or milk chocolate†		1 *pound*	454 *grams*

*Or 1 teaspoon vanilla extract or ⅓ a Tahitian vanilla bean.
†Couverture, available in specialty stores (page 382), has more cocoa butter and creates a thinner, glossier coating of chocolate.

Have ready near the stove a 2-cup heatproof glass measure.

In a medium heavy saucepan (preferably with a nonstick lining), stir together the sugar, honey, and vanilla bean. Heat, stirring constantly, until the sugar dissolves and the syrup is bubbling. Stop stirring and reduce the heat to the lowest setting. (If you are using an electric range, remove it from the heat.)

In a mixing bowl, beat the egg whites until foamy. Add the cream of tartar, and beat until stiff peaks form when the beater is raised slowly.

Increase the heat under the syrup and boil it until a thermometer registers 246° to 248°F. (firm ball stage—syrup dropped into ice water may be formed into a firm ball that does not flatten upon removal from the water). Immediately pour the syrup into the glass measure (to stop the cooking).

If you are using a hand-held electric mixer, beat the syrup into the whites in a steady stream. To keep the syrup from spinning onto the sides of the bowl, avoid pouring the syrup onto them.

CHOCOLATE TRUFFLES AND CANDIES

If you are using a stand mixer, pour a small amount of syrup over the whites with the mixer in the "off" position. Immediately beat at high speed for 5 seconds. Then stop the mixer and add a larger amount of syrup. Beat at high speed for 5 seconds. Continue with the remaining syrup. With the last addition use a rubber scraper to remove the syrup clinging to the measure. Remove the vanilla bean.

Beat at medium speed until cool (about 2 minutes). The mixture will be very stiff and glossy. Add the almonds and pistachio nuts, and briefly beat them into the mixture. (If you are using vanilla extract instead of the vanilla bean, add it now.)

Dust a marble, Formica, or other smooth surface with powdered sugar. Scrape the mixture onto the surface, flatten it with your hands, and dust the top with powdered sugar. Immediately, before the nougat begins to harden, use a heavy rolling pin to roll the nougat into a rectangle about 3/8-inch thick. Allow it to cool and harden for several hours. When it is very firm, cut the nougat into little rectangles about 1½ by 3/4-inch in size. (If necessary, refrigerate the nougat until it is firm enough to cut well.)

TO COAT THE NOUGAT WITH CHOCOLATE

Line baking sheets with smooth aluminum foil or wax paper. Break the chocolate into pieces and place all but about 4 ounces in the top of a double boiler set over very hot water (but no hotter than 160°F.). The water must not simmer or touch the bottom of the double boiler insert.

Stir until the chocolate is fully melted. Return the pan to low heat if the water cools, but be careful that it does not get too hot. The water must not start to simmer. (The chocolate may be melted in a microwave oven if stirred every 15 seconds.)

Remove the double boiler insert from the base and add the reserved unmelted chocolate. Stir continuously until the temperature of the chocolate reaches 88° to 91°F. (84° to 87°F. if milk chocolate). (If you are not using a thermometer, dab a small amount on your upper lip. It should feel cool.) Remove any unmelted

A PASSION FOR CHOCOLATE

chocolate when the mixture reaches the correct temperature.*

If the nougat is a little soft or sticky, it helps to dip each piece in powdered sugar before dipping it in the chocolate.

Dip each nougat into the melted chocolate so that the chocolate entirely surrounds it. Using a fork (preferably a dipping fork), lift it out, tapping the fork against the side of the pan to drain off any excess chocolate. Place the chocolate-covered nougat on the prepared baking sheets. Allow them to cool until the chocolate dulls and they can be lifted from the sheets without sticking. Store airtight.

KEEPS

Several weeks, unrefrigerated, in an airtight container.

NOTES FROM ROSE

Use ordinary supermarket honey, not specialty honey, or the honey flavor is too overwhelming.

If you are not planning to dip the nougat, the syrup can be brought to 250°F. It will be thicker and very sticky but will result in firmer nougat. Be sure to use an accurate thermometer (page 382) or the ice-water test; 250°F. is the beginning of the "hard ball" stage: syrup dropped into ice water may be formed into a hard ball that holds its shape upon removal but is still plastic.

If you have inadvertently brought the temperature of the syrup up too high, add a little hot water to bring it down and the syrup to the proper consistency. The honey will prevent the usual crystallization problem that occurs when stirring a sugar syrup.

The nougat can be lightly chilled before dipping. If it's too cold, the chocolate coating will be thick and less shiny.

---

*To maintain this temperature, place the pan of chocolate on a heating pad set on "low." (Plastic wrap helps to keep it free of chocolate!)

CHOCOLATE TRUFFLES AND CANDIES

LES NOISETTES
TROIS-FRÈRES

CHOCOLATE-COVERED
HAZELNUTS

MAKES ABOUT 100 CANDIES

This simple, charming confection is named "Three Brothers Hazelnuts" because three nuts are encased and held together by gleaming
dark chocolate. Toasted hazelnuts and bittersweet chocolate
are a universally applauded marriage.

INGREDIENTS MEASURE		WEIGHT	
	VOLUME	POUNDS/OUNCES	GRAMS
hazelnuts	3¼ *cups*	1 *pound*	454 *grams*
baking soda	½ *cup*	4 *ounces*	60 *grams*
bittersweet or milk chocolate		1 *pound*	454 *grams*

Baking sheets lined with smooth aluminum foil or wax paper.

In a large saucepan, place 6 cups of water and bring it to a boil. Add the nuts and the baking soda, and boil for 3 minutes. Test a nut by running it under cold water. If the skin is not easy to remove with slight pressure from the fingers, return the nuts to the heat for a minute or so more. Drain and peel the nuts. **BLANCH THE HAZELNUTS**

Toast the hazelnuts in a 350°F. oven for 10 to 15 minutes or until golden brown. Cool completely.

Break the chocolate into pieces and place all but about 4 ounces in the top of a double boiler set over very hot water (but no hotter than 160°F.). The water must not simmer or touch the bottom of the double boiler insert. **TO COAT THE HAZELNUTS WITH CHOCOLATE**

Stir until the chocolate is fully melted. Return the pan to low heat if the water cools, but be careful that it does not get too hot. The water must not start to simmer. (The chocolate may be melted in a microwave oven if stirred every 15 seconds.) Remove the double boiler insert from the base and add the reserved unmelted chocolate. Stir continuously until the temperature of the chocolate reaches 88° to 91°F. (84° to 87°F. if milk chocolate). (If you are not using a thermometer, dab a small amount on your upper lip. It should feel cool.) Remove any unmelted chocolate when the mixture reaches the correct temperature.*

Stir the hazelnuts into the melted chocolate a handful at a time, and using a spoon, lift out three

*To maintain this temperature, place the pan of chocolate on a heating pad set on "low." (Plastic wrap helps to keep it free of chocolate!)

257

CHOCOLATE TRUFFLES AND CANDIES

nuts at a time, together with some of the chocolate. Spoon them onto the prepared baking sheets. Allow the chocolate-and-nut mounds to cool until the chocolate dulls and they can be lifted from the sheets without sticking. The hardened chocolate will encapture each set of three nuts. Store airtight.

KEEPS Several weeks, unrefrigerated, in an airtight container.

NOTE FROM ROSE The baking soda treatment for hazelnuts not only makes it a simple matter to peel the nuts, it also gives them a rich golden color when toasted.

LES PALETS MOKA

CHOCOLATE CREAM COINS
FLAVORED WITH COFFEE AND FROSTED
WITH MILK CHOCOLATE

MAKES ABOUT 60 CANDIES

A paper-thin coating of milk chocolate gives these delightful little coins of tangy mocha ganache a *café-au-lait* flavor.

INGREDIENTS MEASURE		WEIGHT	
	VOLUME	POUNDS/OUNCES	GRAMS
bittersweet chocolate	*4 (3-ounce) bars*	*12 ounces*	*340 grams*
Medaglia d'Oro instant espresso powder	*2 table-spoons*		
crème fraîche (page 348) or heavy cream	*1½ cups*	*12 ounces*	*340 grams*
unsalted butter, softened	*4 table-spoons*	*2 ounces*	*56 grams*
milk chocolate*		*1 pound 8 ounces*	*680 grams*

*Couverture, available in specialty stores (page 382), contains more cocoa butter and creates a thinner, glossier coating of chocolate. Any leftover chocolate can be spread out on foil, hardened, and remelted for future use.

Break the bittersweet chocolate into pieces and process, with the espresso powder, in a food processor until ground very fine.

Heat the crème fraîche to the boiling point, and with the motor running, pour it through the feed tube in a steady stream. Process a few seconds until smooth. Transfer the mixture to a bowl and allow to cool for several hours or overnight, until frosting consistency.

Cut the butter into small pieces and allow it to soften.

When you are ready to make the *palets*, stir the butter into the ganache until it is completely incorporated. Using a pastry bag (or a heavy-duty quart zip-seal bag with one corner cut off) fitted with a number 6 (½-inch) large round tube, pipe little 1-inch balls onto a baking sheet, or use a melon baller dipped in powdered sugar. With your finger or the back of a spoon, flatten the balls into discs. Refrigerate them only if necessary for the chocolate to be firm enough for dipping. (The discs should not be too cold when dipped, as they could cool the dipping chocolate, resulting in a coat that is too thick and dull.)

A PASSION FOR CHOCOLATE

Line baking sheets with smooth aluminum foil or wax paper.

Break the milk chocolate into pieces and place all but about 4 ounces in the top of a double boiler set over very hot water (but no hotter than 160°F.). The water must not simmer or touch the bottom of the double boiler insert.

Stir until the chocolate is fully melted. Return the pan to low heat if the water cools, but be careful that it does not get too hot. The water must not start to simmer. (The chocolate may be melted in a microwave oven if stirred every 15 seconds.) Remove the double boiler insert from the base and add the reserved unmelted chocolate. Stir continuously until the temperature of the chocolate reaches 84° to 87°F. (If you are not using a thermometer, dab a small amount on your upper lip. It should feel cool.) Remove any unmelted chocolate when the mixture reaches the correct temperature.*

Dip each *palet* into the melted chocolate so that the chocolate entirely surrounds it. Using a fork (preferably a dipping fork), lift it out, tapping the fork against the side of the pan to drain off any excess chocolate. Invert the *palets* onto the prepared baking sheets. Allow them to cool until the chocolate dulls and they can be lifted from the sheets without sticking.

Two weeks, at cool room temperature, in an airtight container.

KEEPS

---

*To maintain this temperature, place the pan of chocolate on a heating pad set on "low." (Plastic wrap helps to keep it free of chocolate!)

LES PALETS D'OR

GOLD-FLECKED CHOCOLATE COINS

MAKES ABOUT 100 CANDIES

These tangy, creamy, chocolatey little coins flecked with 22-carat gold are the jewels in Bernachon's confectionery crown. They are what I longed for most after my visit to Lyon. Of course the Bernachon chocolate and crème fraîche are major factors in the *palets d'ors'* distinctive taste, but any fine-quality chocolate and homemade crème fraîche (page 348) will give excellent results. These would make fabulous Christmas gifts, so I am offering the large-quantity recipe, but of course it easily can be divided in half or quarters.

INGREDIENTS MEASURE		WEIGHT	
	VOLUME	POUNDS/OUNCES	GRAMS
bittersweet chocolate		*1 pound 6 ounces*	*600 grams*
crème fraîche	*2 ¼ cups*	*17.5 ounces*	*500 grams*
unsalted butter	*7 table-spoons*	*3.5 ounces*	*100 grams*
bittersweet or milk chocolate*		*2 pounds*	*907 grams*
22k gold leaf (optional) (page 381)			

*Couverture, available in specialty stores (page 382), contains more cocoa butter and creates a thinner, glossier coating of chocolate. Any leftover chocolate can spread out on foil, hardened, and remelted for future use.

Baking sheets lined with heavy-duty plastic or smooth aluminum foil.*
Small hairbrush and comb for the gold leaf.†

Break the chocolate into pieces and process in a food processor until very fine.

Heat the cream to the boiling point, and with the motor running, pour it through the feed tube in a steady stream. Process a few seconds until smooth. Transfer the mixture to a bowl and allow to cool for several hours or overnight, until frosting consistency. In cool weather ganache can remain unrefrigerated for at least 3 days and as long as 2 weeks. At room temperature it remains spreadable.

Cut the butter into small pieces and allow it to soften.

When you are ready to make the *palets*, stir the butter into the ganache until it is completely incorporated. Using a pastry bag (or a heavy-duty quart zip-seal bag with one corner cut off) fitted with a number 6 (½-inch) large round tube, pipe little 1-inch balls onto a baking sheet, or use a melon baller dipped in powdered sugar. With your finger or the back of a spoon,

*Heavy-duty plastic sheeting, available in hardware stores, is an ideal surface to hold the gold flecks and give a bright shiny finish to the chocolate. Alternatively, smooth aluminum foil also gives a high shine.
†To scatter the gold, use a small hairbrush, (preferably natural bristle) reserved for this purpose. Lift up a sheet of gold leaf with the brush, and use a comb (also reserved for this purpose) to flick little bits of gold all over the sheet.

CHOCOLATE TRUFFLES AND CANDIES

flatten the balls into discs. Refrigerate them only if necessary for the chocolate to be firm enough for dipping. (The discs should not be too cold when dipped, as they could cool the dipping chocolate, resulting in a coat that is too thick and dull.)

TO COAT THE *PALETS* WITH CHOCOLATE Scatter the gold over two of the prepared baking sheets. (More can be added as needed.) Break the chocolate into pieces and place all but about 4 ounces in the top of a double boiler set over very hot water (but no hotter than 160°F.). The water must not simmer or touch the bottom of the double boiler insert.

Stir until the chocolate is fully melted. Return the pan to low heat if the water cools, but be careful that it does not get too hot. The water must not start to simmer. (The chocolate may be melted in a microwave oven if stirred every 15 seconds.)

Remove the double boiler insert from the base and add the reserved unmelted chocolate. Stir continuously until the temperature of the chocolate reaches 88° to 91°F. (84° to 87°F. if milk chocolate). (If you are not using a thermometer, dab a small amount on your upper lip. It should feel cool.) Remove any unmelted chocolate when the mixture reaches the correct temperature.*

Dip each *palet* into the melted chocolate so that the chocolate entirely surrounds it. Using a fork (preferably a dipping fork), lift it out, tapping the fork against the side of the pan to drain off any excess chocolate. Invert the *palets* onto the lined baking sheets without the gold. Allow them to cool until the chocolate dulls and they can be lifted from the sheets without sticking. Immediately place each *palet*, bottom side down, on the gold-flecked sheets. (If the *palets* sit too long, the chocolate hardens and does not attract the gold as well.) Store airtight.

KEEPS Two weeks, at cool room temperature, in an airtight container.

*To maintain this temperature, place the pan of chocolate on a heating pad set on "low." (Plastic wrap helps to keep it free of chocolate!)

LES TRUFFES
AU CHOCOLAT

CHOCOLATE TRUFFLES

MAKES ABOUT 60 TRUFFLES

Chocolate truffles are the foundation of any great European chocolate house. They are simple creations, really, composed of ganache, which is pure chocolate and heavy cream or crème fraîche, sometimes flavored with nuts, cinnamon, coffee, liqueur, or even tea. The basic technique for truffles is always the same: Make the ganache, pipe it into various shapes, dip them into melted chocolate, and sometimes roll them in cocoa, powdered sugar, or nuts. It is easy to create your own variations with your favorite flavors. Any of the ganaches on pages 334–44 will make wonderful truffles.

INGREDIENTS	MEASURE	WEIGHT	
	VOLUME	POUNDS/OUNCES	GRAMS
any recipe for ganache (pages 334–44)			
powdered sugar	*2 tablespoons*	*0.5 ounce*	*14 grams*
*bittersweet or milk chocolate**		*2 pounds*	*907 grams*
unsweetened cocoa	*4 cups (lightly spooned)*	*12.75 ounces*	*367 grams*

*Couverture, available in specialty stores (page 382), contains more cocoa butter and creates a thinner, glossier coating of chocolate. Any leftover chocolate can be spread out on foil, hardened, and remelted for future use.

Using a pastry bag (or a heavy-duty quart zip-seal bag with one corner cut off) fitted with a number 6 (½-inch) large round tube, pipe little 1-inch balls of the ganache onto a baking sheet. Alternatively, you can use a melon baller, dipped in powdered sugar, to scoop out the balls, or a star tube to pipe out 1½-inch oblongs.

Refrigerate for a few hours (or freeze briefly) to firm them for rolling and dipping.

Place some powdered sugar in the palms of your hands, and roll each ganache ball into as round an orb as possible. Or you may vary the shape by rolling the ganache into oblongs.

TO MELT THE CHOCOLATE Break the chocolate into pieces and place all but about 4 ounces in the top of a double boiler set over very hot water (but no hotter than 160°F.). The water must not simmer or touch the bottom of the double boiler insert.

Stir until the chocolate is fully melted. Return the pan to low heat if the water cools, but be careful that it does not get too hot. The water must not start to simmer. (The chocolate may be melted in a microwave oven if stirred every 15 seconds.)

Remove the double boiler insert from the base and add the reserved unmelted chocolate. Stir steadily until the temperature of the chocolate reaches 88° to

A PASSION FOR CHOCOLATE

91°F. (84° to 87°F. if milk chocolate). (If you are not using a thermometer, dab a small amount on your upper lip. It should feel cool.) Remove any unmelted chocolate when the mixture reaches the correct temperature.*

If you are planning to coat the dipped truffles with cocoa, place the cocoa in an 8-inch square baking pan and make several 1-inch troughs in it to hold the truffles.

TO DIP THE TRUFFLES

Using your fingers or a dipping loop, dip the truffles, one at a time, into the melted chocolate, tossing them to coat evenly. Lift out the truffle, tapping the loop on the side of the pan to remove any excess chocolate, or using your fingers to scissor off the excess. Drop the truffle into the cocoa trough, or onto a baking sheet lined with aluminum foil or wax paper if you aren't using the cocoa. Spoon enough cocoa over the top to cover the truffle.

When the chocolate coating on the truffles has set, refrigerate them for 5 minutes to give the final "snap" to the coating. (If they were buried in cocoa, first lift them out of the cocoa and place them in a cake pan.)

As you are dipping the truffles, if the chocolate gets too cool and thick, return it very briefly to the heat, stirring constantly.

NOTE FROM ROSE

Two weeks, at cool room temperature, in an airtight container. They can be frozen for up to 3 months and thawed overnight in the refrigerator to prevent condensation.

KEEPS

---

*To maintain this temperature, place the pan of chocolate on a heating pad set on "low." (Plastic wrap helps to keep it free of chocolate!)

Les Truffettes

Chocolate Truffles
Filled with Hazelnuts and Candied
Orange Peel

MAKES ABOUT 70 TRUFFLES

This marvelous truffle variation contains centers of browned, chopped hazelnuts, candied orange peel, and Grand Marnier. After they are dipped in dark bittersweet chocolate, the tartness is tempered with a coating of powdered sugar.

INGREDIENTS MEASURE		WEIGHT	
	VOLUME	POUNDS/OUNCES	GRAMS
candied orange peel (page 248)	1 tablespoon	1 ounce	28 grams
hazelnuts	¾ cup	4 ounces	116 grams
baking soda	3 tablespoons	1.5 ounces	43 grams
bittersweet chocolate	6 (3-ounce) bars	1 pound 2 ounces	510 grams
crème fraîche (page 348) or heavy cream	1 liquid cup	8 ounces	232 grams
Grand Marnier*	½ cup	4.25 ounces	120 grams
bittersweet or milk chocolate†		1 pound 8 ounces	680 grams
powdered sugar	4 cups	1 pound	454 grams

*If you prefer a less pronounced flavor of Grand Marnier, use 1 ¼ cups of cream and ¼ cup of Grand Marnier.
†Couverture, available in specialty stores (page 382), contains more cocoa butter and creates a thinner, glossier coating of chocolate. Any leftover chocolate can be spread out on foil, hardened, and remelted for future use.

Using a greased sharp knife or a food processor, finely chop the orange peel. Set aside.

In a medium saucepan, place 2 cups of water and bring it to a boil. Add the nuts and the baking soda, and boil them for 3 minutes. Test a nut by running it under cold water. If the skin is not easy to remove with slight pressure from the fingers, return to the heat for a minute or so more. **BLANCH THE HAZELNUTS**

Toast the hazelnuts in a 350°F. oven for 10 to 15 minutes, or until golden brown. Cool the nuts completely and chop them fine, but not powder-fine. (Use the medium grater on a food processor and then pulse with the metal blade.) Set aside.

Break the chocolate into pieces and process it in a food processor until ground very fine.

Heat the crème fraîche to a full boil, and with the motor running, pour it through the feed tube in a steady stream. Process a few seconds until smooth. Cool slightly, then add the Grand Marnier, hazelnuts, and orange peel. Pulse just to combine. Transfer the

CHOCOLATE TRUFFLES AND CANDIES

mixture to a bowl and allow to cool for several hours, until frosting consistency. In cool weather ganache can remain unrefrigerated for at least 3 days or as long as 2 weeks. At room temperature it remains spreadable.

Using a pastry bag (or a heavy-duty quart zip-seal bag with one corner cut off) fitted with a number 6 (½-inch) round tube, pipe little 1-inch balls onto a baking sheet. Alternatively, you may use a melon baller, dipped in powdered sugar, to scoop out the balls.

Place some powdered sugar in the palms of your hands, and roll each ganache ball into as round an orb as possible. Refrigerate them only if necessary for the chocolate to be firm enough for dipping. (The *truffettes* should not be too cold when dipped, as they could cool the dipping chocolate, resulting in a coat that is too thick and dull.)

Break the chocolate into pieces and place all but about 4 ounces in the top of a double boiler set over very hot water (but no hotter than 160°F.). The water must not simmer or touch the bottom of the double boiler insert.

Stir until the chocolate is fully melted. Return the pan to low heat if the water cools, but be careful that it does not get too hot. The water must not start to simmer. (The chocolate may be melted in a microwave oven if stirred every 15 seconds.)

Remove the double boiler insert from the base and add the reserved unmelted chocolate. Stir continuously until the temperature of the chocolate reaches 88° to 91°F. (84° to 87°F. if milk chocolate). (If you are not using a thermometer, dab a small amount on your upper lip. It should feel cool.) Remove any unmelted chocolate when the mixture reaches the correct temperature.*

TO DIP THE TRUFFETTES Place the powdered sugar in an 8-inch square baking pan and make several 1-inch troughs in it to hold the truffles.

---

*To maintain this temperature, place the pan of chocolate on a heating pad set on "low." (Plastic wrap helps to keep it free of chocolate!)

Using your fingers or a dipping loop, dip the truffles, one at a time, into the melted chocolate, tossing them to coat evenly. Lift out the truffle, tapping the loop on the side of the pan to remove any excess chocolate, or using your fingers to scissor off the excess. Drop the truffle into the sugar trough, and spoon enough over the top to cover it.

When the chocolate coating on the truffles has set, lift them out of the powdered sugar, place them in a cake pan, and refrigerate them for 5 minutes to give the final "snap" to the chocolate coating.

As you are dipping the truffles, if the chocolate gets too cool and thick, return it very briefly to the heat, stirring constantly.

NOTE FROM ROSE

Two weeks, at cool room temperature, in an airtight container. They can be frozen for up to 3 months and thawed overnight in the refrigerator to prevent condensation.

KEEPS

FRUITS D'AUTOMNE

CHOCOLATE CANDIES WITH CHESTNUT BUTTERCREAM CENTERS AND A COATING OF MARZIPAN

MAKES 12 CANDIES

The ultimate show-off confection, these "chestnuts" consist of several layers: dark chocolate discs topped with mounds of chestnut buttercream, which are then dipped in more dark chocolate and covered with pistachio-flavored marzipan. The whole assembly is then dipped into dark chocolate and a dipping fork is used to form the characteristic peaks. A little wedge is cut in each to reveal the chocolate-covered chestnut center, which completes the image of a chestnut in a shell.

These celestial creations are recommended for the more experienced candy maker. Actually, they are more time-consuming than difficult. But the taste and appearance make them well worth the effort.

CHESTNUT BUTTERCREAM*

INGREDIENTS	MEASURE	WEIGHT	
	VOLUME	OUNCES	GRAMS
canned chestnuts, packed in water		15.5 ounces	439 grams
powdered sugar	⅓ cup (lightly spooned)	1.25 ounces	38 grams
unsalted butter, softened	½ cup	4 ounces	113 grams
dark rum	1 tablespoon		

*From *The Cake Bible*, William Morrow and Company, 1988.

Drain the chestnuts and process them in a food processor until smooth. Then press the chestnuts through a fine strainer into a 2-cup glass measure.

Place ½ cup (4.75 ounces/132 grams) of the purée in a medium bowl. Add the powdered sugar, butter, and rum and stir until smooth. (This recipe makes 1½ cups. The leftover buttercream can be frozen for several months.)

INGREDIENTS	MEASURE	WEIGHT	
	VOLUME	POUNDS/OUNCES	GRAMS
bittersweet or milk chocolate		1 pound	454 grams
pistachio extract*	½ teaspoon		
marzipan	1 cup	10.5 ounces	298 grams
bittersweet or milk chocolate†		1 pound	454 grams

*La Cuisine (page 382), or use a few drops of green food coloring.
†Couverture, available in specialty stores (page 382), contains more cocoa butter and creates a thinner, glossier coating of chocolate. Any leftover chocolate can be spread out on foil, hardened, and remelted for future use.

A baking sheet lined with smooth aluminum foil or wax paper.

Break the chocolate into pieces and place them in the top of a double boiler set over very hot water (but no hotter than 160°F.). The water must not simmer or touch the bottom of the double boiler insert.

TO MAKE THE CHOCOLATE DISCS

Stir until the chocolate is fully melted. Return the pan to low heat if the water cools, but be careful that it does not get too hot. The water must not start to simmer. (The chocolate may be melted in a microwave oven if stirred every 15 seconds. Remove it from the oven before the chocolate has fully melted and stir constantly until the residual heat melts the chocolate). Stir continuously until the temperature of the chocolate reaches 88° to 91°F. (84° to 87°F. if milk chocolate). (If you are not using a thermometer, dab a small amount on your upper lip. It should feel cool.)

Spoon little pools of the chocolate onto the prepared baking sheet, and flatten them into discs about 1¼ inches in diameter. Refrigerate for 5 minutes.

THE CHESTNUT CENTERS Use a pastry bag (or a heavy-duty quart zip-seal bag with one corner cut off) fitted with a number 6 (½-inch) plain round tube, or a spoon, to form 1-inch balls of chestnut buttercream on top of the chocolate discs. Refrigerate until the chestnut buttercream is very firm.

THE MARZIPAN DISCS Knead the pistachio extract into the marzipan and roll it out between sheets of plastic wrap to about ¼-inch thickness. Stamp out 2¾-inch-diameter discs (a small plastic cup or biscuit cutter works well). Knead the marzipan trimmings together, reroll, and cut out enough discs to make a total of twelve. Keep the marzipan discs covered with plastic wrap so that they stay moist and supple.

TO MELT THE CHOCOLATE FOR DIPPING Break the chocolate into pieces and place all but about 4 ounces in the top of a double boiler set over very hot water (but no hotter than 160°F.). The water must not simmer or touch the bottom of the double boiler insert.

Stir until the chocolate begins to melt. Return the pan to low heat if the water cools, but be careful that it does not get too hot. The water must not start to simmer. (The chocolate may be melted in a microwave oven if stirred every 15 seconds.) Remove the double boiler insert from the base and add the reserved unmelted chocolate. Stir continuously until the temperature of the chocolate reaches 88° to 91°F. (84° to 87°F. if milk chocolate). (If you are not using a thermometer, dab a small amount on your upper lip. It should feel cool.) Remove any unmelted chocolate when the mixture reaches the correct temperature.*

TO DIP THE CHESTNUT CENTERS

Use your fingers to drop the chestnut centers into the melted chocolate, buttercream side down. Allow the chocolate to completely cover the chocolate disc as well. Remove the centers with your fingers, or two forks, scissoring off any excess chocolate, and set them on their bases on the lined baking sheet. Refrigerate for at least 5 minutes, or until the chocolate has set firmly. Keep the melted chocolate warm, stirring occasionally to equalize the temperature.

TO COVER THE CENTERS WITH MARZIPAN

Drape the marzipan discs over the chocolate-covered chestnut buttercream centers, and with your fingers, curve the marzipan against the sides of the mounds. The marzipan should reach just about to the base.

TO DIP THE MARZIPAN-COVERED MOUNDS

Using your fingers, drop the marzipan-covered centers into the melted chocolate, chestnut buttercream side down, and twirl them to cover them completely. Gently remove them with your fingers, or two forks, scissoring off any excess chocolate, and set them on fresh sheets of foil or wax paper. As the chocolate begins to thicken and set, use a dipping fork or skewer to create little peaks by tapping the fork on the surface of the chocolate and lifting sharply away. (Monsieur Raymond, the head chocolatier at Bernachon, laughingly calls this process *"pic-pic"*!)

With a very sharp knife, cut a small V-shaped incision through the outer chocolate shell and marzipan.

KEEPS

About three days at cool room temperature, in an airtight container.

---

*To maintain this temperature, place the pan of chocolate on a heating pad set on "low." (Plastic wrap helps to keep it free of chocolate!)

275

CHOCOLATE TRUFFLES AND CANDIES

CHOCOLATE DRINKS

Le Chocolat Chaud

Hot Chocolate

Hot Cinnamon Chocolate
Hot Tea Chocolate

SERVES 6 TO 8

Hot chocolate is a favorite wintertime drink in Lyon. This perfect
balance of milk to cream is the Bernachons' classic hot
chocolate recipe, with several intriguing variations.

INGREDIENTS	MEASURE	WEIGHT	
	VOLUME	OUNCES	GRAMS
milk	3 *liquid cups*	1 *pound 9.5 ounces*	726 *grams*
heavy cream	1 *liquid cup*	8 *ounces*	232 *grams*
bittersweet chocolate, broken into pieces	3 *(3-ounce) bars*	9 *ounces*	255 *grams*

In a medium saucepan, bring the milk and cream to the boiling point. Remove the pan from the heat and add the chocolate. Whisk until the chocolate is fully melted and the mixture is uniform. Ladle into cups and serve at once.

VARIATION:
Hot Cinnamon
Chocolate

For a bit of cinnamon and spice, after adding the chocolate to the milk and cream, sprinkle on 1 ¼ teaspoons of cinnamon and a pinch of black pepper.

VARIATION:
Hot Tea
Chocolate

When I first read about the Bernachons' tea chocolate, I could not imagine what it would be like. But when I tasted the chocolate bar I found it to be a strangely wonderful combination. Not everyone will love it, but for those who do, Bernachon offers this unusual hot chocolate drink: After adding the chocolate to the milk and cream, add 1 tablespoon of strongly brewed black tea.

LE LAIT
DE POULE AU
CHOCOLAT

CHOCOLATE EGGNOG

SERVES 8 TO 10

The Bernachons recommend this invigorating chocolate drink to fortify students during final exams. It could easily be considered a reward as well! This is the ideal solution for those who prefer their ice cream melted.

| INGREDIENTS | MEASURE | WEIGHT | |
	VOLUME	OUNCES	GRAMS
milk	3 cups	1 pound 9.5 ounces	726 grams
heavy cream	1 cup	8 ounces	232 grams
bittersweet chocolate, broken into pieces	3 (3-ounce) bars	9 ounces	255 grams
9 large egg yolks	⅔ liquid cup	5.75 ounces	167 grams

In a medium saucepan, bring the milk and cream to the boiling point. Remove it from the heat and add the chocolate. Whisk until the chocolate is fully melted and the mixture is uniform.

Place the yolks in a large bowl. Whisk in the hot chocolate mixture, very gradually at first. Continue whisking until the mixture is very frothy. Ladle into cups and serve at once.

NOTE FROM ROSE If final exams are over, by all means add a jigger or two of Cognac or rum.

LE CHOCOLAT VIENNOIS

VIENNESE HOT CHOCOLATE

SERVES 6 TO 8

The combination of piping-hot bittersweet chocolate and cold, billowy whipped cream is a cherished one. The heavy cream is decreased in the beverage to balance the luxurious topping.

SWEETENED WHIPPED CREAM

INGREDIENTS	MEASURE	WEIGHT	
	VOLUME	OUNCES	GRAMS
heavy cream	1½ liquid cups	12 ounces	340 grams
superfine sugar	2 tablespoons	1 ounce	25 grams
vanilla	1 teaspoon		4 grams

In a large mixing bowl, combine the cream, sugar, and vanilla and refrigerate for at least 15 minutes. (Chill the beater alongside the bowl.)

Beat until stiff peaks form when the beater is raised. Refrigerate.

INGREDIENTS	MEASURE	WEIGHT	
	VOLUME	OUNCES	GRAMS
milk	3 liquid cups	1 pound 9.5 ounces	726 grams
heavy cream	½ cup	4 ounces	116 grams
bittersweet chocolate	3 (3-ounce) bars	9 ounces	255 grams
superfine sugar (optional)			

In a medium saucepan, bring the milk and cream to the boiling point. Remove the pan from the heat and add the chocolate. Whisk until the chocolate is fully melted and the mixture is uniform. Whisk in superfine sugar to taste.

Ladle the hot chocolate into mugs, and spoon or pipe a generous dome of whipped cream on top.

THE BASICS
OF THE
BERNACHON
KITCHEN

LA GÉNOISE

MAKES ONE 9½-INCH CAKE

Golden génoise is a classic French sponge cake used in many of Bernachon's cakes and confections. It is usually moistened with a syrup made of equal parts sugar and water and flavored with a liqueur.

THE BASICS OF THE BERNACHON KITCHEN

INGREDIENTS	MEASURE	WEIGHT	
ROOM TEMPERATURE	VOLUME	OUNCES	GRAMS
unsalted butter	¼ *cup*	2 ounces	60 grams
vanilla	1½ *teaspoons*		6 grams
7 large eggs	1½ *liquid cups*	14 ounces	400 grams *(weighed in the shells)*
superfine sugar	¾ *cup + 2 tablespoons*	6 ounces	170 grams
honey (optional)	1 *tablespoon*	.75 ounce	21 grams
sifted cake flour	2 *cups*	7 ounces	200 grams

One 10 by 3-inch round baking pan or springform pan, greased, bottom lined with parchment or wax paper, and then greased again and floured.

Preheat the oven to 400°F.

In a small saucepan, melt the butter and add the vanilla. Set it aside to keep it warm.

In a large mixing bowl set over a pan of simmering water, heat the eggs, sugar, and optional honey for extra moistness until just lukewarm, stirring constantly to prevent curdling. (The eggs may also be heated by placing them *still in their shells* in a large mixing bowl in an oven with a pilot light for 3 hours or up to overnight.) Using the whisk attachment, beat the mixture on high speed for 5 minutes or until tripled in volume. (A hand beater may be used, but it will be necessary to beat for at least 10 minutes.)

Remove 1 cup of the egg mixture and thoroughly whisk it into the warm melted butter.

Sift half the flour over the remaining egg mixture, and fold it in *gently* but rapidly with a large balloon whisk, slotted skimmer, or rubber spatula until almost all the flour has disappeared. Repeat with the remaining flour, folding just until the flour has disappeared completely. Fold in the butter mixture until just incorporated.

Pour immediately into the prepared pan, and bake 20 to 30 minutes or until the cake is golden brown and has started to shrink slightly from the sides of the pan. (No need for a cake tester. Once the sides shrink, the cake is done.) Avoid opening the oven door before the minimum time or the cake could fall. Toward the end of the baking time, open the door slightly, and if at a quick glance the cake does not appear done, close the door at once and check again in 5 minutes.

Loosen the sides of the cake with a small metal spatula, and unmold at once onto a lightly greased rack. Reinvert it to cool.

Génoise cuts more easily when made ahead and **NOTE** chilled.

GÉNOISE FOR
A CAKE ROLL OR
SQUARE CAKE

MAKES ONE 16 BY 11-INCH
SHEET CAKE OR ONE
7½-INCH SQUARE

This amount of génoise batter is perfect for making either a cake
roll, such as for the Christmas log (Bûche de Noël) or a square
cake such as for the Sévillan (page 115).

INGREDIENTS	MEASURE	WEIGHT	
ROOM TEMPERATURE	VOLUME	OUNCES	GRAMS
unsalted butter	**3 tablespoons**	**1.5 ounces**	**40 grams**
vanilla	**1 teaspoon**		**4 grams**
4 extra-large eggs	**7 fluid ounces**	**9 ounces**	**260 grams**
		(weighed in the shells)	
superfine sugar	**½ cup + 1 tablespoon**	**4 ounces**	**114 grams**
honey (optional)	**2 teaspoons**	**0.5 ounce**	**14 grams**
sifted cake flour	**1⅓ cups**	**4.5 ounces**	**130 grams**

One 17 by 12-inch jelly-roll pan, greased, bottom lined with parchment or foil (extending slightly over the long sides), and then greased again and floured. Or one 8 by 8 by 2-inch baking pan, greased, bottom lined with parchment or wax paper, then greased again and floured.

Preheat the oven to 400°F.

In a small saucepan, melt the butter and add the vanilla. Set aside to keep warm.

In a large mixing bowl set over a pan of simmering water, heat the eggs, sugar, and optional honey for extra moisture until just lukewarm, stirring constantly to prevent curdling. (The eggs may also be heated by placing them *still in their shells* in a large mixing bowl in an oven with a pilot light for 3 hours or up to overnight.) Using the whisk attachment, beat the mixture on high speed for 5 minutes or until tripled in volume. (A hand beater may be used, but it will be necessary to beat for at least 10 minutes.)

Remove 1 cup of the egg mixture and thoroughly whisk it into the warm melted butter.

Sift half the flour over the remaining egg mixture, and fold it in *gently* but rapidly with a large balloon whisk, slotted skimmer, or rubber spatula until almost all the flour has disappeared. Repeat with the remaining flour, folding just until the flour has disappeared completely. Fold in the butter mixture until just incorporated. Pour the batter immediately into the

THE BASICS OF THE BERNACHON KITCHEN

prepared pan, spreading it evenly with a spatula, and bake 10 minutes or until the cake is golden brown (20 to 30 minutes if baked in an 8-inch square pan or until the cake has started to shrink from the sides of the pan).

Loosen the sides of the cake with a small metal spatula, and unmold at once onto a clean towel that has been lightly sprinkled with powdered sugar. Starting from one long edge, roll cake, towel and all, and allow to cool completely.

Unmold the cake baked in the square pan onto a lightly greased rack. Reinvert it to cool.

A PASSION FOR CHOCOLATE

LA GÉNOISE
AU CHOCOLAT

This chocolate version of the classic génoise is fine-textured and
dense enough to facilitate cutting into the thin layers used
for many of the Bernachon cakes.

INGREDIENTS	MEASURE	WEIGHT	
	VOLUME	OUNCES	GRAMS
unsalted butter	¼ *cup*	2 *ounces*	60 *grams*
vanilla	1½ *teaspoons*		6 *grams*
7 large eggs	1½ *liquid cups*	14 *ounces*	400 *grams* *(weighed in the shells)*
superfine sugar	¾ *cup + 2 tablespoons*	6 *ounces*	170 *grams*
honey (optional)	1 *tablespoon*	.75 *ounce*	21 *grams*
unsweetened cocoa	⅓ *cup (lightly spooned)*	1 *ounce*	30 *grams*
sifted cake flour	1¾ *cups*	6.25 *ounces*	180 *grams*

One 10 by 3-inch round springform pan, greased, bottom lined with parchment or wax paper, then greased again and floured.

Preheat the oven to 400°F.

In a small saucepan, melt the butter and add the vanilla. Set aside to keep warm.

In a large mixing bowl set over a pan of simmering water, heat the eggs, sugar, and optional honey for extra moistness until just lukewarm, stirring constantly to prevent curdling. (The eggs may also be heated by placing them *still in their shells* in a large mixing bowl in an oven with a pilot light for 3 hours or up to overnight.) Using the whisk attachment, beat the mixture on high speed for 5 minutes or until tripled in volume. (A hand beater may be used, but it will be necessary to beat for at least 10 minutes.)

While the eggs are beating, sift together the cocoa and flour.

Remove 1 cup of the egg mixture and thoroughly whisk it into the warm melted butter.

Sift half the flour mixture over the remaining egg mixture, and fold it in *gently* but rapidly with a large balloon whisk, slotted skimmer, or rubber spatula until almost all the flour has disappeared. Repeat with the remaining flour, folding just until the flour has

A PASSION FOR CHOCOLATE

disappeared completely. Fold in the butter mixture until just incorporated.

Pour immediately into the prepared pan, and bake 25 to 35 minutes or until the cake has started to shrink slightly from the sides of the pan. (No need for a cake tester. Once the sides shrink, the cake is done.) Avoid opening the oven door before the minimum time or the cake could fall. Toward the end of the baking time, open the door slightly, and if at a quick glance the cake does not appear done, close the door at once and check again in 5 minutes.

Loosen the sides of the cake with a small metal spatula, and unmold at once onto a lightly greased rack. Reinvert it to cool.

Génoise cuts more easily when made ahead and chilled. **NOTE**

LA GÉNOISE AU CHOCOLAT (LOAF)

LOAF-SHAPED GÉNOISE

MAKES ONE 8½ × 4½-INCH LOAF

This is the same recipe as the preceding one but proportioned for a loaf shape.

INGREDIENTS	MEASURE	WEIGHT	
	VOLUME	OUNCES	GRAMS
unsalted butter	*2 tablespoons*	1 ounce	*30 grams*
vanilla	*1 teaspoon*		*4 grams*
4 large eggs	*¾ liquid cup*	8 ounces	*227 grams* *(weighed in the shells)*
superfine sugar	*½ cup*	3.5 ounces	*100 grams*
honey (optional)	*2 teaspoons*	0.5 ounce	*14 grams*
sifted cake flour	*1 cup*	3.5 ounces	*100 grams*
unsweetened cocoa	*3 tablespoons*	0.5 ounce	*18 grams*

One 9 by 5 by 3-inch (8-cup) loaf pan, greased, bottom lined with parchment or wax paper, then greased again and floured.

Preheat the oven to 400°F.

In a small saucepan, melt the butter and add the vanilla. Set aside to keep warm.

In a large mixing bowl set over a pan of simmering water, heat the eggs, sugar, and optional honey for extra moistness until just lukewarm, stirring constantly to prevent curdling. (The eggs may also be heated by placing them *still in their shells* in a large mixing bowl in an oven with a pilot light for 3 hours or up to overnight.) Using the whisk attachment, beat the mixture on high speed for 5 minutes or until tripled in volume. (A hand beater may be used, but it will be necessary to beat for at least 10 minutes.)

While the eggs are beating, sift together the flour and cocoa.

Remove 1 cup of the egg mixture and thoroughly whisk it into the warm melted butter. Sift half the flour mixture over the remaining egg mixture, and fold it in *gently* but rapidly with a large balloon whisk, slotted skimmer, or rubber spatula until almost all the flour has disappeared. Repeat with the remaining flour, folding just until the flour has disappeared completely. Fold in the butter mixture until just incorporated.

Pour immediately into the prepared pan, and bake 25 to 35 minutes or until the cake has started to shrink slightly from the sides of the pan. (No need for a cake tester. Once the sides shrink the cake is done.) Avoid opening the oven door before the minimum time or the cake could fall. Toward the end of the baking time, open the door slightly, and if at a quick glance the cake does not appear done, close the door at once and check again in 5 minutes.

Loosen the sides of the cake with a small metal spatula, and unmold at once onto a lightly greased rack. Reinvert it to cool.

NOTE   Génoise cuts more easily when made ahead and chilled.

LA GÉNOISE
AU CHOCOLAT
(SQUARE)

CHOCOLATE GÉNOISE
IN THE SHAPE OF A SQUARE

MAKES ONE 7½-INCH SQUARE

Mixing the butter with a small amount of the batter makes it easier to incorporate with less loss of volume.

| INGREDIENTS | MEASURE | WEIGHT | |
	VOLUME	OUNCES	GRAMS
unsalted butter	**3 tablespoons**	**1.5 ounces**	**43 grams**
vanilla	**1 ½ teaspoons**		**6 grams**
6 large eggs	**9.5 fluid ounces**	**12 ounces**	**340 grams** *(weighed in the shells)*
superfine sugar	**¾ cup**	**5.25 ounces**	**150 grams**
honey (optional)	**1 tablespoon**	**.75 ounce**	**21 grams**
sifted cake flour	**1 ½ cups**	**5.25 ounces**	**150 grams**
unsweetened cocoa	**¼ cup (lightly spooned)**	**0.75 ounce**	**21 grams**

One 8 by 8 by 2-inch baking pan, greased, bottom lined with parchment or wax paper, then greased again and floured.

Preheat the oven to 400°F.

In a small saucepan, melt the butter and add the vanilla. Set aside to keep warm.

In a large mixing bowl set over a pan of simmering water, heat the eggs, sugar, and optional honey for extra moistness until just lukewarm, stirring constantly to prevent curdling. (The eggs may also be heated by placing them *still in their shells* in a large mixing bowl in an oven with a pilot light for 3 hours or up to overnight.) Using the whisk attachment, beat the mixture on high speed for 5 minutes or until tripled in volume. (A hand beater may be used, but it will be necessary to beat for at least 10 minutes.)

While the eggs are beating, sift together the flour and cocoa.

Remove 1 cup of the egg mixture and thoroughly whisk it into the warm melted butter.

Sift half the flour mixture over the remaining egg mixture, and fold it in *gently* but rapidly with a large balloon whisk, slotted skimmer, or rubber spatula until almost all the flour has disappeared. Repeat with the remaining flour, folding just until the flour has disappeared completely. Fold in the butter mixture until just incorporated.

Pour immediately into the prepared pan, and bake 25 to 35 minutes or until the cake has started to shrink slightly from the sides of the pan. (No need for a cake tester. Once the sides shrink the cake is done.) Avoid opening the oven door before the minimum time or the cake could fall. Toward the end of the baking time, open the door slightly, and if at a quick glance the cake does not appear done, close the door at once and check again in 5 minutes.

Loosen the sides of the cake with a small metal spatula, and unmold at once onto a lightly greased rack. Reinvert it to cool.

Génoise cuts more easily when made ahead and **NOTE** chilled.

LA PÂTE
À BISCUIT

BISCUIT

MAKES ABOUT 60 PUFFS

This biscuit (a butterless génoise) recipe comes from my book *The Cake Bible*, as the batter most reliably holds its shape for piping in a home kitchen. One tablespoon of honey, however, replaces the 1 tablespoon of water, for additional moistness. This batter can be used to pipe the classic ladyfingers, but the Bernachons more often use it to pipe little puffs.

A PASSION FOR CHOCOLATE

| INGREDIENTS | MEASURE | | WEIGHT |
	VOLUME	OUNCES	GRAMS
6 large eggs, separated			
yolks	3.5 fluid ounces	4 ounces	112 grams
whites	¾ liquid cup	6.25 ounces	180 grams
superfine sugar	¾ cup	5.25 ounces	150 grams
vanilla	2½ teaspoons		10 grams
honey	1 tablespoon	0.75 ounce	21 grams
sifted cake flour	1½ cups	5.25 ounces	150 grams
cream of tartar	¾ teaspoon		

Two large baking sheets, buttered and floured or lined with parchment or foil.

Preheat the oven to 400°F.

In a large mixing bowl, beat the yolks and ½ cup of the sugar on high speed for 5 minutes, or until the mixture is very thick and forms ribbons when dropped from the beater. Lower the speed and beat in the vanilla and honey. Increase to high speed and beat for 30 seconds or until thick again. Sift the flour over the yolk mixture without mixing it in, and set aside.

In another large mixing bowl beat the whites until foamy. Add the cream of tartar and beat until soft peaks form when the beater is raised. Gradually beat in the remaining ¼ cup sugar, beating until very stiff peaks form when the beater is raised slowly. Add one third of the whites to the yolk mixture, and with a large rubber spatula fold until all the flour is incorporated. Gently fold in the remaining whites. Working quickly so that the batter does not lose volume, scoop the batter into a pastry bag (or a heavy-duty gallon zip-seal bag with one corner cut off) fitted with a number 6 (½-inch) round tip and pipe about sixty 1-inch discs about ⅜-inch high onto the prepared baking sheets. Space them at least 1 inch apart, as they will spread slightly.

THE BASICS OF THE BERNACHON KITCHEN

Bake 10 to 15 minutes, or until light golden brown and springy to the touch. Cool for a few minutes on the baking sheets, on wire racks. Remove from the baking sheets and finish cooling on the wire racks. Store airtight for 1 day or freeze until ready to fill.

NOTE FROM ROSE

The Bernachons pipe this batter onto ⅛-inch-thick heavy-duty cardboard. Jean-Jacques explained that cardboard does not absorb heat the way metal does, so the biscuit cooks from the top only and remains moister. Using baking sheets manufactured with double thickness and a layer of air between also works well. Or use two baking sheets—one on top of the other—as insulation.

LA PÂTE
À BABA

BABA

SERVES 10 TO 12

The Bernachon version of this yeast cake is exceptionally
buttery and tender.

INGREDIENTS	MEASURE	WEIGHT	
	VOLUME	OUNCES	GRAMS
water	2 tablespoons	1 ounce	30 grams
sugar	1 tablespoon	0.5 ounce	15 grams
fresh yeast or	2 packed teaspoons	0.5 ounce	11 grams
dry yeast, not rapid-rise	1½ teaspoons		4.5 grams
bread flour	2 cups (lightly spooned)	8.75 ounces	250 grams
5 large eggs	1 liquid cup	10 ounces	284 grams (weighed in the shells)
unsalted butter	9 tablespoons	4.5 ounces	125 grams
salt	¾ teaspoon		6 grams
golden raisins	1 cup	5 ounces	142 grams

One lightly buttered 6-cup ring mold.

PROOF THE YEAST In a small bowl combine the water (100°F. if using fresh yeast, 110°F. if using dry), ½ teaspoon of the sugar, and the yeast. If you are using fresh yeast, crumble it slightly while adding. Set it aside in a draft-free spot for 10 to 20 minutes. By this time, the mixture should be full of bubbles. If not, the yeast is too old to be useful.

In a mixing bowl, combine the flour, eggs, and yeast mixture. Beat (number 6 on a KitchenAid mixer) about 1 minute, or until smooth and well combined. Cut the butter into thin slices and place on top of the dough. Cover with plastic wrap and allow to rise for 2 hours.

Sprinkle the salt, remaining sugar, and raisins over the dough, and mix on low speed just until incorporated and dough is smooth.

Scrape the mixture into the prepared mold, filling it only half full. Cover it loosely with lightly buttered plastic wrap, and allow it to rise in a warm, draft-free area about 1 or 2 hours, or until dough reaches top of mold.

Preheat the oven to 450°F. Bake the baba 5 minutes, lower the temperature to 350°F., and continue baking 20 to 25 minutes or until golden brown and a skewer inserted in the center comes out clean.

RUM SYRUP

INGREDIENTS	MEASURE	WEIGHT	
	VOLUME	POUNDS/OUNCES	GRAMS
sugar	2 cups	14 ounces	400 grams
water	4 cups	2 pounds 1.25 ounces	944 grams
dark rum	½ cup	3.75 ounces	110 grams

Prepare shortly before using and keep warm: In a medium saucepan, bring the sugar and water to a full rolling boil, stirring constantly. Remove from the heat and cool for a few minutes before adding the rum.

Unmold the baba onto a rack, and place it in a large pan or on foil (to catch the dripping syrup). Poke it all over with a cake tester or skewer, and spoon on the hot syrup until as much as possible is absorbed (a poultry baster works well). Reserve the remaining syrup to pass on the side. Allow it to rest for several hours, until firm enough to transfer to a serving plate.

THE BASICS OF THE BERNACHON KITCHEN

LA PÂTE À BRIOCHE MOUSSELINE

BRIOCHE MOUSSELINE

MAKES 3¼ POUNDS / 1½ KILOGRAMS

This is an exceptional brioche. It contains so much butter that it is as fine-textured and as buttery-tasting as a pound cake! The large amount of butter makes the dough very delicate so the butter must be added with your fingers. (The term "mousseline" is used in French confectionery to describe very delicate mixtures.)

In addition to making little chocolate-filled rolls (Les Briochins, page 138), Bernachon also makes many brioche loaves. The loaves are fashioned out of four separate pieces that are easy to pull apart.

INGREDIENTS MEASURE		WEIGHT	
ROOM TEMPERATURE	VOLUME	POUNDS/OUNCES	GRAMS
water	2 table-spoons	1 ounce	30 grams
superfine sugar	2 ½ table-spoons	1 ounce	30 grams
fresh yeast* or	2 packed teaspoons	0.5 ounce	11 grams
dry yeast, not rapid-rise	1 ½ teaspoons		4.5 grams
bread flour	4 cups (lightly spooned)	1 pound 1.5 ounces	500 grams
salt	1 ¾ teaspoons	0.5 ounce	12 grams
10 large eggs	2 liquid cups	1 pound 4 ounces (weighed in the shells)	570 grams
unsalted butter	1 ¾ cups	14 ounces	400 grams
1 extra-large egg for glaze, lightly beaten			

*In cool weather use 16 grams fresh (1 packed tablespoon) or 7 grams dry (1 package, 2 ¼ teaspoons).

PROOF THE YEAST

In a small bowl combine the water (100°F. if using fresh yeast, 110°F. if using dry), ½ teaspoon of the sugar, and the yeast. If using fresh yeast, crumble it slightly while adding. Set aside in a draft-free spot for 10 to 20 minutes. By this time, the mixture should be full of bubbles. If not, the yeast is too old to be useful.

In a mixing bowl, on low speed mix together the flour, the proofed yeast, remaining sugar, salt, and 6 of the eggs. When the ingredients are incorporated, add the remaining eggs, one at a time. Raise speed to medium (4 on a KitchenAid mixer), and beat about 5 minutes or until the dough is smooth, shiny, and very elastic. Using your fingertips, gently mix in the butter, 1 tablespoon at a time. The dough will be very soft and sticky.

Sprinkle the dough lightly with flour (to keep a crust from forming). Cover the bowl tightly and allow the dough to rise at room temperature for 1½ hours.

With lightly greased hands or a rubber spatula, very gently deflate the dough by stirring it or flattening it and turning it over a few times. Sprinkle it lightly with flour, cover it tightly, and refrigerate it for 6 hours or up to 2 days, gently deflating the dough every 45 minutes during the first 4 hours, after which it becomes cold enough to prevent rising. Wrap it loosely but securely in plastic wrap and then foil, and refrigerate.

To make loaves: Butter the loaf pans. For an 8-cup loaf, roll a scant cup (7.5 ounces/200 grams) of dough into a cylinder. Make a total of four cylinders and place them in the prepared pan (it will be half full). For a 6-cup pan, each cylinder should be a scant ¾ cup (5.25 ounces/150 grams).

Cover the pans lightly with buttered plastic wrap, and allow the dough to rise for 2 hours or until it reaches the top of the pans.

Preheat the oven to 425°F. Brush the brioche with the lightly beaten egg. Bake for 5 minutes, lower the heat to 375°F., and continue baking 30 to 40 minutes (the smaller loaf will bake a little faster than the larger one) or until golden brown and a skewer inserted into the middle comes out clean.

NOTE FROM ROSE

For the best flavor and texture, it is important to keep the yeast from over-raising the dough by deflating it at regular intervals. Bernachon calls this very important process "remprage." It keeps the dough from developing a sour flavor and uneven texture. Making the dough a day ahead of baking allows for the best flavor development. The unbaked dough can be frozen for up to 3 months.

LA PÂTE FEUILLETÉE

CLASSIC PUFF PASTRY

MAKES 1¼ POUNDS / 570 GRAMS

This king of French pastries is still prepared mainly by hand at the Bernachons' bakery.

INGREDIENTS	MEASURE	WEIGHT	
ROOM TEMPERATURE	VOLUME	OUNCES	GRAMS
unsalted butter	1 cup	8 ounces	227 grams
all-purpose unbleached flour, preferably Heckers	2 cups minus 2 table-spoons (dip and sweep)	8 ounces	227 grams
salt	½ teaspoon		3.5 grams
ice water	½ cup	4 ounces	116 grams

THE DOUGH Remove 1 ounce (2 tablespoons) of butter from the 8 ounces and refrigerate the remainder. Place the butter in a mixing bowl and add 7 ounces (1⅔ cups) of the flour and the salt. Rub this mixture between your fingers until it is very fine and grainy and no lumps of butter are discernible (about 5 minutes). Add 6 tablespoons of the water and stir gently with a fork to incorporate it. The dough should be soft and clumpy. If necessary, add the remaining water by droplets.

Dump the dough out onto a floured surface and gently knead it, just until the dough holds together and looks fairly smooth. It should not become too elastic or it will be difficult to roll. Cover the dough and allow it to rest 20 minutes at room temperature, or up to 24 hours well wrapped and refrigerated.

THE BUTTER SQUARE Place the remaining 1 ounce (3 tablespoons) of flour on a sheet of plastic wrap, and place the remaining 7 ounces of butter on top. Sprinkle a little of the flour on top of the butter and cover it with the plastic wrap. Pound the butter lightly with a rolling pin to flatten and soften it, then knead it together, using the plastic wrap and your knuckles to avoid touching the butter directly. Work quickly. As soon as the flour is incorporated, shape the butter into a 4½-inch square (no thicker than ¾ inch). At this point the butter should be cool but workable—60°F. Use it at once or keep it cool. Butter must not be colder than 60°F. when rolled into the pastry or it will break through the dough and not distribute evenly.

A PASSION FOR CHOCOLATE

 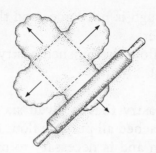 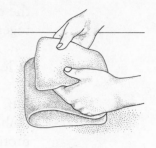

Roll out the dough on a well-floured surface to form a **THE** 6-inch square. Place the butter square diagonally in **DOUGH** the center of the dough square, and lightly mark the **PACKAGE** dough at the edges of the butter with the dull side of a knife. Remove the butter and roll each marked corner of the dough out to form flaps. The dough will be slightly elastic. Moisten these flaps lightly with water and replace the butter on the dough, wrapping securely. Stretch the flaps slightly to reach across the dough package.

On a well-floured surface, keeping the dough seam side up, gently roll the package into a rectangle measuring 6 by 12 inches. Brush off all flour from the surface of the dough, and fold it into thirds as you would fold a business letter. This is the first "turn." Before each subsequent turn, move the dough so the closed end is on your left. Clean the work surface, reflour, and roll and fold a second time exactly the same way, but turn the dough over occasionally to keep seams and edges even. Be sure to roll into all four corners of the dough, and use a pastry scraper to even the edges.

Mark the dough with two fingertips, or knuckles if you have long nails, to indicate that two turns have been completed. Wrap the dough in plastic wrap, then foil, and refrigerate for 30 to 40 minutes. The dough must not chill for longer than 40 minutes, or the butter will never distribute evenly.

Continue to roll and turn the dough, marking the turns with fingertips and resting 30 minutes between turns, until six turns have been completed. It is best to do only one turn at a time now, as dough will become elastic and the best results are obtained when

THE BASICS OF THE BERNACHON KITCHEN

the dough is not forced and the layers are not pressed together.

Allow the finished pastry to rest, refrigerated, for at least 2 hours.

NOTES FROM ROSE

Puff pastry that is given six "turns" has 729 layers. Unbleached all-purpose flour has more gluten-forming protein and is necessary to provide the extra support for the thin, fragile layers of butter and dough. Heckers flour has an especially high protein content. (The protein count is indicated on the side of a bag of flour.)

Single turns, as opposed to the newer double turns, make it easier to control the shaping and layering of the pastry, and it will rise more evenly when baked. Although the actual working time is short, you will need to be around for a 4-hour period to complete the turns. The temperature of the butter is critical to making the best puff pastry. It should be cold but malleable.

It is best if the pastry is used by the next day—or it may be frozen for months.

LA PÂTE
À CROISSANT

CLASSIC CROISSANTS

MAKES 24 CROISSANTS

This is the real thing—the French croissant at its best: buttery, wondrously airy and flaky.

INGREDIENTS MEASURE		WEIGHT	
ROOM TEMPERATURE	VOLUME	POUNDS/OUNCES	GRAMS
water	2 table-spoons	1 ounce	30 grams
superfine sugar	1 table-spoon + 2 teaspoons	0.75 ounce	20 grams
fresh yeast or	2 packed teaspoons	0.5 ounce	11 grams
dry yeast, not rapid-rise	1½ teaspoons		4.5 grams
unbleached all-purpose flour*	3½ cups (dip and sweep)	1 pound 1.5 ounces	500 grams
salt	1¾ teaspoons	0.5 ounce	12 grams
warm milk	1⅓ cups	11 ounces	314 grams
unsalted butter	1 cup + 1½ table-spoons	8.75 ounces	250 grams
2 large eggs, beaten			

*Heckers flour is the ideal choice as it has a high protein count, resulting in very light dough.

Three 11 by 17-inch baking sheets, buttered.

PROOF THE YEAST In a small bowl combine the water (100°F. if using fresh yeast, 110°F. if using dry), ½ teaspoon of the sugar, and the yeast. If using fresh yeast, crumble it slightly while adding. Set aside in a draft-free spot for 10 to 20 minutes. By this time, the mixture should be full of bubbles. If not, the yeast is too old to be useful.

Reserve 3 tablespoons (1 ounce/28 grams) of the flour, and in a large mixing bowl, mix together the remaining flour, salt, and remaining sugar. Add a scant cup of the warm milk and the yeast mixture, and stir just until the dough is smooth, adding more milk if necessary. Place it in a clean, lightly buttered bowl, cover the bowl with plastic wrap, and allow the dough to rise at room temperature for 1½ hours (in summer or if the kitchen is very warm, only 45 minutes). To ensure that the yeast is distributed evenly, while the dough is rising, one or two times gently deflate it by tossing it over and flattening it gently with your hands.

A PASSION FOR CHOCOLATE

Place the remaining 1 ounce (3 tablespoons) of flour on a sheet of plastic wrap and place the butter on top. Sprinkle a little of the flour on top of the butter, and cover with the plastic wrap. Pound the butter lightly with a rolling pin to flatten and soften it, then knead together the butter and flour, using the plastic wrap and your knuckles to avoid touching the butter directly. Work quickly. As soon as the flour is incorporated, shape it into a 5-inch square (no thicker than ¾ inch). At this point the butter should be cool but workable—60°F. Use at once or keep it cool. The butter must not be colder than 60°F. when rolled into the pastry or it will break through the dough and not distribute evenly.

Roll out the dough on a well-floured surface to form an 8-inch square. Place butter square diagonally in center of dough square, and lightly mark dough at edges of butter with the dull side of a knife. Remove butter and roll each marked corner of the dough out to form a flap. Dough will be slightly elastic. Moisten these flaps lightly with water and replace butter on dough, wrapping securely. Stretch flaps slightly to reach across the dough package. Wrap loosely in plastic wrap and refrigerate for 30 minutes.

THE DOUGH PACKAGE

On a well-floured surface, keeping dough seam side up, gently roll dough package into a rectangle measuring 8 by 12 inches. Brush off all flour from the surface of the dough, and fold dough into thirds as you would fold a business letter. This is the first "turn."

Before each subsequent turn, move the dough so that the closed end is on your left. Clean the surface, reflour, and roll and fold a second time exactly the same way—but turn the dough over occasionally to keep seams and edges even. Be sure to roll into all four corners of the dough and use a pastry scraper to even the edges.

Mark dough with two fingertips, or knuckles if you have long nails, to indicate that two turns have been completed. Wrap with plastic wrap, then foil, and refrigerate for 30 to 40 minutes. The dough must not chill for longer than 40 minutes, or the butter will never distribute evenly.

Continue to roll and turn dough, marking the turns with fingertips and resting 30 minutes between turns, until four turns have been completed. It is best to do only one turn at a time now, as the dough will become elastic and the best results are obtained when dough is not forced and layers not pressed together.

Wrap the dough in plastic wrap, then foil, and refrigerate overnight.

The next day, remove the dough and allow it to sit at room temperature for 10 to 15 minutes or until soft enough to roll.

Give the dough one more turn, and then roll it out to form a rectangle about 12 by 36 inches, and ⅛ inch thick. Cut it into two long pieces (each will be 6 by 36 inches). Cut each piece into twelve triangles (each one will measure 3 inches at its base, 6 inches from the center of the base to the point).

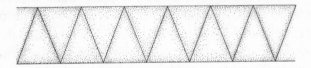

Roll each triangle, starting at the base and working toward the point. Place them 2 inches apart on a buttered pastry sheet, and cover lightly with buttered plastic wrap.

Allow the croissants to rise for 1 hour at room temperature. They will become slightly puffy and lighter when touched with the fingertip, but will not increase greatly in size.

Preheat the oven to 475°F. Brush the croissants lightly with the beaten eggs.

A PASSION FOR CHOCOLATE

Bake for 5 minutes, then lower the heat to 400°F. and continue baking for 7 to 10 minutes or until golden brown and done. (Check by cutting into one to see if the dough in the center is cooked.) Remove immediately from the sheets and cool on racks.

Check carefully toward the end of the baking time, as some may be done before others. **NOTE**

When making the dough, it is important that the butter remain cool though malleable. Beating it with a rolling pin helps to soften it without melting it.

NOTES FROM ROSE

The frozen croissants taste like fresh-baked when they are reheated (but do not use a microwave oven as they could toughen and will not crisp).

If oven space does not allow for adequate air circulation between the pans, bake one sheet at a time.

Two days at room temperature, 3 months frozen. Reheat for 3 to 5 minutes in a 300°F. oven to crisp the outside and freshen the inside. **KEEPS**

LA PÂTE
À CHOUX

CREAM-PUFF PASTRY

MAKES 48 PUFFS

Bernachon's recipe for cream-puff pastry has less milk and butter
than most, and more egg, which makes it both
lighter and crisper.

INGREDIENTS	MEASURE		WEIGHT	
	VOLUME	OUNCES	GRAMS	
milk	⅔ cup	5.5 ounces	160 grams	
unsalted butter	5 tablespoons	2.5 ounces	71 grams	
sugar	1½ teaspoons		7 grams	
salt	½ teaspoon			
all-purpose flour	1 cup (lightly spooned)	4.25 ounces	121 grams	
5 large eggs	1 liquid cup	10 ounces	284 grams (weighed in the shells)	
1 large egg for glaze, lightly beaten				
slivered almonds	scant ½ cup	1.75 ounces	50 grams	

One 11 by 17-inch baking sheet, lined with parchment or greased.

Preheat the oven to 400°F.

In a medium saucepan, combine the milk, butter, sugar, and salt, and bring the mixture to a full rolling boil. Remove it immediately from the heat, and add the flour all at once. Stir with a wooden spoon until the mixture forms a ball, leaves the sides of the pan, and clings slightly to the spoon. Return it to low heat and cook, stirring and mashing continuously, for about 3 minutes (to cook the flour). Without scraping the pan, transfer the mixture to the bowl of a food processor fitted with the metal blade.

Process 15 seconds with the feed tube open (to allow steam to escape). With the motor running, pour in the eggs and continue processing for 30 seconds. The mixture should be smooth, shiny, and too soft to hold peaks. (If you are using an electric mixer, allow the flour mixture to cool for 5 minutes in the bowl. Then beat in the eggs, one at a time, beating after each addition until incorporated.)

If you are using parchment, place a small dot of dough at each corner to attach it to the baking sheet.

To make one large puff ring: Spoon the batter into a large ring, about 9 inches in diameter, on the baking sheet. Bake 45 minutes. To prevent the pastry from deflating, do not open the oven door until shortly before baking time is over. Remove the pastry from the oven and brush it immediately with the beaten egg. Place the almonds on top, and return it to the oven for about 5 minutes or until the almonds and the ring are a deep golden brown.

Use a long metal spatula or knife to dislodge the pastry ring and two pancake turners to lift it onto a rack, and cool completely. Store the pastry in an airtight plastic bag up to 1 week refrigerated, 6 months frozen. Recrisp it in a warm oven, then cool and fill it before serving.

To make individual puffs: Fill a pastry bag (or a 1-gallon zip-seal bag with one corner cut off) with the mixture, fit it with a ½-inch tip, and pipe puffs about 1½ inches in diameter about 1 inch apart.

Bake 20 minutes, or until puffs are golden brown and do not yield to pressure when squeezed gently. Turn off the oven and prop a wooden spoon in the door to keep it slightly ajar for 1 hour. Then remove puffs to a rack and cool completely. Store them in an airtight plastic bag or container up to 1 week refrigerated, 6 months frozen.

TO FILL Use a pastry bag fitted with a Bismarck tube (or plain round ¼-inch tube) to pipe lightly sweetened whipped cream into the hollow center of each cream puff. Then dip the tops of the puffs into chocolate glaze if desired.

LA PÂTE BRISÉE

PIE DOUGH

MAKES PASTRY FOR
ONE 10-INCH TART

This recipe makes a flaky and tender pastry, perfect for tarts and pies. It is easy and reliable.

INGREDIENTS	MEASURE	WEIGHT	
	VOLUME	OUNCES	GRAMS
unsalted butter	*9 tablespoons*	*4.5 ounces*	*125 grams*
all-purpose flour	*1¾ cups (dip and sweep)*	*8.75 ounces*	*250 grams*
salt	*¼ teaspoon*		
1 extra-large egg		*2.25 ounces*	*65 grams*
ice water	*1 to 2 tablespoons*		

Cut the butter into small pieces and allow it to soften slightly.

In a bowl, combine the flour, salt, and butter. Rub between the fingertips until coarse and crumbly—don't overdo or it will be too tender.

Add the egg and mix lightly with the fingertips or a fork until the flour mixture is moistened. Sprinkle on the water, 1 teaspoon at a time, until all the particles are moistened and the mixture begins to hold together. Dump the dough out onto a work surface and "fraiser": smear it in front of you with the palm of the hand two or three times, but don't overwork it. The dough should feel slightly elastic. Flatten it into a disc, wrap it in plastic wrap, and refrigerate it for at least 2 hours.

Roll out the pastry ⅛ inch thick, about 14 inches in diameter. Transfer it to a 10-inch tart pan. Trim the extra pastry so that it is about 1 inch higher than the edges of the pan. Fold it inward to create a double layer of pastry at the sides to give it extra strength. Prick the bottom if you will be prebaking it.

LA PÂTE SUCRÉE

SWEET PIE DOUGH

MAKES PASTRY FOR
ONE 10-INCH TART

This sweet, tender pastry is just sturdy enough to support rolling for a crust.

INGREDIENTS	MEASURE	WEIGHT	
ROOM TEMPERATURE	VOLUME	OUNCES	GRAMS
unsalted butter, softened	9 tablespoons	4.5 ounces	125 grams
superfine sugar	½ cup + 2 tablespoons	4.5 ounces	125 grams
salt	¼ teaspoon		
all-purpose flour	1¾ cups (dip and sweep)	8.75 ounces	250 grams
1 extra-large egg			
milk	1 tablespoon		

In a mixing bowl, beat the butter with the sugar and salt. Add the flour and mix for a few seconds. Then rub the mixture between your palms until it is coarse and crumbly—don't overdo or it will be too tender. Add the egg and milk to a well in the center of the flour, and stir with a fork or your fingers until the dough is moistened and will form a ball. Dump the dough onto a sheet of plastic wrap and press it gently to shape into a ball. Then press it into a disc and wrap it in the plastic. Let it rest 1 hour, refrigerated, before rolling. Roll out the pastry ⅛ inch thick, about 14 inches in diameter. Transfer it to a 10-inch tart pan. Trim the extra pastry so that it is about 1 inch higher than the edges of the pan. Fold it inward to create a double layer of pastry at the side to give it extra strength.

LA PÂTE À
PIQUE-NIQUE

SWEET COCOA-CINNAMON
PIE DOUGH WITH ALMONDS

MAKES PASTRY FOR
ONE 10-INCH TART

This chocolatey, cinnamon-perfumed pastry is crisp and delicious enough to eat by itself as a cookie. In fact, the Bernachons created it as a cookie to take on picnics! It also, however, makes a great base for tarts such as nut tarts and the famous Linzer tart.

INGREDIENTS	MEASURE	WEIGHT	
ROOM TEMPERATURE	VOLUME	OUNCES	GRAMS
1 *extra-large egg*			
milk	1 *tablespoon*		
unsalted butter, softened	9 *tablespoons*	4.5 *ounces*	125 *grams*
superfine sugar	1 *cup*	7 *ounces*	200 *grams*
salt	¼ *teaspoon*		
all-purpose flour	1¾ *cups (dip and sweep)*	8.75 *ounces*	250 *grams*
unsweetened cocoa	¼ *cup (lightly spooned)*	1 *ounce*	25 *grams*
sliced almonds, chopped fine	½ *cup + 1½ tablespoons*	1.75 *ounces*	50 *grams*
cinnamon (optional)	½ *teaspoon*		

Two 11 by 17-inch baking sheets, lightly buttered.

Preheat the oven to 350°F.

In a small bowl, mix together the egg and the milk. Set aside.

In a large mixing bowl, beat the butter with the sugar and salt for about 30 seconds. Add the flour and mix for a few seconds. Continue to mix the dough by rubbing it together with the palms of your hands until it looks like coarse grains. Do not overdo this or the dough can become too tender and fragile.

Make a well in the center of the dough and add the egg and milk mixture, stirring with a fork until the dough is moistened and will begin to form a ball. Dump the dough onto a sheet of plastic wrap.

Stir together the cocoa, almonds, and cinnamon and sprinkle this mixture over the dough. Use the plastic wrap to knead it into the dough until evenly incorporated.

Flatten the dough into a disc, wrap it in the plastic, and refrigerate it for at least 1 hour or up to overnight.

Roll out the dough between sheets of plastic wrap to about ⅛-inch thickness (about 14 inches in diameter). Transfer it to a 10-inch tart pan. Trim the extra pastry so that it is about 1 inch higher than the edges of the pan. Fold it inward to create a double layer of pastry at the sides to give it extra strength. Prick the bottom if you will be prebaking it.

LA PÂTE
À SUCCÈS

SUCCÈS

MAKES THREE 9-INCH DISCS

A succès, like a meringue, is made up of egg whites and sugar, but some of the sugar is replaced with ground nuts. This not only results in a great deal of added flavor but also significantly reduces sweetness. Unlike the crisp meringue, a succès is slightly chewy, but tender and cake-like. It is traditionally used in place of cake layers.

INGREDIENTS	MEASURE	WEIGHT	
	VOLUME	OUNCES	GRAMS
sliced almonds	*2 cups*	*6.25 ounces*	*180 grams*
superfine sugar	*¾ cup + 2 table-spoons*	*6.25 ounces*	*180 grams*
7 large egg whites, room temperature	*7 fluid ounces*	*7.25 ounces*	*210 grams*
cream of tartar	*1 teaspoon*		*3 grams*

Two baking sheets, buttered and floured or lined with parchment, marked with three 8-inch circles.

Preheat the oven to 350°F.

In a food processor, place the almonds and ¾ cup sugar and process until the almonds are finely grated.

In a mixing bowl, beat the egg whites until foamy, add the cream of tartar, and beat until soft peaks form when the beater is raised slowly. Gradually add the remaining 2 tablespoons sugar, beating until stiff peaks form when the beater is raised slowly. Fold in the grated almond mixture.

Using a pastry bag (or a 1-gallon zip-seal bag with one corner cut off) fitted with a large plain number 6 (½-inch) tip, pipe the batter onto the prepared baking sheets to form three 8-inch circles, starting at the outer perimeter and spiraling inward toward the center. Use a small metal spatula to fill in any gaps with leftover batter and to smooth the surface. Bake for 15 to 20 minutes, or just until the discs begin to brown. Remove the baking sheets to a rack. Loosen the succès from the sheets and allow them to cool completely on the sheets on racks before transferring them to a work surface or serving plate. They will have expanded to about 9 inches.

To obtain a perfect circle, invert a cake pan over the succès and trim any excess with a sharp knife.

Use superfine sugar for the best texture. It is not actually necessary to use flour on the baking pan to keep it from sticking; however, the flour does keep the succès from spreading.

NOTES FROM ROSE

LA MERINGUE

MERINGUE

This meringue is sometimes baked for confections such as the Rochers (page 195), or used to frost a cake and then browned under the broiler, or folded into whipped cream and frozen, as for the Chocolate Dauphin (page 231).

INGREDIENTS	MEASURE	WEIGHT	
	VOLUME	POUNDS/OUNCES	GRAMS
10 *large egg whites*	1 ¼ *cups*	10.5 *ounces*	300 *grams*
superfine sugar	3 *cups*	1 *pound 5 ounces*	600 *grams*
1 *vanilla bean, split* *			

*You may substitute 1 teaspoon vanilla extract for the vanilla bean, but the bean offers a fuller, more aromatic flavor. If using extract, add it at the very end. If using a Tahitian bean, use only ½ bean.

In a large mixing bowl, place the egg whites, sugar and vanilla bean and set over a large pan of simmering water. (The bottom of the bowl should not touch the water.) Stir constantly with a whisk until the mixture is warm. Then beat, preferably with the whisk attachment, until meringue is stiff and shiny. Remove the vanilla bean.

Vanilla bean can be rinsed, dried in a warm oven, and reused.

NOTES FROM ROSE

Separate each egg into two small cups before adding the egg white to the rest of the whites. Even a speck of yolk will prevent the whites from beating. A speck of yolk can be removed using a half an eggshell to scoop it out.

THE BASICS OF THE BERNACHON KITCHEN

LA GANACHE

This chocolate-and-cream frosting and filling is one of the best ways known to enjoy chocolate.

| INGREDIENTS | MEASURE | WEIGHT | |
	VOLUME	OUNCES	GRAMS
bittersweet chocolate	*4 (3-ounce) bars*	*12 ounces*	*340 grams*
crème fraîche* (page 348) or heavy cream	*1¼ liquid cups*	*10 ounces*	*290 grams*

*The crème fraîche adds a slightly tangy flavor to the ganache.

Break the chocolate into pieces and process in a food processor until very fine.

Heat the crème fraîche to the boiling point, and with the motor running, pour it through the feed tube in a steady stream. Process a few seconds until smooth. Transfer to a bowl and cool for several hours, until frosting consistency.

NOTE FROM ROSE

The Bernachons always prepare ganache at least 12 hours ahead, refrigerating it in warm weather. This allows the flavors to develop and ripen fully. If it has been refrigerated, they soften it by gently stirring it in a double boiler over simmering water. This can also be done in a microwave, stirring every 10 seconds. In any case, it is important to stir only as much as necessary to equalize the melting process, or the ganache will aerate and lighten in color. In cool weather ganache can remain unrefrigerated for at least 3 days or as long as 2 weeks. At room temperature it remains spreadable.

LA GANACHE
ANTILLAISE

MAKES ABOUT 3½ CUPS

Browned hazelnuts and dark rum blend magnificently with bittersweet chocolate and cream.

INGREDIENTS	MEASURE	WEIGHT	
	VOLUME	OUNCES	GRAMS
hazelnuts	*1 ¼ cups*	*6 ounces*	*170 grams*
baking soda	*¼ cup*	*2 ounces*	*60 grams*
*bittersweet chocolate**	*5 (3-ounce) bars*	*15 ounces*	*425 grams*
heavy cream	*1 liquid cup*	*8 ounces*	*232 grams*
dark rum	*¼ cup*	*2 ounces*	*55 grams*

*If you would like to use the Bernachon hazelnut chocolate, omit the hazelnuts and replace the chocolate with 15 ounces/425 grams of chocolate with hazelnuts and 6 ounces/170 grams of bittersweet chocolate.

BLANCH THE HAZELNUTS

In a medium saucepan, place 3 cups of water and bring it to a boil. Add the nuts and the baking soda, and boil for 3 minutes. Test a nut by running it under cold water. If the skin is not easy to remove with slight pressure from the fingers, return to the heat for a minute or so more. Drain well and peel.

Toast the hazelnuts in a 350°F. oven for 10 to 15 minutes or until golden brown. Cool completely and chop fine, but not powder-fine. (Use the medium grater on a food processor and then pulse with the metal blade.) Set aside.

Break the chocolate into pieces and process in a food processor until very fine.

Heat the cream to the boiling point, and with the motor running, pour it through the feed tube in a steady stream. Process a few seconds until smooth. Cool slightly before adding the rum and the hazelnuts. Pulse just to combine. Transfer to a bowl and cool for several hours, until frosting consistency. In cool weather ganache can remain unrefrigerated for at least 3 days or as long as 2 weeks. At room temperature it remains spreadable.

VARIATIONS

Amaretto, Frangelico, and whiskey are all fine replacements for the rum.

LA GANACHE
CINGHALAISE

The lovely cinnamon flavor in this delicious chocolate-and-cream mixture comes through following the chocolate. It is strongly reminiscent of the best homemade chocolate pudding of childhood—only better.

INGREDIENTS	MEASURE	WEIGHT	
	VOLUME	OUNCES	GRAMS
*bittersweet chocolate**	*4 (3-ounce) bars*	*12 ounces*	*340 grams*
cinnamon	*½ teaspoon*		
heavy cream†	*1½ liquid cups*	*12 ounces*	*340 grams*

*If you would like to use the Bernachon cinnamon chocolate, simply omit the cinnamon.
†The Bernachons use crème fraîche for this ganache, but I find the combination with the cinnamon too tart for my taste.

Break the chocolate into pieces and process with the cinnamon in a food processor until very fine. Heat the cream to the boiling point, and with the motor running, pour it through the feed tube in a steady stream. Process a few seconds until smooth. Transfer to a bowl and cool for several hours, until frosting consistency. In cool weather ganache can remain unrefrigerated for at least 3 days or as long as 2 weeks. At room temperature it remains spreadable.

THE BASICS OF THE BERNACHON KITCHEN

LA GANACHE MOKA

MOCHA GANACHE

MAKES ABOUT 2½ CUPS

This frosting and filling is for the coffee lover. It has the unmistakable flavor of Höpje candy, and it is especially delicious when made with crème fraîche. For a more subtle note, decrease the amount of coffee.

INGREDIENTS	MEASURE	WEIGHT	
	VOLUME	OUNCES	GRAMS
*bittersweet chocolate**	*4 (3-ounce) bars*	*12 ounces*	*340 grams*
Medaglia d'Oro instant espresso powder	*2 tablespoons*		
crème fraîche† (page 348) or heavy cream	*1½ liquid cups*	*12 ounces*	*340 grams*

*If you would like to use the Bernachon mocha chocolate, simply omit the espresso.
†The crème fraîche adds a slightly tangy flavor to the ganache.

Break the chocolate into pieces and process, with the espresso powder, in a food processor until very fine. Heat the cream to the boiling point, and with the motor running, pour it through the feed tube in a steady stream. Process a few seconds until smooth. Transfer to a bowl and cool for several hours, until frosting consistency. In cool weather ganache can remain unrefrigerated for at least 3 days and as long as 2 weeks. At room temperature it remains spreadable.

LA GANACHE
PRÉSIDENT

MAKES ABOUT 2¾ CUPS

This is the filling and frosting used for the cake called Le Président.
The Bernachons love the pure flavors of the bittersweet
chocolate, cream, and toasted hazelnuts.

INGREDIENTS	MEASURE	WEIGHT	
	VOLUME	OUNCES	GRAMS
hazelnuts	*1 cup*	*5 ounces*	*142 grams*
baking soda	*¼ cup*	*2 ounces*	*60 grams*
bittersweet chocolate*	*3⅓ (3-ounce) bars*	*10 ounces*	*284 grams*
crème fraîche† (page 348) or heavy cream	*1 liquid cup + 2 tablespoons*	*9 ounces*	*260 grams*

*If you would like to use the Bernachon hazelnut chocolate, omit the hazelnuts and replace the chocolate with 13 ounces/375 grams of chocolate with hazelnuts and 2 ounces/57 grams of bittersweet chocolate.
†The crème fraîche adds a slightly tangy flavor to the ganache. In cool weather ganache can remain unrefrigerated for at least 3 days or as long as 2 weeks. At room temperature it remains spreadable.

BLANCH THE HAZELNUTS

In a medium saucepan, place 3 cups of water and bring them to a boil. Add the nuts and the baking soda, and boil them for 3 minutes. Test a nut by running it under cold water. If the skin is not easy to remove with slight pressure from the fingers, return to the heat for a minute or so more. Drain well.

Toast the hazelnuts in a 350°F oven for 10 to 15 minutes or until golden brown. Cool completely and chop fine, but not powder-fine. (Use the medium grater on a food processor and then pulse with the metal blade.) Set aside.

Break the chocolate into pieces and process in a food processor until very fine. Heat the cream to the boiling point, and with the motor running, pour it through the feed tube in a steady stream. Process a few seconds until smooth. Add the hazelnuts and pulse just to combine. Transfer to a bowl and cool for several hours, until frosting consistency.

LA GANACHE
AU THÉ

TEA GANACHE

MAKES ABOUT 2½ CUPS

If you love tea, this will likely be your favorite chocolate frosting and filling. The tea produces an intriguingly sharp floral background taste against the bittersweet chocolate. If you keep this ingredient secret, no one will ever guess.

INGREDIENTS	MEASURE	WEIGHT	
	VOLUME	OUNCES	GRAMS
bittersweet chocolate	*4 (3-ounce) bars*	*12 ounces*	*340 grams*
*instant tea**	*1 tablespoon*		
crème fraîche† (page 348) or heavy cream	*1½ liquid cups*	*12 ounces*	*340 grams*

*Instant lemon tea adds a wonderful, almost berry-like, flavor. If you would like to use Bernachon's *chocolat au thé*, simply omit the instant tea. The tea used in the Bernachons' chocolate is a very floral and delicious flavor component.
†The crème fraîche imparts a slightly tangy flavor to the ganache.

Break the chocolate into pieces and process it, together with the instant tea, in a food processor until very fine. Heat the cream to the boiling point, and with the motor running, pour it through the feed tube in a steady stream. Process a few seconds until smooth. Transfer to a bowl and cool for several hours, until frosting consistency. In cool weather ganache can remain unrefrigerated for at least 3 days or as long as 2 weeks. At room temperature it remains spreadable.

THE BASICS OF THE BERNACHON KITCHEN

SAUCE AU CHOCOLAT CHAUDE

HOT CHOCOLATE SAUCE

SERVES 6 TO 8

This chocolate sauce could be called a light ganache. Only the proportions of cream to chocolate have been changed, making the sauce less fudgy when poured atop a frozen dessert. It has the pure taste of chocolate, enriched and softened to pouring consistency.

INGREDIENTS MEASURE		WEIGHT	
	VOLUME	POUNDS/OUNCES	GRAMS
bittersweet chocolate	*2 (3-ounce) bars*	*6 ounces*	*170 grams*
crème fraîche (page 348) or heavy cream	*2 cups*	*1 pound*	*464 grams*

Break the chocolate into small pieces.

In a small saucepan, bring the cream to a boil, stirring constantly. Remove it from the heat, add the chocolate, and stir until the chocolate is fully melted and the sauce is smooth. Use at once or reheat when ready to serve.

CRÈME FRAÎCHE

MAKES 1 CUP

This recipe* produces a crème fraîche with a gentle tang. Use it for
recipes calling for crème fraîche; it will add a subtle
depth and complexity.

*From *The Cake Bible*, William Morrow and Company, 1988.

| INGREDIENTS | MEASURE | WEIGHT | |
	VOLUME	OUNCES	GRAMS
heavy cream	*1 liquid cup*	*8 ounces*	*232 grams*
buttermilk	*1 tablespoon*	*0.5 ounce*	*15 grams*

Combine the cream and buttermilk in a jar with a tight-fitting lid and place it in a warm spot, such as the top of the refrigerator or near a stove. Allow it to sit undisturbed for 12 to 14 hours, or until thickened but still pourable. (Ultra-pasteurized cream may take as long as 36 hours.)

This recipe produces a crème fraîche reminiscent of the enchanting varieties found in France. I prefer it to any of the available commercial products.

    It is also wonderful for finishing sauces, not only because of its delicious flavor, but also because it does not curdle like sour cream.

NOTES FROM ROSE

LA CRÈME
CHANTILLY

SWEETENED WHIPPED CREAM

LA CRÈME CHANTILLY AU CHOCOLAT
CHOCOLATE WHIPPED CREAM

MAKES 2 CUPS

Lightly sweetened whipped cream, flavored with vanilla.
The chocolate version is also light as a cloud, and
deliciously bittersweet.

INGREDIENTS	MEASURE	WEIGHT	
	VOLUME	OUNCES	GRAMS
heavy cream	*1 liquid cup*	*8 ounces*	*232 grams*
superfine sugar	*2 tablespoons*	*1 ounce*	*26 grams*
vanilla	*½ teaspoon*		

In a large mixing bowl, place all the ingredients and stir well. Refrigerate covered for at least 15 minutes (chill beater alongside bowl).

Beat until stiff peaks form when the beater is raised.

VARIATION:
La Crème
Chantilly
Au Chocolat
(Chocolate
Whipped Cream)

Increase the sugar to ⅓ cup (2.25 ounces/66 grams), and stir in ¼ cup lightly spooned (1 ounce/25 grams) unsweetened cocoa.

Refrigerate the mixture for at least 1 hour before beating (to dissolve the cocoa).

Keeps refrigerated for several days.

La Crème Pâtissière

Pastry Cream

Chocolate Pastry Cream

MAKES ABOUT 6 CUPS

This exceptional pastry cream is satiny-smooth, fragrant with vanilla, and has none of the rubberyness so often associated with pastry cream.

INGREDIENTS MEASURE		WEIGHT	
	VOLUME	POUNDS/OUNCES	GRAMS
milk	5 cups	2 pounds 10.5 ounces	1 kilogram 210 grams
2 vanilla beans, split*			
salt	1½ teaspoons		10 grams
10 large egg yolks	¾ liquid cup	6.5 ounces	186 grams
superfine sugar	1½ cups	10.5 ounces	300 grams
all-purpose flour	¾ cup + 1 tablespoon (lightly spooned)	3.5 ounces	100 grams

*You may substitute 2 teaspoons vanilla extract for the vanilla beans, but the beans offer a fuller, more aromatic flavor. If you are using extract, add it after the pastry cream has cooled. If using a Tahitian bean, use only 1 bean.

In a saucepan, place 4 cups of the milk, the vanilla beans, and the salt. Bring it to a full boil, then remove it from the heat.

In a medium bowl, whisk together the egg yolks and sugar until thoroughly combined. Whisk in the flour, and then the remaining 1 cup of cold milk (to prevent curdling). Whisking constantly, gradually add the hot milk.

Return the mixture to the saucepan and bring it to a boil, whisking constantly. Simmer it for 3 minutes, whisking constantly.

Transfer the mixture to a bowl, press plastic wrap directly onto the surface (to prevent a skin from forming), and cool. Store refrigerated up to 5 days. Remove the vanilla beans before serving.

VARIATION: Chocolate Pastry Cream

After the mixture has simmered for 3 minutes, remove it from the heat and add 3 ounces/85 grams of chopped bittersweet chocolate. Whisk until melted.

NOTE FROM ROSE

Pastry cream can be frozen for up to one month.

LA CRÈME
AU BEURRE

BUTTERCREAM FILLING

CHOCOLATE BUTTERCREAM
MOCHA BUTTERCREAM
PRALINE BUTTERCREAM

MAKES ABOUT 3½ CUPS

P astry cream is the base for this delicious and unusually light
buttercream. It is more creamy and less buttery
than most buttercreams.

INGREDIENTS MEASURE		WEIGHT	
	VOLUME	POUNDS/OUNCES	GRAMS
milk	2½ cups	1 pound 5.25 ounces	605 grams
1 vanilla bean, split*			
salt	¾ teaspoon		5 grams
5 large egg yolks	3 fluid ounces	3.25 ounces	93 grams
superfine sugar	¾ cup	5.25 ounces	150 grams
all-purpose flour	½ cup (dip and sweep)	2.5 ounces	70 grams
unsalted butter, softened	⅓ cup	2.5 ounces	75 grams

*You may substitute 1 teaspoon vanilla extract for the vanilla bean, but the bean offers a fuller, more aromatic flavor. If you are using extract, add it after the buttercream has cooled. If using a Tahitian bean, use only ½ bean.

In a saucepan, place 2 cups of the milk, the vanilla bean, and the salt. Bring it to a full boil, then remove from the heat.

In a medium bowl, whisk together the egg yolks and sugar until thoroughly combined. Whisk in the flour, and then the remaining ½ cup of cold milk (to prevent curdling). Whisking constantly, gradually add the hot milk and vanilla bean. Return the mixture to the saucepan and bring to a boil, whisking constantly. Simmer for 3 minutes, whisking constantly.

Transfer the mixture to a bowl, press plastic wrap directly onto the surface (to prevent a skin from forming), and cool unrefrigerated. In a small bowl, mash the butter with a fork to ensure that it is soft and creamy throughout. Remove the vanilla bean, and when the cream is almost cold, whisk in the butter just until smooth. Return the plastic to the surface, and store refrigerated up to 5 days.

VARIATIONS: Chocolate Buttercream

After the milk and vanilla mixture has come to a boil, remove it from the heat and add 3 ounces/85 grams of chopped bittersweet chocolate. Whisk until melted.

THE BASICS OF THE BERNACHON KITCHEN

Mocha Buttercream Dissove 1 tablespoon Medaglia d'Oro instant espresso powder in ½ teaspoon of boiling water and gently beat it into the finished buttercream.

Praline Buttercream Reduce the amount of sugar by 1 tablespoon when preparing the buttercream. Beat 3 tablespoons (1.75 ounces/50 grams) of praline paste (available in specialty stores, page 382) into the butter before beating it into the pastry cream.

NOTES FROM ROSE Pastry cream must not be cold when batter is added or it will separate. If separation should occur, warm the bottom of the bowl over hot water for 2 to 3 seconds before continuing to beat. Overbeating will also cause cream to break down.

The completed buttercream can be frozen for up to one month. Allow it to come to room temperature before whisking *lightly* or it will break down.

The buttercream will continue to thicken after refrigeration. If you are planning to make the buttercream a day or more ahead of completing the cake, it's fine to decrease the flour to 2 ounces/58 grams (½ cup sifted, i.e., sift the flour directly into a ½-cup measuring cup with an unbroken rim and level it off with a knife or metal spatula). You may also use this smaller amount of flour if you are using the buttercream between layers of lighter cake such as the succès as opposed to a genoise with syrup.

LA GLACE À LA VANILLE

VANILLA ICE CREAM

MAKES ABOUT 1 QUART

Smooth, creamy ice cream, perfumed with flecks of real vanilla bean, with real old-fashioned flavor—the kind that can't be bought. For a richer, even creamier version see the note.

It's a known fact that vanilla ice cream makes chocolate taste even more delicious. Serve it with a good chocolate sauce (page 226) or, for a fudgier effect, a hot ganache of your choice (pages 334–44).

INGREDIENTS	MEASURE	WEIGHT	
	VOLUME	POUNDS/OUNCES	GRAMS
7 large egg yolks	½ liquid cup	4.5 ounces	128 grams
superfine sugar	1 cup	7 ounces	200 grams
salt	pinch		
heavy cream	1 cup	8 ounces	232 grams
milk	2¼ cups	1 pound 3 ounces	540 grams
2 vanilla beans, split*			

*You may substitute 2 teaspoons vanilla extract for the vanilla beans, but the beans offer a fuller, more aromatic flavor. If you are using extract, add it after the mixture has cooled. If using a Tahitian bean, use only 1 bean.

Place a fine strainer near the stove, suspended over a medium mixing bowl.

In a medium-size, heavy, noncorrodible saucepan, stir together the yolks, sugar, and salt until well blended, using a wooden spoon.

In another saucepan (or heatproof glass measure if using a microwave on high power), heat the cream, milk, and vanilla beans to the boiling point. Stir a few tablespoons into the yolk mixture; then gradually add the remainder, stirring constantly.

Heat the mixture to just below the boiling point (170°F. to 180°F.), stirring constantly. Steam will begin to appear and the mixture will be slightly thicker than heavy cream. It will leave a well-defined track when a finger is run across the back of a spoon that has been dipped in the mixture. Immediately remove the pan from the heat and pour the mixture into the strainer, scraping up any thickened cream that has settled on the bottom of the pan. Remove the vanilla beans and scrape the seeds into the sauce. Stir until the seeds separate. Return the pod to the sauce until ready to freeze.

Cool the mixture in an ice-water bath or the refrigerator until cold. Freeze in an ice cream maker. Allow it to ripen for 2 hours in the freezer before serving. Store up to 3 days.

I find that a higher percentage of cream to milk results in a smoother ice cream. I recommend 2½ cups of cream and ¾ cup of milk. I also prefer to use only ¾ cup of sugar. Adding 1 tablespoon of vodka before freezing also helps to keep the ice cream creamy.

HONEYED GOLDEN ALMONDS

PRALINE

MAKES 1 CUP

Bathing sliced almonds in a honeyed syrup and then toasting them produces almonds with a very delicious flavor, delightfully crisp texture, and a nostalgic golden color. They are great to use for decorating cakes.

| INGREDIENTS | MEASURE | WEIGHT | |
	VOLUME	OUNCES	GRAMS
water	1 ¼ *cups*	10.5 *ounces*	290 *grams*
sugar	1 *cup*	7 *ounces*	200 *grams*
½ vanilla bean, split			
honey	2 *teaspoons*	0.5 *ounce*	14 *grams*
sliced almonds	1 *cup*	3 *ounces*	85 *grams*

A baking sheet.

Preheat the oven to 400°F.

In a large saucepan, combine the water, sugar, vanilla bean, and honey. Bring it to a boil, stirring constantly.

Add the almonds and boil undisturbed for about 3 minutes.

Using a strainer, drain the almonds. Place them in one layer on the baking sheet and bake, stirring gently occasionally, for 6 to 10 minutes, or until golden in color. They will be sticky but become dry when cool. Cool, and store airtight.

Several weeks at room temperature; several months **KEEPS** refrigerated.

DECORATIONS

Decorating with Cocoa

FOR DECORATING A CAKE
OF 8 TO 10 SERVINGS

A dusting of cocoa provides an elegantly easy finish for a cake. The cocoa powder creates a velvety dimensional quality.

| INGREDIENTS | MEASURE | WEIGHT | |
	VOLUME	OUNCES	GRAMS
unsweetened cocoa	¼ cup (lightly spooned)	1 ounce	25 grams

A dredger or fine strainer.

Place the cocoa in a dredger or fine strainer.

Place the cake to be decorated on a rack or sheet of wax paper. Dust the cocoa evenly over the surface of the cake to form a fine coating. Lift the cake with a heavy-duty pancake turner and place it on a serving plate. For a fancier effect, place a doily or template on top of the cake before dusting it with cocoa. Remove the doily carefully so as not to disturb the design.

If desired, add chocolate curls (page 367), leaves (page 373), or candied orange peels (page 248).

NOTE Powdered sugar can be used in the same way to provide contrast against a dark chocolate cake. For a startlingly beautiful effect, cover the surface of the cake with cocoa; place a doily or template gently on top; dust with powdered sugar, and then carefully lift away the doily.

NOTES FROM ROSE If using a strainer, use a spoon to tap against the sides for a finer coating.

For an unusual effect, after coating the surface of the cake with cocoa, use a long serrated knife to mark lined patterns into the surface. Use a light touch to make several lines, first going in one direction and then at right angles to it.

A cake rack can also be used to mark the surface by lightly pressing it into the cocoa (see Le Succès, page 125).

A PASSION FOR CHOCOLATE

CHOCOLATE CURLS

Small shiny curls of chocolate make a simple but attractive cake decoration.

INGREDIENTS	MEASURE		WEIGHT	
	VOLUME		OUNCES	GRAMS
*bittersweet chocolate**	1⅓ (3-ounce) bars		*4 ounces*	*113 grams*

*Couverture, available in specialty stores (page 382), contains more cocoa butter and creates a thinner, glossier coating of chocolate.

Chocolate can be curled with a melon-baller or sharp potato peeler.

In one hand, hold the chocolate block against a wad of paper toweling so that the heat of your hand doesn't melt the chocolate. Hold the peeler against the upper edge of the chocolate and, digging in one edge of the cutter, bring the blade toward you. Greater pressure forms thicker, more open curls. Lighter pressure makes tighter curls.

NOTE When handling the chocolate curls or placing them on a cake, use the tip of a knife or a small spoon or tweezers because the heat of your fingers will melt the curls.

NOTE FROM ROSE If the chocolate is too cold, it will splinter or lighten in cooler; if too warm, it will come off in soft strips that will not curl. To soften chocolate, leave it in an 80°F. room, such as the kitchen, for several hours. Chocolate can also be softened by placing it briefly under a lamp or in a microwave oven using a 3-second burst of high power. It takes a few tries to get the chocolate soft enough without oversoftening it, but once this point is reached, it will last for at least 10 minutes.

CHOCOLATE CIGARETTES

These are actually long curls. To make cigarettes, break the chocolate into pieces and place them in the top of a double boiler set over very hot water (but no hotter than 160°F.). The water must not simmer or touch the bottom of the double boiler insert.

Stir until the chocolate begins to melt. Return the pan to low heat if the water cools, but be careful that it does not get too hot. (The chocolate may be melted in a microwave oven if stirred every 15 seconds.)

Using either method, remove it from the heat source before the chocolate has fully melted and stir constantly until the residual heat melts the chocolate. Stir continuously until the temperature of the chocolate reaches 88 to 91°F. (84 to 87°F. if milk chocolate). (If you are not using a thermometer, dab a small amount on your upper lip. It should feel cool.)

Spread the chocolate into a long band ⅛ inch thick on a smooth marble or Formica counter and allow it to set. Don't wait too long or the chocolate will harden too much and will not curl. Test small sections at the edges to see when the consistency is perfect.

Using a knife or pizza wheel, score the chocolate to determine the desired length of the cigarette. Using a triangular scraper held at a 45° angle to the chocolate, push firmly against the counter, starting at the bottom of the chocolate band and pushing away from you. The higher the angle and the thinner the chocolate, the tighter the curl.

Use a pancake turner to lift the cigarettes and store airtight, refrigerated, or at cool room temperature for up to several months.

NOTE Long, even chocolate cigarettes take a great deal of practice. To elongate shorter ones, place one smaller end into a larger end of a second one in telescoping fashion.

Summer coating (also known as compound chocolate), which contains palm kernel oil instead of cocoa butter, is much easier to use for "cigarettes." To melt it, use hot water from the tap (no hotter) in the bottom of the double boiler. Stir occasionally until the chocolate is completely melted.

CHOCOLATE PETALS

Thes wide swatches of chocolate are used to compose large chocolate flowers to decorate the tops of cakes.

Break the chocolate into pieces and place them in the top of a double boiler set over very hot water (but no hotter than 160°F.). The water must not simmer or touch the bottom of the double boiler insert.

Stir until the chocolate begins to melt. Return the pan to low heat if the water cools, but be careful that it does not get too hot. (The chocolate may be melted in a microwave oven if stirred every 15 seconds.)

Using either method, remove it from the heat source before the chocolate has fully melted and stir constantly until the residual heat melts the chocolate. Stir continuously until the temperature of the chocolate reaches 88° to 91°F. (84° to 87°F. if milk chocolate). (If you are not using a thermometer, dab a small amount on your upper lip. It should feel cool.)

Spread the chocolate into a long band 1/8-inch thick on a smooth marble or Formica counter and allow it to set. Don't wait too long or the chocolate will harden too much and will not curve. Test small sections at the edges to see when the consistency is perfect.

Use a long-bladed metal spatula (hold it in a slightly curved position) or a large round biscuit cutter (about 3 inches in diameter) to scrape wide curved pieces of chocolate. Set them aside to continue hardening.

Store airtight, refrigerated, or at cool room temperature. When you are ready to compose the flower, start by placing the widest chocolate petals in position to form the outside of the ring. For the next ring, use smaller petals, slightly overlapping the first ring. Continue this way, saving the smallest petals for the center.

CHOCOLATE LEAVES

FOR DECORATING A CAKE
OF 8 TO 10 SERVINGS

Chocolate molded onto real leaves makes one of the most elegant and beautiful of all chocolate decorations. Chocolate leaves are especially attractive when intermingled with fruit such as brandied or candied cherries or chestnuts.

| INGREDIENTS | MEASURE | | WEIGHT |
	VOLUME	OUNCES	GRAMS
fresh leaves	8 to 12		
sweetened chocolate	2 (3-ounce) bars	6 ounces	170 grams

Break the chocolate into pieces and place them in the top of a double boiler set over very hot water (but no hotter than 160°F.). The water must not simmer or touch the bottom of the double boiler insert.

Stir until the chocolate begins to melt. Return the pan to low heat if the water cools, but be careful that it does not get too hot. (The chocolate may be melted in a microwave oven if stirred every 15 seconds.)

Using either method, remove it from the heat source before the chocolate has fully melted and stir constantly until the residual heat melts the chocolate. Stir continuously until the temperature of the chocolate reaches 88° to 91°F. (84° to 87°F. if milk chocolate). (If you are not using a thermometer, dab a small amount on your upper lip. It should feel cool.)

Keep the chocolate at the proper temperature by placing the pan of chocolate on a heating pad set on "low." To keep the pad free of melted chocolate, cover it first with plastic wrap.

Holding a leaf by its stem and supporting it underneath with a finger or the palm of your hand, use a small metal spatula or artist's brush to smooth an even layer of chocolate on the underside of the leaf. (Be sure to use the veiny underside as all the delicate lines will be imprinted on the chocolate.) Don't allow the chocolate to get on the other side of the leaf or it may break when peeling off the leaf.

To remove the chocolate from the leaf, peel back the stem end, touching the chocolate as little as possible. If chocolate adheres to the leaf, it has not set long enough.

Carefully place the chocolate leaf on a baking sheet lined with foil, parchment, or wax paper and refrigerate or freeze for 3 minutes, until set and no longer shiny. If using large leaves, add a second coat of chocolate for stability. White chocolate and couverture also require second coats as the chocolate is thinner when melted and light may shine through in spots when the leaf is placed on the cake.

Choose attractive sturdy leaves with pronounced veins, such as rose, geranium, nasturtium, maple, or lemon.

Couverture chocolate makes the most delicate and glossy leaves.

Tweezers are great for picking up the leaves without melting them.

NOTES FROM ROSE

CHOCOLATE GLAZE

FOR DECORATING A CAKE
OF 6 TO 8 SERVINGS

A chocolate glaze is an ideal adornment for a cake. It is easy to make and creates a flawless, shiny finish while sealing in freshness.

INGREDIENTS	MEASURE	WEIGHT	
	VOLUME	OUNCES	GRAMS
bittersweet or milk chocolate	3 (3-ounce) bars	9 ounces	255 grams

Brush all crumbs from the surface of the cake and place it on a cardboard round the same size as the cake. Suspend the cake on a rack set on a baking sheet to catch the excess glaze.

PREPARE THE CAKE FOR GLAZING

Break the chocolate into pieces and place them in the top of a double boiler set over very hot water (but no hotter than 160°F.). The water must not simmer or touch the bottom of the double boiler insert.

PREPARE THE GLAZE

Stir until the chocolate begins to melt. Return the pan to low heat if the water cools, but be careful that it does not get too hot. (The chocolate may be melted in a microwave oven if stirred every 15 seconds.)

Using either method, remove it from the heat source before the chocolate has fully melted and stir constantly until the residual heat melts the chocolate. Stir continuously until the temperature of the chocolate reaches 88° to 91°F. (84° to 87°F. if milk chocolate). (If you are not using a thermometer, dab a small amount on your upper lip. It should feel cool.)

Pour the chocolate onto the center of the cake, allowing the excess to flow down the sides. Using a large metal spatula, smooth the glaze quickly and evenly, moving the spatula lightly back and forth across the top until smooth. If any spots on the sides remain unglazed, use a small metal spatula to lift up some chocolate that has fallen onto the baking sheet and apply to uncovered area.

Lift the rack and tap it lightly on the counter to settle the glaze. Lift the cake from the rack using a broad spatula or pancake turner and set it on a serving plate.

PIPED DECORATIONS

P iped decorations of melted chocolate, ganache, plain or chocolate whipped cream, or even chocolate *crème pâtissière* do wonders for making a cake look festive.

PURE CHOCOLATE

| INGREDIENTS | MEASURE | WEIGHT | |
	VOLUME	OUNCES	GRAMS
bittersweet or milk chocolate	*1 (3-ounce) bar*	*3 ounces*	*85 grams*

Break the chocolate into pieces and place it in the top of a double boiler set over very hot water (but no hotter than 160°F.). The water must not simmer or touch the bottom of the double boiler insert.

MELT THE CHOCOLATE

Stir until the chocolate begins to melt. Return the pan to low heat if the water cools, but be careful that it does not get too hot. (The chocolate may be melted in a microwave oven if stirred every 15 seconds.)

Using either method, remove it from the heat source before the chocolate has fully melted and stir constantly until the residual heat melts the chocolate. Stir continuously until the temperature of the chocolate reaches 88° to 91°F. (84° to 87°F. if milk chocolate). (If you are not using a thermometer, dab a small amount on your upper lip. It should feel cool.)

To pipe pure chocolate, it must be thickened slightly so that it will fall smoothly from the piping bag. Glycerine (available in drug stores and candy supply stores) is ideal. (Stock syrup will also work: Bring an equal volume of water and sugar to a full rolling boil, cover, and cool.) Add only 1 drop of glycerine or stock syrup at a time, stirring and testing the thickness by allowing the chocolate to drop from a height of 4 inches. If it falls in a smooth string, the thickness is right.

PIPING PURE CHOCOLATE

A heavy-duty freezer zip-seal bag makes an ideal, disposable pastry bag for piping. For piping chocolate, simply cut off a small corner, or make a parchment cone. (Do not use a metal tip as the chocolate will harden in it.)

NOTES FROM ROSE

A zip-seal bag can even be used to melt the chocolate. Mini morsels or chips melt quickly and need no glycerine to thicken the melted chocolate. Simply place them in the bag (a quart size is perfect, and it must be heavy-duty to prevent any water from seeping in), close it tightly, and submerge it up to the top of the chocolate in water hot from the tap. After 5 minutes, knead the chocolate to mix it and speed the melting. If the water has cooled, add fresh hot water and let the chocolate sit for a few more minutes or until completely melted.

For ganache or buttercream, cut off a scant ½-inch semicircle from one of the corners and insert a decorating tube (or plastic coupler available in cake decorating supply stores if you wish to change tubes without emptying the bag).

A number 22 star tip can be used to make a wide variety of decorative designs and borders.

GOLDEN HIGHLIGHTS

Tiny flecks of 22-carat gold are quite simply the most extravagant enhancement to the soft deep-brown color of chocolate.

Gold leaf is available in sign-painter supply stores and some art supply stores. To scatter the gold, use a small hairbrush, reserved for this purpose. Lift up a sheet of gold leaf with the brush and use a comb (also reserved for this purpose) to flick little bits of gold over the chocolate.

SOURCES

Bernachon chocolate: *Bernachon*, 42 cours Franklin-Roosevelt, 69006 Lyon, France. Telephone: (33)78.24.37.98.

Lindt cocoa, couverture chocolate for dipping and summer coating: *Maid of Scandinavia*, 3244 Raleigh Avenue, Minneapolis, Minnesota 55416. Telephone: 800/328–6722.

Maestrani Kosher Chocolate: *Taam-Tov Food, Inc.*, 188 Twenty-eighth Street, Brooklyn, New York 11232. Telephone: 718/788–8880.

Pernigotti Cocoa: *Williams-Sonoma*, Mail Order Department, P.O. Box 7456, San Francisco, California 94120–7456. Telephone: 415/421–4242.

Special ingredients such as pistachio extract, praline paste, canned chestnuts: *La Cuisine*, 323 Cameron Street, Alexandria, Virginia 22314. Telephone: 800/521–1176.*

Special equipment such as cake pans, dipping forks, the Cordon Rose chocolate and sugar thermometers: *The Broadway Panhandler*, 520 Broadway, New York, New York 10012. Telephone: 212/966–3434. *Dean & DeLuca*, 560 Broadway, New York, New

---

*La Cuisine also carries a variety of equipment, including densimeters and the Cordon Rose chocolate and sugar thermometers.

York 10012. Telephone: 212/431–1691; outside New York, 800/221–7714, Monday-Friday, 9 A.M.–5 P.M. *Fante*: 1006 South Ninth Street, Philadelphia, Pennsylvania 19147, Telephone: 215/922–5557. *Maid of Scandinavia*, 3244 Raleigh Avenue, Minneapolis, Minnesota 55416. Telephone: 800/328–6722.

INDEX

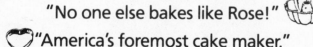